Disasters and Vulnerable Populations

Lisa R. Baker, PhD, LCSW, is an associate professor of social work at the University of Alabama at Birmingham (UAB). Dr. Baker has a strong clinical background in perinatal and pediatric health care social work and mental health experience providing crisis services to children and families. She is a disaster mental health responder and has conducted research and published in the areas of disaster preparedness, evidence-based practice, and perinatal health care.

Loretta A. Cormier, PhD, is an associate professor of anthropology at UAB. In addition to her work on disaster preparedness, her research has involved work in the fields of cultural and biological anthropology. She is the author of two research monographs, *Kinship with Monkeys: The Guajá Foragers of Eastern Amazonia* (2003) and *The Ten Thousand Year Fever: Rethinking Human and Wild Primate Malaria* (2011), and is the coauthor of a textbook, *Introductory Cultural Anthropology: An Interactive Approach* (2010). She has conducted fieldwork with the Amazonian Guajá hunter–gatherers, the Navajo, the Choctaw, and the Fiji Islanders. She also serves as the director of the anthropology graduate student program and the peace studies program at UAB.

Disasters and Vulnerable Populations

Evidence-Based Practice for the Helping Professions

Lisa R. Baker, PhD, LCSW
Loretta A. Cormier, PhD

SPRINGER PUBLISHING COMPANY
NEW YORK

Springer Publishing Company, LLC
11 West 42nd Street
New York, NY 10036
www.springerpub.com

Acquisitions Editor: Stephanie Drew
Composition: Exeter Premedia Services Private Ltd.

ISBN: 978-0-8261-9845-7
e-book ISBN: 978-0-8261-9848-8

14 15 16 17 / 5 4 3 2 1

The author and the publisher of this Work have made every effort to use sources believed to be reliable to provide information that is accurate and compatible with the standards generally accepted at the time of publication. The author and publisher shall not be liable for any special, consequential, or exemplary damages resulting, in whole or in part, from the readers' use of, or reliance on, the information contained in this book. The publisher has no responsibility for the persistence or accuracy of URLs for external or third-party Internet websites referred to in this publication and does not guarantee that any content on such websites is, or will remain, accurate or appropriate.

Library of Congress Cataloging-in-Publication Data
Baker, Lisa R.
Disasters and vulnerable populations : evidence-based practice for the helping professions / Lisa R. Baker, PhD, LCSW, Loretta A. Cormier, PhD.
    p. ; cm.
  ISBN 978-0-8261-9845-7—ISBN 978-0-8261-9848-8 (ebook)
 1. Emergency management.   2. Disaster relief.   3. Disaster victims.   I. Cormier, Loretta A.
  II. Title.
  HV551.2.B35 2015
  363.34'8—dc23

                                                                                    2014015474

Printed in the United States of America by Gasch Printing.

For the helpers

Contents

Introduction

When I was a boy and I would see scary things in the news, my mother would say to me, "Look for the helpers. You will always find people who are helping." To this day, especially in times of "disaster," I remember [those] words.
—Rogers (2003)

WHY THIS BOOK?

As a social work professor, I often tell my students that responding to someone at a point of vulnerability is a privilege. Being with someone when he or she is hurt, afraid, or alone requires a defined skill set, a capacity to be near human suffering, and a desire to make things better. Nowhere else is this more true than in the field of disaster preparedness and response, where "helpers" abound. Preparedness involves helping individuals, groups, and families take an active role in preventing harmful effects. Response means stepping in when preparedness was not enough, or the effects were too devastating to be handled on one's own. Both require a defined skill set and an appreciation that no disaster goes as planned.

Disasters affect millions of people each year across the globe, indifferent to age, race, socioeconomic status (SES), or level of preparedness. Ranging from small to large, they inhibit people's ability to function in their daily life due to physical and emotional damage. Disasters may be naturally sourced, such as tornados, hurricanes, tsunamis, or earthquakes, or man-made, such as bombings, nuclear disasters, and shootings. Responders are faced with the task of helping pick up the pieces, whether that be physically in the form of medical aid, psychologically in the form of psychosocial support and therapeutic interventions, or even in concrete ways such as providing a meal, restoring electricity, or rebuilding a community. However, responding to a diverse population means recognizing important differences when considering the best way to intervene. Some populations, for varying reasons, tend to be at greater risk than others. We call these populations *vulnerable*.

The purpose of this book is to provide a tool kit for helping professions responding to vulnerable populations and preparing populations prior to a disaster. The intent is a compilation of the best available evidence for working with these populations. This book is not meant to be an exhaustive manual, although we try to gather as much available evidence as possible to provide guidelines grounded in empirical research. When empirical evidence is not available (which can be most of the time), we move to evidence that is guided by empirical principles, or is put forth by those known to be experts in the field, all in the hope that the information we gather is useful in the field.

DEFINING VULNERABLE

Disasters, whether man-made or natural, can affect anyone, but the effects are not always equal. Some populations are more vulnerable to the effects of a disaster than others, making it more difficult for them to prepare, evacuate, shelter, respond, and recover in the event of a disaster or emergency. Providing assistance to such populations post-event consumes a greater amount of resources than those required by the general population, or those without special needs and circumstances. Considering the needs of these groups requires special knowledge essential to preparedness, response, and recovery planning.

But just who makes up a vulnerable population? There are different lenses through which to frame the answer. The Centers for Disease Control and Prevention (CDC) broadly defines vulnerable populations by SES, geography, gender, age, disability, and risk status related to sex and gender (Office of Minority Health and Health Equity/CDC, 2014). One estimate reports that over 49% of the population has some sort of special need requiring specialized planning and response (Kailes & Enders, 2007). These categories broadly include children aged 15 and younger, adults aged 65 and older, non-English-speaking or little-English-speaking people, and persons with a disability. However, even these broad categories do not paint a complete picture.

In circumstances where there is mass evacuation, such as during Hurricanes Katrina and Sandy, there is always frequent media coverage of large-scale evacuations, including evacuation of medical facilities and nursing homes. Those with chronic medical conditions and older adults are two of the many categories worthy of consideration. Vulnerable populations also include pregnant women, prisoners, the homeless, those with functional mental health issues or addiction issues, those with transportation issues, persons in poverty, minorities, persons who are obese, and those who have special supervision needs (Hoffman, 2008; Murray & Monteiro, 2012; Zoraster, 2010). Population variability results in complex challenges in planning and service provision, including legal issues. For example, while the needs of persons with disabilities are often protected under civil rights laws, unfortunately these laws make little provision for how to address such needs during a disaster situation (Hoffman, 2008).

SES has recently been recognized as a significant vulnerability factor. Persons of a lower SES are highly susceptible to negative sequelae. They often have greater health and medical needs, suffer from lack of resources to engage in personal preparedness planning, have transportation issues that can hinder evacuation, have limited support systems, and often live in areas with dense populations. Their homes may be overcrowded, housing is less secure, and construction quality inferior to those in higher SES neighborhoods, amplifying the effects of damage and safety (Zoraster, 2010).

Evacuation can also be an issue for those of a lower SES due to limited financial resources. A person from a middle or higher SES may be better able to absorb the effects of temporary loss of income or the expense of having to locate alternative housing arrangements. Those living with less financial means will need to depend on temporary government assistance or the generosity of others to help bridge the financial gap. Even when assistance is available, the application process may be complicated and difficult to navigate, delaying receipt of assistance. Persons of a lower SES may have lower education levels, affecting their ability to know what avenues to pursue to obtain aid. English may not be their primary language, increasing the communication barrier and compounding cultural issues.

Previous large-scale disasters such as Hurricanes Andrew and Ivan demonstrated the significance a lack of personal transportation can have for helping those of lower economic means to evacuate (Zoraster, 2010). However, transportation in large cities can also be an issue for those without economic difficulties. Flooding from Superstorm Sandy created transportation issues for people from all SES levels, as public transportation was cut off from those who had the financial means to obtain alternative transportation but relied on the public system for convenience and economy.

SUMMARY

Meeting the needs of diverse and complex populations requires both a general perspective and specific knowledge guiding the responder. Effective resource utilization, unity of response, and shared understanding begin with acknowledging the special requirements of those populations most vulnerable. Those who engage in disaster preparedness and response with vulnerable populations should be aware of the characteristics that make those populations vulnerable and make special considerations during planning, response, and recovery. This book aims to highlight some of those characteristics, providing responders with necessary guidelines to assess and intervene with those who are especially vulnerable.

REFERENCES

Hoffman, S. (2008). Preparing for disasters: Protecting the most vulnerable in emergencies. Retrieved March 12, 2014, from http://ssrn.com/abstract=1268277

Kailes, J. I., & Enders, A. (2007). A function-based framework for emergency management and planning. *Journal of Disability Policy Studies*, 17(4), 230–237.

Murray, J. S., & Monteiro, S. (2012). Disaster risk and children part I: Why poverty-stricken populations are impacted most. *Journal for Specialists in Pediatric Nursing*, 17(2), 168–170. doi:10.1111/j.1744-6155.2011.00317.x

Office of Minority Health and Health Equity/Centers for Disease Control and Prevention (2014, updated February). Other at risk/vulnerable populations. Retrieved March, 7, 2014, from http://www.cdc.gov/minorityhealth/populations.html#Other

Rogers, F. (2003). *The world according to Mister Rogers: Important things to remember*. New York, NY: Hyperion.

Zoraster, R. M. (2010). Vulnerable populations: Hurricane Katrina as a case study. *Prehospital Disaster Medicine*, 25(1), 74–78.

Overview of Disaster Preparedness and Response

When Disaster Strikes: Disaster Response

CASE STUDY: Heeding the Warning

Elizabeth, a 26-year-old mother of two, kissed her husband and young sons goodbye as they loaded into the car to head to her parents' house 75 miles away. The family had been hearing reports on the radio that bad weather with possible tornados was coming; however, the blue sky did little to support the urgent warnings. Anxious for a little quiet time before heading out, Elizabeth stayed behind to finish the dinner she was taking to a family friend, intending to join her family in a couple of hours. As she lost track of time, Elizabeth noticed that the weather outside was beginning to take a more threatening turn. The sky was becoming darker and the wind was intensifying. She turned on the television and was met by scrolling warning information and meteorologists pointing to threatening pockets of color on the radar. As she reached for her cell phone to call her husband, she noticed several missed calls and wondered whether she should leave immediately to try to join him. Her question was answered as she heard the ominous cry of the warning siren and the unnerving quietness outside. She quickly went to the basement and waited in panic as the EF-4 tornado descended on her neighborhood. Her house groaned and cracked under the strain of the winds. When the noise was replaced with silence, Elizabeth made her way out of the basement and entered the kitchen where she had been only moments earlier, now the only room remaining.

Hurricane Sandy, one of the most devastating and destructive hurricanes in U.S. history, slammed into the northeast coastline in October 2012. Estimates as of summer 2013 assess the amount of damage to be over $68 billion, a number that to date is only surpassed by damage estimates of Hurricane Katrina in 2005 (U.S. National Oceanic and Atmospheric Administration, 2012). Developing as a tropical wave in the Caribbean Sea, the storm travelled through the warm waters and made initial landfall near Kingston, Jamaica, as a hurricane. The storm spread destruction throughout Cuba as a Category 3 hurricane on the Saffir–Simpson Hurricane Wind Scale, moving through the Bahamas, and weakening to a Category 1 storm. Sandy spent days in the water of the Atlantic as it moved its way up the northeast coast of the United States before making landfall near Brigantine, New Jersey. At this point, the storm was classified as a post-tropical cyclone with hurricane-force winds. The effects of the storm intensified as it merged with a winter storm system traveling from the west, warranting many to nickname the storm "Superstorm" Sandy (Nolan, 2012). As early as October 26, governors from across the northeast began declaring states of emergency and requesting pre-disaster declarations from President Obama days before the October 29 land-fall in New Jersey (Campbell, 2012; Federal Emergency Management Agency [FEMA], 2012c; The White House Office of the Press Secretary, 2012). In spite of pre-positioning of resources, the negative effects of the storm impacted millions. At least 117 deaths were reported from the American Red Cross (ARC) track-ing system. The majority of the fatalities involved older adults, as many who were unable to escape the floodwater drowned (Casey-Lockyer et al., 2013). The response for Superstorm Sandy was tremendous, although much different from another devastating storm that occurred 7 years earlier.

In August 2005, one of the deadliest hurricanes in recent history, Hurricane Katrina, made landfall on the Louisiana–Mississippi border as an extremely dan-gerous and extraordinarily large Category 3 hurricane, at times reaching Category 5 status. Hurricane-force winds stretched over 75 miles from the center, impacting 90,000 square miles and over 15 million people (The White House, 2006; Zimmerman, 2012). Although not *the* deadliest storm in U.S. history, Hurricane Katrina claimed 1,836 lives, with 705 people still reported missing. In contrast to similar Category 3 storms, Louisiana not only dealt with the direct impact, but received a double dose of disaster when levees designed to keep water from New Orleans and surrounding areas failed under the unprecedented storm surge. In spite of a significant flood protection system, including 350 miles of levees, flooding destroyed New Orleans, leaving surrounding areas 80% underwater and thousands stranded and in need of evacuation (The White House, 2006). News reports in the weeks and months that followed cited numerous errors in the response, culminating in what many refer to as one of the greatest failures of the George W. Bush presidency (Ahlers, 2006; Hsu, 2006; Walsh, 2008). However, the nature of the storm and the special circumstances of the area impacted created another "perfect storm" in the response effort. While each storm, and corresponding response, is truly different from the next, Hurricane Katrina presented responders and officials with challenges not present in previous events. The response was unique, providing information that would change the future of disaster response across the United States.

AFTER THE DISASTER

It is said that all disasters begin locally and end locally. Local and community first responders establish initial incident command (the system used to control and oversee the response effort) in or nearby the impacted area. The incident command system is responsible for providing coordination and execution of the response effort for any one incident or disaster. In most cases, this occurs through local fire and police jurisdictions or emergency managers. However, leadership of the system may change as the dynamics of the response change and as higher level resources (state and federal) are called in to assist. In the case of Hurricane Katrina, local response was significantly impacted when fire and police departments suffered total destruction, resulting in a lack of clear incident command. The communication infrastructure was essentially nonexistent for days due to the extent of the storm damage. Emergency personnel were unable to receive information or report to work as a result of the inability to establish local incident command structures. Loss of the capability to establish incident command hindered coordination of effort and the ability to assess resources required for the response. Federal search-and-rescue response, including that from the Coast Guard, FEMA Urban Search and Rescue Task Force, and the Department of Defense, was available; however, resources were mobilized only after a significant delay caused by lack of communication on multiple levels. The initial deployment of military support was hindered in part by a resulting breakdown in the chain of command.

Hurricane Katrina posed problems that were different from those presented in previous disasters such as Hurricane Andrew in 1992. The large-scale evacuation effort was complicated first by geography and second by the impact of the storm surge. Tens of thousands of citizens self-migrated or were evacuated to the Superdome post-impact; however, it was soon evident that floodwaters were making it difficult, if not impossible, to resupply basic necessities and coordinate a large-scale evacuation (The Associated Press, 2005). At the time, the magnitude of the Hurricane Katrina response exceeded the capability of FEMA and resulted in fragmented and disorganized service delivery (The White House, 2006).

In the months that followed, the federal government used a critical eye to review the response, making recommendations for improvement in numerous areas. Clarifications in the process were implemented. Roles were delineated and restructured, providing a more efficient system for distribution and assignment of resources. State and local governments were recognized as being in the best position to respond and assess the needs of their communities.

When needs exceed the available resources, responsibility shifts to the federal government to supply local and state forces to handle the response. A successful response is the result of a clear, unified effort that involves suitable integration of services and resources. The investigation after Hurricane Katrina resulted in the creation of a system of national preparedness that integrates the federal, state, local, and private sectors, including the use of Voluntary Organizations Active in Disaster (VOADs) to achieve a unified response (The White House, 2006).

But how does the response work? Who is in charge? Who makes decisions, and ultimately, who determines the success or failure? These are all questions that need to be answered in order to fully understand the complexities of disaster response. The truth is that disaster response is initiated well before an actual event. Processes are pre-established utilizing a response framework comprising federal, state, local, and private resources to meet the unique needs of the population. These processes not only take into account how to proceed after an event, but also look at ways to prevent and lessen the effects of an event. This cyclical approach of considering all aspects of a disaster, referred to as the *disaster life cycle*, allows for multiple points of intervention.

The Disaster Life Cycle

The disaster life cycle highlights phases of a disaster (Figure 1.1). As a cycle there is no clear beginning or ending point, with each phase influencing the next. It is a continuous loop illustrating the relationship among phases and allowing room for overlap. Interventions intersecting at any point in the cycle influence the entire chain. While there are slightly varying elements to the cycle, the most recent edition of the National Response Framework (NRF; FEMA, 2013) outlines five distinct areas in the cycle, including *Prevention*, *Preparedness*, *Response*, *Recovery*, and *Mitigation*.

Prevention

In a perfect world, all disasters could be prevented. However, we know that at least with natural disasters this is rarely the case. *Prevention* capabilities, being able to prevent an event from happening, are in a constant state of development as more is learned about disaster etiology. Advances in meteorological technology and weather tracking systems greatly improved the warning time for certain natural disasters, enabling pre-positioning of resources and implementation of preparedness plans, preserving life and property; however, not every disaster is predictable.

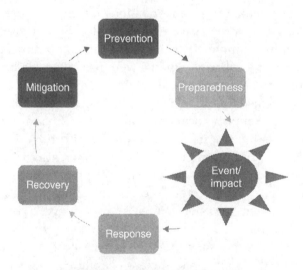

FIGURE 1.1 The disaster life cycle.

In spite of technological advances, some natural disasters, such as earthquakes, are more difficult to predict, and very few man-made disasters are predictable. The terrorist attacks on multiple cities on September 11, 2011, the Deepwater Horizon oil spill in April 2010, and the bombing of the Alfred P. Murrah building in Oklahoma City in 1995 are just a few examples of large-scale disasters that had little or no warning (Call & Pfefferbaum, 1999; Young, 2013). However, improved national and local security enabling the targeted prevention of man-made disasters such as bombings and acts of terrorism has influenced the occurrence of events. Heightened security and vigilance at local and community levels may have also prevented local acts of mass violence such as school shootings (Gallardo, 2012).

Preparedness

As we know that most disasters are not preventable, the next identified phase in the life cycle is *preparedness*. Preparedness consists of individuals, families, and communities anticipating personal needs in the event of a disaster and acting on ways to meet those needs by increasing awareness; establishing a plan; obtaining physical supplies such as food, water, and health-related items; and identifying shelter options. Federal, state, and local governments have provided vast resources to assist individuals and communities to become prepared. Personal preparedness builds response capacity, helping individuals to meet their own needs without the assistance of external resources. Plans and preparation activities conducted prior to an event allow for a more efficient use of resources post-event, and contribute to saving lives and property.

Response

Prevention and preparedness activities can only go so far in anticipating needs. Since each disaster is unique, each *response* to a disaster must also be unique, dependent upon information that is only fully understood after the event occurs. Disaster response involves post-event activities aimed to limit loss of life and property, assisting a population in regaining a pre-event level of functioning. The scale of the response varies greatly but is in direct proportion to the magnitude of the disaster, the geographic and population vulnerabilities of the region, and the availability of resources. Response efforts (as opposed to recovery efforts) are generally short term and receive the most attention in the media. Immediate response efforts center on providing crisis intervention services and stabilizing the community. The general public oftentimes confuses response activities with longer phase work that occurs in recovery. While there is some overlap, the goal of response is stabilization as opposed to restoration of pre-event functioning, the goal of recovery.

Recovery and Mitigation

Recovery activities commonly receive less attention in the media even though such activities can take place months or years after the event, depending on the level of devastation. The recovery period includes damage and risk assessment by authorities, resulting in plans for *mitigation*, or actions taken in order to lessen the effects of future events. Recovery and mitigation go hand in hand as efforts made to restore communities involve changes that make areas less vulnerable to future risk. For example, the lengthy recovery process in New Orleans following Hurricane Katrina has left the region better prepared against future storms that bring accompanying storm surges. Houses are rebuilt with more stringent building codes and the public becomes better informed about its role in securing homes and safeguarding families from possible effects. Communication and command infrastructures are strengthened and system gaps are identified.

The National Incident Management System

Since disasters begin and end locally, it would be logical to initiate a discussion of response by beginning at the local level. But in fact, when most people think of disaster response they think about the federal level, with organizations such as the FEMA and the Department of Homeland Security. While these organizations do in fact play a pivotal role in response, they do so only at the request of the lower levels of government.

The National Incident Management System (NIMS) is a framework implemented by departments and agencies at all levels of government, including nongovernmental organizations (NGOs) and the private sector. NIMS employs key concepts of disaster response in an effort to manage incidents of any scale. The concepts are as applicable to small-scale events, such as community fires, chemical exposures, or ice storms, as they are to larger scale events such as widespread tornado outbreaks or mass shootings. The approach was developed by applying known best practices from previous experience to develop a unified framework applicable for any level of jurisdiction.

By applying the principles set forth by NIMS, responders can be assured that everyone is working from the same viewpoint. For example, since communication is key in any response effort, NIMS provides a common set of terminology and standardized organizational structures to allow responders to work from a shared set of objectives. When objectives are established in advance, postevent efforts are coordinated and streamlined. Components of the NIMS framework include specifics about preparedness, communications and information, resources, command and management, and ongoing maintenance. NIMS functions under the larger umbrella of the NRF, a directorate from the federal government providing guidance and structure to incident management. Components of NIMS support response and standardize incident command and management across all levels, resulting in coordinated, flexible, and adaptable efforts (Department of Homeland Security [DHS], 2008).

The National Response Framework

The NRF is a set of guidelines developed by the federal government that identifies current best practices for managing incidents. These guidelines can be scaled to fit disaster events of any size, from small to catastrophic. The NRF was developed in order to clearly define the principles, roles, and responsibilities of responders at all levels. In addition, it defines how these roles and responsibilities are integrated among responders. For example, an incident response could involve local municipalities such as fire and medical response, state resources such as the National Guard, and local and regional private organizations and NGOs such as the ARC, the Lutheran Disaster Response network, and the Salvation Army. In order to maximize the acquisition and distribution of different types of resources, and avoid duplication of effort and resources, these responders need to follow the same rules and guidelines for response. The NRF provides such standardized guidelines utilizing principles from NIMS.

As mentioned earlier, the post-event phases of disaster response and recovery are very different in spite of overlapping at points. The NRF provides guidance during immediate response and in the recovery phase, addressing what is needed to save lives, protect personal property and surrounding environment, stabilize the area, and restore basic community services. Restoring basic services is a necessary component of establishing area safety and security in order for communities to move forward in recovery with a solid foundation.

The federal government is highly involved in providing guidance to aid the disaster response and recovery process. In March 2011, Presidential Policy Directive 8 (PPD-8): National Preparedness was signed by President Barack Obama in order to establish priorities and policies to be addressed at the federal level. PPD-8 defines five areas to be addressed by national policy guidelines: Prevention, Protection, Mitigation, Response, and Recovery (Obama, 2011). These areas may sound familiar and are delineated above as components of the disaster life cycle. The NRF is a major component of PPD-8 identifying key roles and responsibilities of persons at multiple levels involved in response. Identifying roles and delineating responsibilities enable integration of resources and allow multilevel support of response at all levels, including local, state, tribal, and federal governments.

One of the key elements of the NRF is its ability to consider the different levels of support and recognize that resources may be generated from multiple sources. Lessons learned from responses such as those after Hurricane Katrina stress that the private sector and other NGOs such as volunteer agencies can provide tremendous assistance in meeting the needs of a community or region. Previously such resources were not integrated in the national response plan, a miscalculation that was corrected in subsequent disaster plans.

Guiding Principles of the National Response Framework

There are several guiding principles of the NRF outlining necessary factors evident in any response effort. Such principles include maintaining an *engaged partnership*, creating a *tiered response*, exhibiting *scalable and flexible operational capabilities*, demonstrating *unity of effort*, and establishing *readiness to act*. These principles guide response efforts and ensure an integrated and efficient plan of action. These principles are not mutually exclusive, but rather build upon and complement each other.

There are countless agencies—governmental, nongovernmental, and private—that provide services to aid in response. An *engaged partnership* assesses and recognizes capacity for all members of the community to provide services that are unique and integral components of the response process. These resources vary greatly from service to service and may include medical and mental health support, sheltering and feeding, housing and infrastructure support, long-term recovery, and so on. In order to effectively and efficiently utilize these resources, they are "layered" with services from other organizations to provide a supportive network. An engaged partnership recognizes that services may be unified with services from other sources while respecting individual agency governance and objectives. Much like pieces of a puzzle, each resource fills a specialized need that contributes to the whole. These resources include individual efforts, community efforts, the private sector, volunteer special interest groups, and all levels of the government. Working within a supportive network provides an opportunity for agencies to build a web of resources that does not drain or deplete any one entity.

A *tiered response* (see Figure 1.2) is also imperative to coordinate well-delivered effort. The foundation of a tiered response begins at the local level. Whenever possible, local agencies and organizations take the lead in response tasks. Comprising the lowest and most substantial tier, local agencies provide the basis for the response. The vast majority of disasters can be handled at the local

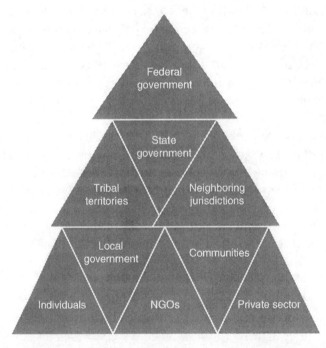

FIGURE 1.2 A tiered response. Most disasters are resourced adequately at the local level. A small portion of disasters require assistance from the state government and neighboring jurisdictions, while an even smaller proportion require the full resources of the federal government.

NGO, nongovernmental organization.

level. City and county infrastructure are generally equipped to handle the needs of response and recovery; however, when the need is greater than the capacity of local resources, assistance is requested from the next higher level. Neighboring communities, state, and tribal territories comprising the second tier may be approached when local and community resources are deemed insufficient. In rare circumstances, both local- and state-level resources are not enough. In the case of catastrophic or extremely large-scale disaster, resources are requested at the federal level. These resources comprise the smallest top tier; however, due to the magnitude of the precipitating event, greater attention is given when they are employed.

With the multitude of agencies and organizations from all levels providing resources, it is imperative that any response possesses *flexible, scalable, and adaptable operational capabilities*. Resources vary and can include concrete service delivery, materials and supplies, food and basic necessities, shelter capabilities, transportation, rescue and recovery operations, health care services, utility restoration, and so on. With such a variance in the type, amount, and source of resources, there must be uniformity in the plan and delivery of those services. Responses adapt to the changing needs of an incident, whether that means scaling up to obtain more resources or scaling down as the response moves into recovery. Regardless, resources need to be able to expand or adapt as needed. Some resources are only needed during the response, while others may bridge response and recovery or only be necessary during the recovery phase. Throughout this process, it is critical that resources are utilized efficiently and are not duplicated or wasted. Having an engaged partnership is one way to safeguard against duplication or waste in resources.

One of the most important concepts to consider is *unity of effort*. Working together and delineating mutually developed and unified objectives requires unity of effort among responders. The incident command system (a component of NIMS) clearly outlines the chain of command during an incident and discusses how organization of command is to be maintained throughout an event. Individual agencies and organizations contribute to the response effort while maintaining their own individual authority and responsibility, preserving the integrity of their own mission. Unity of effort guided by the incident command system allows the local government, private sector, NGOs, and other agencies to consolidate resources and maximize response.

However, none of these agencies would be able to effectively respond if they did not heed the final principle of the NRF, *readiness to act*. The principle of readiness to act stipulates that all responders, agencies, and organizations need to be responsible for anticipating and managing their response efforts while appreciating their own level of risk. Risk must be anticipated and a plan for managing risk must be in place prior to the initiation of a response. As with any good response plan, a great deal of work is completed before the actual event. Training, planning, and organizing resources prior to deploying them for a response are critical to ensure smooth service delivery and integrated response.

Roles of Key Players

The NRF recognizes that there are key players in disaster response and recovery at every level. These players range from individuals and families to large government organizations. In learning from past events, the NRF seeks to identify the roles of players and stakeholders in order to streamline resource delivery and optimize response.

Individuals, Families, and Households

While it may seem like there is little an individual can do in light of a large-scale disaster, there is actually a great deal that individuals, families, and households can contribute to disaster response. As mentioned earlier, a key element of the disaster life cycle is to intervene prior to the event through preparedness efforts. Individuals, families, and households that are prepared lessen the burden on response resources by ensuring self-sufficiency and resiliency, reducing the drain of limited resources. Families can do their part to reduce hazards in their households that may make them vulnerable in a disaster. For example, they should be aware of natural gas and water main emergency shut-off valves. Flammable liquids and materials should be placed in a safe location and escape routes from their home, neighborhood, and communities identified. Individuals, families, and households should be aware of the types of natural disasters that are prevalent in their areas and plan accordingly. For example, families living in southern coastal regions may need to prepare for weather disasters such as flooding and hurricanes, while northern households should be aware of potential risks from snow and ice.

FEMA and the ARC encourage an "all-hazards" approach to preparedness that includes general preparedness activities suitable for a variety of disasters. The all-hazards approach recommends that people be able to be self-sustaining for a period of 3 days following an event without the assistance of outside help or resources (FEMA, ARC). The 3-day rule is the general guideline for how long it may take for emergency personnel and rescue workers to enter an area in the event of a large-scale disaster. Households should be familiar with emergency plans that include communicating with family members in case of separation or if mechanisms such as telephone and electronic transmissions are compromised. Emergency plans should include stipulations for reunification if household members are separated from their homes, neighborhoods, or communities during evacuation. All household emergency plans should include provisions for members who are more vulnerable, such as those with special health or mental health needs, physical challenges, mobility challenges, children, older adults, and pets. Whenever possible, households should be aware of neighbors who have similar high-risk factors that may make them more vulnerable during a disaster. Neighbors are the true first responders in any emergency scenario.

In addition to preparing their household, individuals may also wish to volunteer at a larger level by becoming a trained disaster volunteer. There are numerous opportunities for individuals to maximize their skills through joining a VOAD (Box 1.1) or other disaster response organizations. For instance, those

BOX 1.1

Voluntary Organizations

Voluntary organizations are key players in disaster response and recovery. Voluntary Organizations Active in Disaster (VOADs) are local-, state-, and national-level nonprofit, faith-based, advocacy-based, and social community groups and organizations that provide a variety of services for disaster victims and communities impacted by disasters. National VOAD (NVOAD) has over 100 members, including organizations such as the American Red Cross (ARC), All Hands Volunteers, AmeriCares, Catholic Charities U.S.A., Churches of Scientology Disasters Response, Habitat for Humanity, HOPE Animal-Assisted Crisis Response, The Jewish Federation of North America, Samaritan's Purse, and Save the Children, to name a few. These organizations are recognized as an integral part of the National Response Framework and National Disaster Recovery Framework. Working from their key principles of cooperation, communication, coordination, and collaboration, they provide a multitude of services such as food and shelter, family reunification, medical and mental health services, spiritual support, financial assistance, and rebuilding and recovery services. Organizations are present at the local, state, and national levels to provide support to government response and recovery efforts. Comprising mostly volunteers, VOADs are able to participate in national responses while maintaining their own authority, responsibility, and accountability within their specific mission and objectives. To find out more about VOADs, visit www.nvoad.org

with medical training may decide to volunteer their time as a member of the Medical Reserve Corps. The Medical Reserve Corps utilizes specialists such as physicians, nurses, therapists, pharmacists, and public health professionals to respond to disasters and emergencies in a given community. Members of the Medical Reserve Corps provide not only crisis services but also long-term support services to local clinics and shelters (Office of the Surgeon General, 2013). Community Emergency Response Teams (CERTs) are another example of an avenue that individuals can take to become involved. CERT members are trained in basic disaster preparedness and response skills and use those skills to respond in their community (FEMA, 2013). Like other responders, CERT members are a valuable part of an integrated response.

Every individual, however, can assist in the response by paying careful attention during the disaster. This includes monitoring situations closely for any significant changes in status that require action on the part of the individual, and following the guidance of authorities when given instructions about preparing, evacuating, and resuming activities post-event. Whatever avenue individuals decide to take, it is critical that they participate in training. Box 1.2 outlines the importance of becoming a trained responder and how unsolicited or "untrained"

BOX 1.2

Why Is Training Necessary?

The news of a disaster, especially one that is local, generates the need to help among others in a community. While the use of trained volunteers is critical to the response and recovery effort, unsolicited or untrained volunteer responders often pose a greater hazard and can actually impede efforts. Large-scale disasters such as the Loma Prieta earthquake, the 9/11 attacks, Hurricane Katrina, and Superstorm Sandy saw tens of thousands of unsolicited volunteers show up on the disaster site (Fernandez, Barbera, & van Dorp, 2006a). While the efforts and willingness to help were appreciated, a surge of untrained volunteers can bog down an already compromised response system and demand a shift in attention from those in command.

Being able to respond effectively requires advance training and preparation in order to maximize the efficient use of resources and work in conjunction with larger organizations and volunteer agencies. This training is not only important to streamline a coordinated response, but also to protect the volunteer from the physical dangers and possible psychological issues that arise in a response scenario. Unsolicited volunteers can quickly overwhelm agencies and result in resources being pulled away from the response effort in order to manage and "crashtrain" volunteers. In addition, such volunteers at the disaster site often place themselves in risk of physical danger, drawing resources away from response to actual victims (Merchant, Leigh, & Lurie, 2010).

Citizens and neighbors are often the true first responders to a local crisis, merely helping those in their community (Fernandez, Barbera, & van Dorp, 2006b). For the volunteer, such efforts can reduce stress, and impart a sense of purpose and connection to those dealing with the effects of a disaster. However, volunteers who have not received prior training can often place themselves in physical danger, suffer health consequences due to conditions and circumstances, and be unprepared to handle the emotional consequences of being in the midst of profound suffering (Harman & Pinto, 2007). Even trained professionals who have not had prior disaster experience can find themselves unsure as they provide services in austere conditions, find disruption in provision of their own basic needs, and suffer compassion fatigue (Adams, 2007; Bartley, 2007).

Persons interested in responding should first register with an existing volunteer organization through local, regional, or government avenues. Second, persons should participate in training opportunities provided by those agencies to heighten skills in disaster response and prepare volunteers to function within the boundaries of those organizations. Once training is complete, volunteers are placed on rosters for resourcing specific needs during a disaster period. Volunteers deployed as a part of a larger organization structure will be an asset, not a liability in the disaster field. In addition, volunteers will find that it will be easier to engage in response work and receive the support they need to be a health responder (Merchant, Leigh, & Lurie, 2010).

volunteers can hinder the response effort. Training ensures that all individuals who choose to help others can do so in a secure and effective manner, aiding instead of jeopardizing the safety of themselves and others.

Communities

In 1996, the then first lady of the United States Hillary Rodham Clinton wrote a book *It Takes a Village*. This book was a discourse on the concept that children are raised by more than just exposure to their immediate families and households. That indeed there are many other people such as extended family, friends, social and religious groups, and community organizations that influence and shape the children of today. If you have not noticed by now, the same can be said about disaster response. Indeed, it does take more than one agency or organization to deliver a comprehensive response that meets everyone's needs. In fact, it often does take a "village" full of responders to address the multitude of concrete and psychosocial needs following a disaster.

While often presented in the framework of a VOAD, faith-based and community organizations provide a tremendous service to meet the needs of individuals following a disaster. Affiliation with a religious or social organization eases the way for individuals to seek help and essential services. Churches and civic organizations provide sheltering and concrete services as well as long-term mental health and recovery opportunities. Schools, universities, and academic groups can also provide resources unique to their setting. After Hurricane Katrina, students at Tulane University found support through partnering campuses that were able to provide access to courses, assisting students in maintaining their academic progress in the midst of recovery. The response of these universities filled a specialized need that may have otherwise been unrecognized as an integral part of recovery.

Faith-based and community organizations can not only provide concrete services but also help through advocacy, organizing community response, training volunteers, and providing people with a sense of connection to others. Communities often combine resources and respond independent of formal mechanisms, initiating the healing and recovery process along with trained responders. The momentum and energy of people joined together for a common purpose should never be underestimated.

Nongovernmental Organizations

By now you should be sensing that identifying the key players in disaster response is a little like trying to decipher alphabet soup. One of the common terms used in disaster response is NGOs. NGOs can take the form of many different types of organizations including faith-based, race- and ethnicity-based, nonprofit, and social organizations. VOADs fall under the category of NGOs. NGOs are a critical component of disaster response and are recognized as such under the NRF.

While NGOs are driven by their own priorities and objectives, they work in partnership with all levels of disaster responders including local, state, and federal resources. NGOs may provide services to victims in general or they may target certain populations. Regardless, NGOs provide essential services that reduce the resource burden for other entities and engage in collaborative efforts to ensure comprehensive services. Some of the services provided include sheltering, immediate and longer term food supplies, clothing, temporary housing assistance, medical and mental health services, family reunification, and assistance with boarding and caring for pets. NGOs can provide assistance with transportation, search and rescue operations, and communications. Organizations targeting minority racial and ethnic groups may provide assistance with translation as well as provide pre-event training on delivering disaster services in a culturally competent manner. In fact, the provision of trained volunteers in general is a significant resource of NGOs, reducing the resource burden on government organizations to train, organize, and deploy volunteers.

Private Sector

The private sector is also a key player in response. Comprising large and small private businesses, commerce, private cultural and educational institutions, and a multitude of different types of industry, the private sector is critical to help support the local economy, which can take a devastating hit after a disaster. In 2010, the Deepwater Horizon/BP oil spill disaster delivered a significant blow to the economy of the coast of the Gulf of Mexico. It was a man-made disaster that spanned the months from April, the time of the initial explosion and beginning of the oil leak, to July 2010, the month that the defective oil well was capped and leaking ceased. The effects of the oil contamination were devastating to the ecosystem, fish, and wildlife of the Gulf, with the oil covering 68,000 square miles of water (Norse & Amos, 2010). There was extensive damage to marine and other wildlife habitats as well as to the fishing and tourism industries of the Gulf coast. In the years immediately preceding the spill, tourism in the Gulf region exceeded $34,000 billion annually and was responsible for the provision of over 400,000 jobs. The estimated impact of the oil spill on the tourism industry in that region is over $22.7 billion for the 3-year recovery period (Oxford Economics, 2009). The private sector response in the Deepwater Horizon oil spill was significant. Unlike natural disasters, which can elicit responses from utility companies, health care facilities, and communication operations, the Deepwater Horizon disaster generated response from universities, scientists, and private corporations that provided insight, expertise, and manpower to stop the spill and aid in the cleanup. The private sector supports local response, local economy during recovery, and community and local infrastructures necessary for preservation of life and property.

Local Government

Perhaps the most critical players in any disaster effort are local governments. As the first-line responders, they are responsible for immediate assessment of needs and evaluation of resources. The local government, composed of elected officials, emergency managers, and mid-level organizations, is responsible for overseeing the day-to-day operations of the response. Emergency managers are tasked with coordinating efforts of all participants during a response. As we know, this can comprise efforts by individuals, community organizations, NGOs, private-sector agencies, and others. In most circumstances, efforts are coordinated from a central hub known as the emergency operations center (EOC). An EOC provides a central location for representatives from key players to meet, receive information, and coordinate efforts.

The local government is also responsible for overseeing communication to all parties and coordinating public awareness. Decisions are made about what information is essential to provide to the public and how that information should be disseminated. This oftentimes takes the form of news briefs, public service announcements, websites, and radio broadcasts. Fire, emergency, and emergency medical services (EMS) take the lead in many instances under guidance from local authorities.

The local government determines when additional resources are needed to supplement efforts. These decisions are made by collecting information and assessing needs and resources at the time of and immediately following an incident. As a part of a tiered response system, the local government initiates the chain of requests to higher authorities to access state and potential national resources.

State Government

If the local government determines that its resources are not sufficient to handle the response, they may request additional assets from the state government. In these circumstances the local resources are either depleted, or anticipated to be depleted as the response effort continues. State resources are available to supplement local efforts when needs exceed local capabilities and resources.

Resources at the state level may come from many different avenues and include state-level branches of national agencies. For example, states may receive resources from not only the office of the governor, but also the State Homeland Security advisor, the State Emergency Management Agency director, and the National Guard. Agencies and organizations at this level may provide national response capabilities that are otherwise not accessible at the local level. Included at the state level are also higher level branches of NGOs such as the ARC and VOADs.

Federal Government

While it is the responsibility of the local government to respond first and provide emergency services, in many instances the local and state governments are not able to meet the capacity or anticipate not being able to meet the capacity of a major event. In those circumstances, assistance may be requested from the federal government. Figure 1.3 outlines the steps involved when a governor determines that the combined resources of local and state governments are not sufficient to accomplish the tasks of the response and recovery. At this point, the governor may request a Presidential Major Disaster Declaration. A Presidential Disaster Declaration requests an assessment from the federal government of the exhibited or projected impact of an event for the purpose of soliciting government

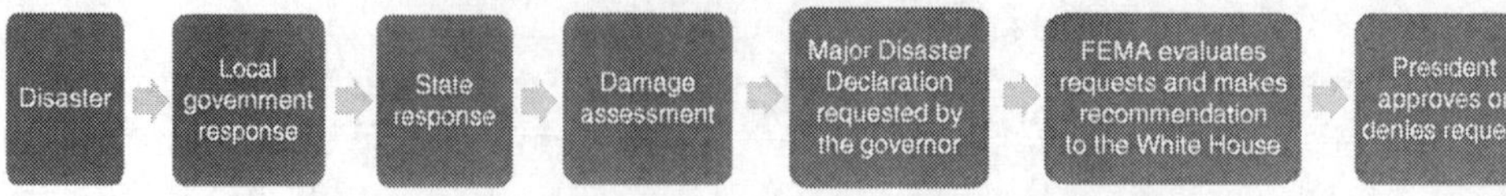

FIGURE 1.3 Steps in a presidential disaster declaration.
Source: FEMA (2012a).

funding. While most declarations occur after the incident, in some circumstances, a declaration may be requested prior to an anticipated disaster if the disaster is expected to exceed the resources of the state. This occurs more often in natural disasters where weather patterns and climate conditions are able to be tracked and monitored prior to land impact, as in the case of hurricanes and other large-scale storms.

Federal assistance is established through the Robert T. Stafford Disaster Relief and Emergency Assistance Act. The Stafford Act is activated and coordinated through FEMA (McCarthy, 2011). States do not relinquish their role when the Stafford Act is initiated. They must continue to commit their full use of resources and validate that state funds will be contributed to the effort.

In 2012, there were over 200 natural disaster events in the United States, including floods, wildfires, tornados, ice storms, and minor earthquakes, with 47 major disaster declarations and 16 emergency declarations (FEMA, n.d.). Both major disaster declarations and emergency declarations result in federal assistance; however, emergency declarations are shorter in duration and more limited in the scope of services provided than a major disaster declaration. A major disaster declaration institutes significant resources to fund response as well as long-term recovery (FEMA, 2012a, 2012b). The economic impact of disaster response and recovery alone for 2012 in the United States was $85.7 billion and the number continues to grow (Center for Disaster Philanthropy, 2013).

SUMMARY AND CONCLUSIONS

Disasters are complicated events, requiring a comprehensive and interconnected response and recovery effort. The disaster life cycle highlights the cyclical nature of prevention, response, recovery, and mitigation, illuminating how intervention at any point has the capability of influencing the entire life cycle. The coordinated efforts of private, local, state, and federal organizations and agencies demonstrate that the assessment and delivery of needs is multifactorial and requires a collective response from all stakeholders.

As each disaster unfolds, we are able to reassess preparedness guidelines, response frameworks, and integrated recovery efforts. Each disaster brings a different set of challenges, but also provides the opportunity to strengthen our knowledge of the nuances that lead to successful response and recovery. Responders and key stakeholders should continue to study response mechanisms in order to implement the most effective and efficient procedures and policies.

REFERENCES

Adams, L. M. (2007). Mental health needs of disaster volunteers: A plea for awareness. *Perspectives in Psychiatric Care, 43*(1), 52–54.

Ahlers, M. (2006, April 14). *Report: Criticism of FEMA's Katrina response deserved.* Retrieved September 25, 2013, from http://www.cnn.com/2006/POLITICS/04/14/fema.ig

Bartley, A. G. (2007). Confronting the realities of volunteering for a national disaster. *Journal of Mental Health Counseling, 29*(1), 4–16.

Call, J. A., & Pfefferbaum, B. (1999). Lessons from the first two years of Project Heartland, Oklahoma's mental health response to the 1995 bombing. *Psychiatric Services, 50,* 7. Retrieved September 25, 2013, from http://journals.psychiatryonline.org/article.aspx?articleid=83123

Campbell, C. (2012). *President Obama signs New York emergency declaration.* Retrieved September 28, 2013, from http://politicker.com/2012/10/president-obama-signs-new-york-emergency-declaration-2

Casey-Lockyer, M., Heick, R. J., Mertzlufft, C. E., Yard, E. E., Wolkin, A. F., Noe, R. S., & Murti, M. (2013, May). Deaths associated with Hurricane Sandy—October–November 2012. *Morbidity and Mortality Weekly Report, 62*(20), 393–397. Retrieved September 28, 2013, from http://www.cdc.gov/mmwr/preview/mmwrhtml/mm6220a1.htm

Center for Disaster Philanthropy. (2013). *Disaster statistics.* Retrieved September 25, 2013, from http://disasterphilanthropy.org/where/disaster-statistics

Department of Homeland Security (DHS). (2008). *The National Incident Management System.* Retrieved September 26, 2013, from http://www.fema.gov/pdf/emergency/nims/NIMS_core.pdf

Department of Homeland Security (DHS). (2013). *National Response Framework.* Retrieved September 25, 2013, from http://www.fema.gov/media-library-data/20130726-1914-25045-1246/final_national_response_framework_20130501.pdf

FEMA. (n.d.). *Disaster declarations by year.* Retrieved September 28, 2013, from http://www.fema.gov/disasters/grid/year

FEMA. (2012a, updated June 13). *The disaster process and disaster aid programs.* Retrieved September 28, 2013, from http://www.fema.gov/disaster-process-disaster-aid-programs

FEMA. (2012b, updated June 13). *Declaration process fact sheet: The emergency response process.* Retrieved September 28, 2013, from http://www.fema.gov/declaration-process-fact-sheet

FEMA. (2012c, updated October 29). President Obama signs New Jersey emergency declaration. Retrieved September 29, 2013, from http://www.fema.gov/news-release/2012/10/29/president-obama-signs-new-jersey-emergency-declaration

FEMA. (2013, March 14). *Community emergency response teams.* Retrieved September 28, 2013, from http://www.fema.gov/community-emergency-response-teams

Fernandez, L. S., Barbera, J. A., & van Dorp, J. R. (2006a). Spontaneous volunteer response to disasters: The benefits and consequences of good intentions. *Journal of Emergency Management, 4*(5), 57–68.

Fernandez, L. S., Barbera, J. A., & van Dorp, J. R. (2006b, October). Strategies for managing volunteers during incident response: A systems approach. *Homeland Security Affairs, 11*(3). Retrieved September 29, 2013, from http://www.hsaj.org/?article=2.3.9

Gallardo, M. (2012, December 16). *Cedar Lake man with 47 guns arrested after school threat.* Retrieved September 25, 2013, from http://abclocal.go.com/wls/story?section=news/local/indiana&id=8922348

Harman, P. L., & Pinto, M. A. (2007, October). Disaster response: Safety and health guidelines for volunteers. *Professional Safety, 52*(10), 61–63.

Hsu, S. S. (2006, February 12). *Katrina report spreads blame.* Retrieved September 25, 2013, from http://www.washingtonpost.com/wpdyn/content/article/2006/02/11/AR 2006021101409.html

Merchant, R. M., Leigh, J. E., & Lurie, N. (2010). Health care volunteers and disaster response—first, be prepared. *New England Journal of Medicine, 362*(10), 872–873. doi:10.1056/NEJMp1001737

McCarthy, F. X. (2011, June 7). Federal Stafford Act Disaster Assistance: Presidential declarations, eligible activities, and funding. *Congressional Research Service.* Retrieved September 29, 2013, from http://www.fas.org/sgp/crs/homesec/RL33053.pdf

Nolan, D. (2012). *Why is Sandy unusual?* Retrieved September 29, 2013, from http://www.cnn.com/2012/10/29/opinion/nolan-hurricane-sandy

Norse, E. A., & Amos, J. (2010). Impacts, perception, and policy implications of the Deepwater Horizon oil and gas disaster. *Environmental Law Reporter.* Retrieved September 27, 2013, from http://mcbi.marine-conservation.org/publications/pub _pdfs/Norse-and-Amos-2010.pdf

Obama, B. (2011). *Presidential policy directive, PPD-8: National preparedness.* Retrieved September 27, 2013, from http://www.dhs.gov/presidential-policy-directive -8-national-preparedness

Office of the Surgeon General. (2013, September 9). *Division of the civilian volunteer Medical Reserve Corp.* Retrieved September 29, 2013, from https://www.medical reservecorps.gov/HomePage

Oxford Economics. (2009). *Potential impact of the Gulf spill on tourism.* Retrieved September 28, 2013, from http://www.ustravel.org/sites/default/files/page/2009/11/Gulf _Oil_Spill_Analysis_Oxford_Economics_710.pdf

The Associated Press. (2005, September 3). Evacuation at Superdome halted; 5,000 remain inside. Retrieved September 25, 2013, from http://usatoday30.usatoday.com /news/nation/2005-09-03-katrina-superdome_x.htm

The White House. (2006). *The federal response to Hurricane Katrina: Lessons learned.* Retrieved September 25, 2013, from http://www.georgewbush-whitehouse.archives.gov /reports/katrina-lessons-learned

The White House Office of the Press Secretary. (2012, October 28). *President Obama signs Maryland emergency declaration.* Retrieved September 25, 2013, from http://www.whitehouse.gov/the-press-office/2012/10/28/president-obama -signs-maryland-emergency-declaration

United States National Oceanic and Atmospheric Administration National Weather Service (NOAA). (2012). *Hurricane/post-tropical cyclone Sandy, October 22–29.* Retrieved September 27, 2013, from http://www.nws.noaa.gov/os/assessments /pdfs/Sandy13.pdf

Young, M. (2013, January 20). *5 worst man-made disasters in history.* Retrieved September 25, 2013, from http://www.policymic.com/articles/23620/5-worst -man-made-disasters-in-history

Walsh, K. T. (2008, December 11). *Hurricane Katrina left a mark on George W. Bush's presidency.* Retrieved September 28, 2013, from http://www.usnews.com/news /articles/2008/12/11/hurricane-katrina-left-a-mark-on-george-w-bushs-presidency

Zimmerman, K. A. (2012). *Hurricane Katrina: Facts, damage and aftermath.* Retrieved September 28, 2013, from http://www.livescience.com/22522-hurricane-katrina -facts.html

Before the Storm: Preparedness

Being prepared for a disaster is a responsibility that falls with individuals, groups, organizations, communities, and all levels of government. While preparedness is a concept that is widespread in the media, the process of initiating behaviors to achieve preparedness is often met with significant personal and societal barriers. Nonetheless, preparedness is a critical component in being able to mediate and moderate negative effects in large- or small-scale events.

On April 15, 2013, two bombs were detonated near the finish line of the Boston Marathon in Boston, Massachusetts, killing several people and injuring hundreds more. The ensuing manhunt for the bombing suspects resulted in almost one million residents in Boston and surrounding neighborhoods being asked to remain indoors and shelter in place until such time as areas were deemed to be safe. Public transportation, businesses, and public institutions were closed as the city went into lockdown (DeLuca, 2013; Ford, Smith, & McShane, 2013; Kotz, 2013). Persons were faced with not being able to travel within their community, access stores and pharmacies, and were unsure about response times from emergency services until the area was secured. While the actual shelter-in-place time was under 24 hours, the incident brought to light issues raised when people are given instructions to remain indoors with little or no anticipation.

On January 28, 2014, Birmingham, Alabama forecasters were predicting that the city and surrounding areas were on the outskirts of a winter storm expecting to bring a "dusting" of snow, with little or no anticipated effects on travel or daily operations. Instead, the Birmingham area received up to 2" of snow during the middle of the work day. The previous days of extremely cold temperatures left the city vulnerable, resulting in precipitation immediately freezing, dropping snow on top of icy roads. Almost immediately, schools and businesses dismissed students and employees, resulting in a treacherous gridlock on streets. In a city of over one million people, thousands of motorists funneled on to frozen streets, hundreds were forced to abandon their cars and walk to homes or hotels, workers were forced to stay at work and shelter in place, families were separated, and emergency workers were unable to pass through blocked streets. Hundreds of elementary, middle, and high school students were stranded at local schools with teachers when parents were unable to make it to pick them up. The city remained in gridlock for days as temperatures stayed low enough to keep the snow and ice from melting (Magee, 2014; West, 2014). In contrast to large-scale events like Hurricane Katrina or the attacks on the World Trade Center in New York City, these incidents are smaller in scale, but nonetheless have a large impact on individuals, families, and communities.

In both of the above scenarios, as well as in larger events, preparing for anticipated needs helps individuals remain self-sufficient after a disaster. The Federal Emergency Management Agency (FEMA), the Department of Homeland Security (DHS), the American Red Cross (ARC), and the Centers for Disease Control and Prevention (CDC) have established guidelines to assist individuals in preparing to protect life and property during a disaster. Current recommendations from these agencies and organizations discuss implementing an "all-hazards" approach, delineating preparedness for any type of natural or man-made disaster. This approach recognizes that the differing nature of events often results in the same issues when it comes to personal safety and protecting life and property.

DEFINING PREPAREDNESS

A study conducted in 2011 by the National Center for Disaster Preparedness at Columbia University found that among those surveyed, 62% felt like it would take first responders less than 3 hours to reach them in the event of a disaster. This number was down slightly from an earlier survey stating that approximately 66% were confident in a response time less than 3 hours (National Center for Disaster

Preparedness, 2011). Anyone who has lived through or witnessed the effects of disasters knows that this assumption is unrealistic. Events like Hurricane Katrina and Superstorm Sandy serve as reminders that it can be days before emergency personnel make it to disaster areas and conduct evacuations. As a result, it is critical that individuals prepare themselves to be able to address their own needs in the event that first responders are unable to arrive immediately. In that respect, guidelines recommend that individuals make plans to be self-sufficient for a time period of at least 72 hours post-disaster (DHS), which is the anticipated time for emergency personnel to be able to access all areas of a disaster site.

The 72-hour guideline includes planning to handle issues of safety, security, comfort, and well-being. This consists of anticipating health and mental health needs, shelter and security, as well as social needs, such as being able to access and locate family members or support networks. These needs are met differently depending on the circumstances of the individual, environment, and available resources. For example, a healthy, single adult may have fewer concerns about taking care of himself or herself than an elderly person who has mobility issues. Families with adequate financial resources may not hesitate to evacuate to another city where they can afford to stay in a hotel for a week or two until they are able to return to their home. The thought of evacuation may be very different for a person with a lower income who is unsure about the ability to secure his or her property, or stay in a hotel if he or she is unable to locate public shelters.

During the hurricane seasons of 2004 (e.g., Hurricane Ivan) and 2005 (e.g., Hurricane Katrina), hundreds of thousands of people along the Gulf Coast were challenged by a set of health threats in the aftermath of the hurricanes. Such threats include dehydration and malnutrition resulting from limited safe food and water supplies and energy loss (Few, 2007). Subsequent food and waterborne illnesses from contamination of food and water sources and supplies are common, leading to exacerbation of existing health problems due to lack of access to medical care, medicines, and other treatments. Threats also include psychosocial stressors as individuals experience distress due to changes in daily routines, disruption of clinical care, loss of personal comfort measures, and overcrowded shelter conditions (Callaghan et al., 2007). These losses can dramatically increase when such events occur in less-developed areas or areas with a high percentage of persons living within a lower socioeconomic status.

Current recommendations frame preparedness utilizing an all-hazards approach. The all-hazards approach recognizes that there are response differences among natural disasters, man-made incidents, nuclear incidents, and health care crises, but that the associated consequences are very similar. Universal effects include threat to personal life and safety, separation of families and caregivers, emotional distress, and loss or damage to property. These aftereffects, although differing in specifics, represent common components central to all disasters.

In addition to providing a standardized guide for individuals, the all-hazards approach provides a common framework for those responsible for establishing preparedness recommendations. Working from a unified perspective provides great benefits when integrating multilevel preparedness and response systems.

A common framework optimizes resources by providing a template for guiding education, information, and training, while maintaining the capability of adapting to individual scenarios (Adini, Goldberg, Cohen, Laor, & Bar-Dayan, 2012).

Disaster response historically has been handled at the local level, with federal assets only being requested in large-scale events. Personal preparedness was a concept initiated within the individual, with little prompting from outside entities. Even large-scale hurricanes like Andrew in 1992 and Floyd in 1999 did little to swing responsibility for preparedness from government to the general public. However, beginning in the early 2000s there began a shift in thinking as attention to preparedness activities increased among all levels of government, as well as community organizations and entities.

Perhaps one of the most significant movements to engage the general public in participating in preparedness activities was in 2003. At that time, FEMA as part of DHS launched the *READY* campaign. Designed to raise public awareness about preparedness, the campaign focused on three simple steps:

1. Be informed
2. Make a plan
3. Build a kit

This campaign provides the groundwork for similar campaigns developing from the ARC, CDC, and local and state health departments, as well as special interest organizations targeting populations such as children, older adults, and those with physical disabilities. Within the larger population, subpopulations such as older adults, families with children, and families with individuals who have special health or mental health needs are considered especially vulnerable (Callaghan et al., 2007; Nick et al., 2009; Uscher-Pines, Hausman, DeMara, Heake, & Hagen, 2009). General preparedness guidelines are applicable, but more detailed plans and kits are often necessary to accommodate special needs and circumstances.

Many natural disasters have seasonal patterns; while not predictable, their likelihood is greater during certain times of the year (e.g., Atlantic hurricanes and Pacific cyclones). In the case of hurricanes, cyclones, and typhoons, the process of storm intensification and movement is gradual enough that meteorologists can give advanced warning so that public alerts can be broadcast to communities at risk to initiate disaster response behaviors. However, even for types of disasters with seasonal patterns and where advanced warning is available, it is clear that citizens are not responding to the mass-media messages on disaster preparedness, even when presented in creative ways (see Box 2.1).

Although the FEMA *READY* campaign was launched years prior to storms such as Hurricane Katrina, very few individuals acted on the information and initiated preparedness behaviors. Mass-media campaigns are the most common method to distribute information; however, there is little evidence to date that indicates such mass-media campaigns are effective in changing behaviors. Existing research on whether public education is effective in helping families

BOX 2.1

Are We Being Invaded by Zombies?

In 2011, the CDC got creative with their marketing of preparedness guidelines. While maintaining standard all-hazards preparedness guidelines, they introduced the "Zombie Preparedness" campaign, a series of resources compiling a preparedness toolkit utilizing a fictitious Zombie Apocalypse as the emergency scenario. The toolkit includes a novella following the experience of a couple and their dog as they face the zombies. All-hazards preparedness information and tools are provided to spread the important message about preparedness. The website includes resources and tools for educators to implement the preparedness information in a fun, classroom environment (http://emergency.cdc.gov/socialmedia/zombies.asp).

maintain current plans and implement preparedness behaviors is inconclusive. Most studies have been conducted with small sample sizes and research designs that measure only immediate knowledge gains (Adams & Canclini, 2008; Eisenman et al., 2009; Lujan & Acevedo, 2009). For example, McCormick, Pevear, and Xie (2013) found that there was no significance difference in preparedness levels among those who reported hearing or seeing mass-media announcements and those who stated they did not.

It is evident that the field of preparedness research is shifting, perhaps in response to previous studies on campaign effectiveness. Researchers and agencies are becoming involved in a concerted, although limited, effort to explore preparedness at a deeper level, asking questions about who is prepared and pondering effective interventions to help increase preparedness levels across multiple populations.

WHO IS PREPARED?

Each disaster brings with it a different set of circumstances, along with an opportunity to learn more about preparedness and response. While the frequency of literature on preparedness is beginning to emerge, unfortunately the knowledge base is still in its infancy and the literature is not rigorous in its design. A 2010 review of literature on public health emergency preparedness revealed that available literature is mostly based on surveys and focus groups, with little empirical literature. Research is primarily anecdotal in nature, focusing on planning aspects of preparedness (Yeager, Menachemi, McCormick, & Ginter, 2010), rather than evaluating interventions to increase preparedness or evaluating whether or not preparedness behaviors influence post-event outcomes. But conversations are at least beginning to emerge about the need for systematic methods of inquiry in these areas.

However limited, the literature consistently reveals that the general population as a whole is not prepared for disasters. In 2007 and 2011, the National Center for Disaster Preparedness and Response at Columbia University conducted population surveys to evaluate levels of public preparedness. In some respects, the results indicate that public preparedness levels may be on the increase. In 2007, 43% of families indicated that they had an emergency plan. That number rose to 49% in 2011. However, the numbers fall dramatically when the question probes further to determine if the emergency plan is a completed plan. The survey found that only 35% of citizens had a complete, basic plan, which for this survey includes 2 days of food and water, a flashlight, a portable radio and batteries, emergency phone numbers, and a communication plan that discusses meeting places for family members in case of evacuation or separation (National Center for Disaster Preparedness, 2011). In spite of low levels of preparedness, respondents shared that they were very concerned about the possibility of another major disaster, with 72% stating that they were concerned or very concerned about another terrorist attack.

Unfortunately these results are not uncommon. A study by the ARC found that only 46% of Americans had enough food, water, and medicine to shelter at home if they became sick with pandemic flu. A 2012 survey by the CDC showed more optimistic results in some areas, revealing that 95% of households had a working flashlight and 83% had a 3-day supply of food; however, only 21% had a written evacuation plan, a critical component of a complete emergency plan (CDC 2012). Results from the CDC appear to be more in line with results from the National Center for Disaster Preparedness when accounting for a complete plan that can meet all basic needs post-disaster. Similar survey results appear to be found even when individuals are a part of a high-risk or vulnerable population. Personal disaster preparedness is critical for ensuring efficient utilization of services and essential in mitigating the negative effects of disasters, especially among vulnerable populations such as children, older adults, and persons with special health care needs (Callaghan et al., 2007; Nick et al., 2009; Uscher-Pines et al., 2009).

A survey of 857 adult patients presenting to the emergency department found that only 53% had a plan that included greater than 75% of basic checklist items, and only 46% had enough food and water to be self-sustaining for 3 days (True, Adedoyin, Shofer, Hasty, & Brice, 2013). Baker and Baker (2010) found that families with children of special health care needs were no more prepared than the general population, even though they are a population more vulnerable to negative outcomes. The findings of this study were consistent with similar studies concluding that most families are not prepared to be self-sufficient for 3 days following a disaster. Specifically, the study found that over 88% of families did not have a personal disaster kit and over 90% did not have a family communication plan. In addition, over 80% of families did not have an emergency medical plan for their children, even though 50% of families included a child who had multiple health care needs. Concern about potential disasters remained high, particularly for severe weather and power outages, even though few families had completed recommended preparedness tasks (Baker & Baker, 2010). When evaluating the behaviors necessary to establish adequate preparedness, personal planning for disasters is more difficult than simply stockpiling resources (Baker & Baker, 2010; Eisenman et al., 2009; Murphy, Cody, Frank, Glik, & Ang, 2009).

As a result of the slowly growing preparedness literature base, we are beginning to appreciate characteristics between those who are prepared and those who are less prepared. Kohn and colleagues (2012) reviewed the literature base on personal preparedness and found common characteristics among persons with higher levels of preparedness. These characteristics are also discussed in similar studies. For example, age is a factor in levels of preparedness. The older the age of the individual, the more likely he or she is to be prepared. However, this factor peaks after age 30, declining as persons progress to elderly ages (True, Adedoyin, Shofer, Hasty, & Brice, 2013). Individuals with a higher education and higher incomes, and married couples with children, are more likely to be prepared (CDC, 2012; McCormick, Pevear, & Xie, 2013), as well as individuals who own their homes. Although minorities are often less prepared prior to an event, some studies indicate that post-event preparedness levels are not influenced by race and ethnicity (True, Adedoyin, Shofer, Hasty, & Brice, 2013).

When it comes to predicting factors that might indicate higher preparedness levels, the literature again provides some insight. It is easy to perceive that the level of concern may motivate individuals to become more prepared; however, we know that is not always the case. As the National Center on Preparedness indicates, individuals are concerned about future disasters, but not always to the point of initiating preparedness behaviors. Baker and Baker (2010) confirmed this finding when they found that perceived risk and level of concern about future disasters was not associated with an increase in completion of preparedness tasks. It appears that individuals recognize the importance of being prepared, but do not initiate the behaviors necessary to become prepared. Even persons who live in areas of greater geographic risk do not demonstrate higher levels of preparedness than the general population (Baker & Cormier, 2013).

Some literature is emerging, however, that indicates a past experience with a devastating disaster may impact preparedness levels. In a survey of over 1,500 Jefferson County, Alabama, residents, researchers found that only 39% of the sample populations had a completed disaster kit (McCormick, Pevear, & Xie, 2013). In 2011, Jefferson County was part of a historic tornado outbreak involving EF-4 and EF-5 category storms that swept throughout the Alabama region. A follow-up study with the same population found that over 86% reported that they had thought more about preparedness after the event and 60% reported taking steps to increase individual preparedness. Results from the follow-up study reflect that 66% of individuals sampled had a completed disaster kit as opposed to the 39% in the early survey (McCormick, Pevear, Rucks, & Ginter, in press). These findings indicate that firsthand experience with devastating storms may have a stronger influence on preparedness behaviors than simply being concerned about potential disasters. A similar study by Chen, Banerjee, and Liu (2012) surveyed individuals in a high-risk geographic area about preparedness levels. Participants were asked whether or not they were aware of potential emergencies and had an evacuation plan and minimal available resources, prior to and 1 year after a major hurricane. Researchers found no differences in pre- and post-preparedness; however, it should be noted that the population reported basic preparedness levels higher than the general population, with 70% of respondents stating that they had an evacuation plan.

BARRIERS TO PREPAREDNESS

The reasons why persons do not take steps to become prepared are complex. They include socioeconomic circumstances, demographic characteristics, social and psychological reasons, and functional limitations. Levac, Toal-Sullivan, and O'Sullivan (2012) discuss that there are many factors that influence individual preparedness levels. Apparent threat and concern do not appear to be significant on their own, but rather influenced by the perceived intensity of the event and personal significance. Persons are influenced by their responsibilities, especially those who are caregivers to others. Caregivers appear to be more likely to engage in preparedness behaviors to protect those that they care for (Diekman, Kearney, O'Neil, & Mack, 2007).

We know that mass-media messaging is not especially effective in increasing preparedness levels, but knowledge itself is a factor. Persons need to have at least minimal exposure to information on becoming prepared. Past general knowledge variables such as self-efficacy and motivation become influencers. Persons with an internal locus of control will perceive that they are capable of taking necessary actions and believe those behaviors will impact their ability to successfully handle a disaster scenario. Persons with an external locus of control will believe that being prepared will not increase their likelihood of a successful outcome and that they have no control over what happens. These belief systems need to be considered in preparedness planning, as they can significantly influence success or failure of interventions.

Taking the steps to become prepared requires significant personal and financial resources. Persons who have difficult social situations and limited resources have a harder time implementing the steps necessary to be prepared. Persons on a limited income oftentimes find it difficult to stockpile extra food and water, and insurance companies may not always pay for extra supplies of medications. While it is ideal to have a complete kit with extra supplies, life circumstances could make that difficult. In such situations, it is important that special assistance be provided to help individuals increase their level of preparedness.

Literature is beginning to emerge that highlights interventions at a personal level to increase preparedness levels, especially among vulnerable populations. Interventions that are most effective include personal elements and individual attention (Adams & Canclini, 2008; Baker & Baker, 2010; Baker, Baker, & Flagg, 2012; Eisenman et al., 2009; Lujan & Acevedo, 2009). Although these studies rely on providing the same education elements as current mass-media campaigns, they provide the information utilizing socially informal contexts. One study in particular evaluated the effectiveness of utilizing small group discussion and social networks moderated by health promoters, in comparison to culturally appropriate media-only delivery, to provide disaster preparedness education to a Latino community. Preparedness levels at follow-up were greater in the group that received information through the health promoter/small group modality as opposed to the media-only group (Eisenman et al., 2009). However, it is important to recognize that other societal barriers need to be addressed before expectations about preparedness are imposed. Honore (2008) discusses that a reduction in health disparities is necessary prior to reducing the challenges faced by the medically disadvantaged in acting on preparedness behaviors.

Is Preparedness Effective?

As mentioned throughout this chapter, there is little research on evidence-based interventions to increase preparedness levels; however, there is even more of a scarcity of research evaluating whether preparedness levels influence outcomes. However, the literature that does exist suggests that preparedness is beneficial. In 2012, researchers conducted a survey of residents of Joplin, Missouri, and Tuscaloosa, Alabama, 1 year after the deadly 2011 tornado outbreak. The outbreak spawned category EF-4 and EF-5 tornados that were responsible for 220 fatalities and over 2,500 injuries. Researchers found that residents who have an emergency preparedness communication plan were more likely to seek shelter prior to the storm as compared to those without a plan. Having a communication plan increased the odds of taking shelter by 76% to 143%, when controlling for other variables such as age, education level, marital status, and functional limitations (Cong, Liang, & Luo, 2014).

Further study needs to be conducted in this area. Significant resources are expended in order to prepare individuals, communities, and governments to self-sustain following a disaster. While common theory implies that preparedness is definitely a factor in improving outcomes, empirical evidence to this effect strengthens the argument.

PREPAREDNESS GUIDELINES

As previously mentioned, the general guidelines indicate that persons should be able to be self-sustaining for a period of 72 hours post-disaster, regardless of the type of disaster. General preparedness involves three significant clusters of behaviors, including being informed, making a plan, and building a kit. The specifics of each of these three components are detailed in Table 2.1. It is important to note that the guidelines presented in this chapter apply to the general population. Populations that fall under the category of "vulnerable" populations will have additional guidelines and recommendations specific to their needs. Specific guidelines for vulnerable populations are discussed in subsequent chapters.

TABLE 2.1 Preparedness Guidelines for the General Population

BE INFORMED

- Be aware of the types of disasters that occur in your area and county warning procedures, evacuation plans, and shelters before disaster strikes
- Learn differences in potential emergencies and how they may impact decisions about how to respond and prepare, including
  - Natural disasters
  - Technological and accidental hazards
  - Terrorism and other acts of violence
  - Pandemic outbreaks such as influenza
  - Home fires
- Identify hazards in your area
- Be aware of alert and warning systems for neighborhood, workplace, schools, and other locations
- Know the difference between disaster alerts and what action to take in each situation
- Be aware of evacuation procedures in your workplace or schools; know the location of fire extinguishers and emergency alarms
- Monitor television, radio, Internet, and social media news reports as able for information from authorities on local conditions and official instructions
- Know your community's response and evacuation plans
- Be aware of ways to safeguard your property ahead of time in case evacuation becomes necessary

MAKE A PLAN

General
- Involve in planning all family and friends who are involved in implementation
- Review plan as needs and circumstances change
- Practice your plan once a year or when circumstances change
- Have at least one person in the household certified in first aid and cardiopulmonary resuscitation (CPR)

Sheltering in Place and Evacuation
- Develop a plan to shelter in place in the event that you are unable to evacuate or are advised by officials to stay where you are
  - Ensure all family members are aware of the shelter-in-place location, including alternate locations if they cannot make it home
  - Know how and when to turn off water, natural gas, and electricity at the main switches; keep needed tools available; provide these instructions to members of your personal support network
  - Keep a disaster kit available
  - Keep closed-toe shoes, bike helmets, and other protective gear in an accessible location

- Develop a plan to evacuate
  - Plan two ways out of every room
  - Always evacuate if you are instructed by official personnel
  - Know how and when to turn off water, natural gas, and electricity at the main switches; keep needed tools available; provide these instructions to members of your personal support network
  - Include contact information for utility companies in your evacuation kit
  - Follow recommendations for mitigating potential impairments for evacuating: bolt bookshelves to walls; anchor outdoor items that can be projectiles in high winds and hurricanes; install hurricane shutters (if appropriate to area); trim trees that overhang roofs; repair cracks in ceilings and foundations; store flammable materials away from heat sources
  - Decide on transportation, route, and points of contact if separated
  - Allow plenty of time
  - Have your disaster kit available and ready to travel
  - Be aware of automobile safety
    - Have car fueled in case evacuation is necessary
    - Do not drive through flooded areas or near fallen power lines

(continued)

TABLE 2.1 Preparedness Guidelines for the General Population (*continued*)

- Make sure each car has a separate emergency kit containing:
  - Jumper cables
  - Flashlights with extra batteries
  - First aid kit
  - Nonperishable food such as canned food (with can opener, snacks, energy bars)
  - Water (1 gallon per person per day)
  - Basic toolkit
  - Shovel, ice scraper
  - Change of clothes
  - Blankets
  - Charged cell phone and car phone charger
  - Flares or reflective triangle
  - Decide beforehand if possible which area shelters are available
  - Register on the American Red Cross (ARC) "Safe and Well" website when you arrive at your destination
  - Be aware of medical needs and special population shelters if applicable
  - Be aware of shelters/vets, etc., that will take animals if you have pets

Communication—Family, Friend, and Neighbor Communication Plan

- Develop a communication plan that outlines how to contact family members and other contacts in case of emergency
  - List phone numbers of all family members
  - List alternate phone numbers of friends and neighbors who may be able to assist
  - List contact information for one out-of-state friend or family member
- Ensure that each family member with a cell phone has designated an "I.C.E." (In Case of Emergency) contact in his or her cell phone contact list
- Pick a meeting spot for joining up with family and friends, including
  - Inside your neighborhood
  - Outside your neighborhood (such as library, church, community center, etc.)
- Review and revise communication plan yearly to update contact information
- Make a copy of the plan for each person that can be folded and put in pocket or wallet

BUILD A KIT

- Build a basic disaster supply kit and store in an accessible location
- Kit should include the following supplies:
  - Water—one gallon per person for at least 3 days
  - Food—3-day supply of nonperishable food items with can opener (if needed)
    - Include paper plates and utensils
  - Battery-powered or hand-crank radio and a National Oceanic and Atmospheric Administration (NOAA) weather radio with extra batteries
  - Flashlight and extra batteries
  - First aid kit
    - Include nonprescription medications (pain relievers, antacids, etc.)
    - Extra prescription medications if applicable
  - Whistle to signal for help
  - Dust mask, plastic sheeting, and duct tape to seal house if needed
  - Personal hygiene items (toothpaste, soap, shampoo, feminine items, etc.)
  - Bathroom tissue, paper towels
  - Moist towelettes, garbage bags, and ties for personal sanitation
  - Supplies for pets (if applicable)
  - Small cash supply
  - Extra clothing
  - Towels, blankets
  - Chlorine bleach

(*continued*)

TABLE 2.1 Preparedness Guidelines for the General Population (*continued*)

○ Fire extinguisher
○ Small repair kit (screwdriver, hammer, or multipurpose tool and nails)
○ Pencil and paper
• Kits should also include the following documents (in secure, waterproof container or on password-protected flash drive):
○ Copies of communication plan
○ Copies of driver's licenses, ID badges, social security cards, birth certificates, and other important identification papers
○ Current photos of family and pets for identification
○ Copies of credit cards with contact phone numbers
○ Copies of prescriptions
○ Immunization records
○ Insurance policies (including auto, home, etc.)
○ Wills and guardianship documents if applicable
○ Bank account information
○ Computer file backup if applicable
○ Deeds and mortgage papers
○ Maps of the area
• Update disaster supply kit at least once a year
○ Review documents and plans for any changes
○ Change out food and water: check for expired items

Sources: Alabama Department of Public Health (2014); American Red Cross (ARC, 2014); Federal Emergency Management Agency (FEMA, 2014).

SUMMARY AND CONCLUSIONS

Disaster preparedness is a necessary component in mediating and moderating negative effects of disasters. However, preparedness is not always an easy task. Implementing all of the recommended tasks necessary for adequate preparedness against any hazard is often met with significant personal, financial, and societal barriers. Some populations have a more difficult time in initiating the steps to preparedness due to their income, health and mental health status, mobility needs, lack of social support network, and limited knowledge of expectations. Persons may not always know where to go for help in order to complete these tasks and access information when the disaster strikes. Research tells us that previous history with a disaster, level of need, geographic locations, and other variables do little to increase behaviors with at-risk populations. While it is clear that mass-media messaging has limited effectiveness in promoting behavior change, we also know that individual and targeted interventions are beginning to make a difference.

Future research in the area of preparedness should continue to establish empirical evidence for the use of interventions increasing preparedness levels, especially with vulnerable populations. Longitudinal studies should be conducted to further investigate how preparedness behaviors pre-event translate to response behaviors, and the significance of the impact post-event. While some beginning steps have been taken, the field is poised for continuation of these important questions.

REFERENCES

Adams, L. M., & Canclini, S. B. (2008). Disaster readiness: A community-university part-nership. *Online Journal of Issues in Nursing, 13*(3). Retrieved February 26, 2014, from http://www.nursingworld.org/MainMenuCategories/ANAMarketplace/ANA Periodicals/OJIN/TableofContents/vol132008/No3Sept08/ArticlePreviousTopic /DisasterReadiness.aspx

Adini, B., Goldberg, A., Cohen, R., Laor, D., & Bar-Dayan, Y. (2012). Evidence-based support for the all-hazards approach to emergency preparedness. *Israel Journal of Health Policy Research.* Retrieved February 16, 2014, from http://www.ijhpr.org /content/1/1/40

Alabama Department of Public Health. (2014). *Are you ready?* Retrieved March 4, 2014, from http://www.adph.org

American Red Cross. (2014). *Plan and prepare.* Retrieved March 4, 2014, from http://www .redcross.org/prepare

Baker, L., & Cormier, L. (2013). Disaster preparedness and families of children with spe-cial needs: A geographic comparison. *Journal of Community Health, 38*(1), 106–112. doi:10.1007/s10900-012-9587-3

Baker, L., & Baker, M. (2010). Disaster preparedness among families of children with spe-cial healthcare needs. *Disaster Medicine and Public Health Preparedness, 4*(3), 240–245. doi:10.1001/dmp.2010.28

Baker, M. D., Baker, L. R., & Flagg, L. E. (2012). Preparing families of children with special healthcare needs for disasters: An education intervention. *Social Work in Health Care, 51*(5), 417–429. doi:10.1080/00981389.2012.659837

Callaghan, W. M., Rasmussen, S. J., Jamieson, D. J., Ventura, S. J., Farr, S. L., Sutton, P., . . . Posner, S. F. (2007). Health concerns of women and infants in times of natural disasters: Lessons learned from Hurricane Katrina. *Maternal and Child Health Journal, 11*, 307–311.

Centers for Disease Control and Prevention. (2012, September 14). Household prepared-ness for public health emergencies-14 states, 2006–2010. *Morbidity and Mortality Weekly Report, 61*(3), 713–722.

Chen, V., Banerjee, D., & Liu, L. (2012). Do people become better prepared in the after-math of a natural disaster? The Hurricane Ike experience in Houston, Texas. *Journal of Public Health Management and Practice, 18*(3), 241–249. doi:10.1097/PHH.0b013e 31822d4beb

Cong, Z., Liang, D., & Luo, J. (2014). Family emergency preparedness plans in severe tornados. *American Journal of Preventive Medicine, 46*(1), 89–93. doi:10.1016/j.amepre .2013.08.020

DeLuca, M. (2013, April 13). Boston transit shut down, nearly 1 million sheltering in place amid terror hunt. Retrieved October 23, 2013, from http://usnews.nbcnews. com/_news/2013/04/19/17822687-boston-transit-shut-down-nearly-1-million -sheltering-in-place-amid-terror-hunt?lite

Diekman, S. T., Kearney, S. P., O'Neil, M. E., & Mack, K. A. (2007). Qualitative study of homeowners' emergency preparedness: Experiences, perceptions and practices. *Prehospital and Disaster Medicine, 22*(6), 494–501. doi:10.1017/S1049023X00005318

Eisenman, D. P., Glik, D., Gonzalez, L., Maranon, R., Zhou, Q., Tseng, C., & Asch, S. (2009). Improving Latino disaster preparedness using social networks. *American Journal of Preventive Medicine, 37*, 512–517. doi:10.1016/j.amepre.2009.07.022

Federal Emergency Management Agency. (2014, February 4). *Ready: Prepare, plan, stay informed.* Retrieved March 4, 2014, from http://www.ready.gov

Few, R. (2007). Health and climatic hazards: Framing social research on vulnerability, response and adaptation. *Global Environmental Change, 17,* 281–295. doi:10.1016/j .gloenvcha.2006.11.001

Ford, B., Smith, G., & McShane, L. (2013). *Police narrow in on two suspects in Boston Marathon bombings.* Retrieved February 2, 2014, from http://www.nydailynews.com/news /national/injury-toll-rises-marathon-massacre-article-1.1319080

Honore, R. L. (2008). Health disparities: Barriers to a culture of preparedness. *Journal of Public Health Management Practice, 14*(6), s5–s7. doi:10.1097/01.PHH.0000338381 .29071.d6

Kohn, S., Lipkowitz Eaton, J., Feroz, S., Bainbridge, A., Hoolachan, J., & Barnett, D. (2012). Personal disaster preparedness: An integrative review of the literature. *Disaster Medicine and Public Health Preparedness, 6*(3), 217–231. doi:10.1001/dmp.2012.47

Kotz, D. (2013, April 24). Injury toll from Marathon bombs reduced to 264. Retrieved October 13, 2013, from http://usnews.nbcnews.com/_news/2013/04/19/17822687- boston-transit-shut-down-nearly-1-million-sheltering-in-place-amid-terror -hunt?lite

Levac, J., Toal-Sullivan, D., & O'Sullivan, T. (2012). Household emergency prepared- ness: A literature review. *Journal of Community Health, 37,* 725–733. doi:10.1007 /s10900-011-9488-x

Lujan, J., & Acevedo, S. (2009). Development and testing of a communication card for emergency and disaster preparedness for monolingual Spanish-speaking individu- als with low literacy. *Internet Journal of Rescue and Disaster Medicine, 8*(2). Retrieved February 16, 2014, from http://ispub.com/IJRDM/8/2/6286

Magee, D. (2014, January 29). Birmingham's perfect (Snow) storm: 5 reasons the region slid to a halt. Retrieved February 2, 2014, from http://blog.al.com/spotnews/2014/01 /birminghams_perfect_snow_storm.html

McCormick, L. C., Pevear, J., Rucks, A. C., & Ginter, P. M. (in press). The effects of the April 2011 Tornado outbreak on personal preparedness in Jefferson County, Alabama. *Journal of Public Health Management and Practice.*

McCormick, L. C., Pevear, J., & Xie, R. (2013). Measuring levels of citizen public health emergency preparedness, Jefferson County, Alabama. *Journal of Public Health Management and Practice, 19*(3), 266–273. doi:10.1097/PHH.0b013e318264ed8c

Murphy, S. T., Cody, M. C., Frank, L. B., Glik, D., & Ang, A. (2009). Predictors of prepared- ness and compliance in natural disasters and terrorist attacks. *Disaster Medicine and Public Health Preparedness, 3,* S1–S9.

National Center for Disaster Preparedness. (2011). The American Preparedness Project: Where the US public stands in 2011 on terrorism, security and disaster prepared- ness. Retrieved February 16, 2014, from http://hdl.handle.net/10022/AC:P:13579

Nick, G. A., Savoia, E., Elqura, L., Crowther, M. S., Cohen, B., Leary, M., Wright, T., . . . Koh, H. K. (2009). Emergency preparedness for vulnerable populations: People with special health-care needs. *Public Health Reports, 124*(2). 338–343.

True, N. A., Adedoyin, J. D., Shofer, F. S., Hasty, E. K., & Brice, J. H. (2013). Level of disaster preparedness in patients visiting the emergency department: Results of the civilian assessment of readiness for disaster (CARD) survey. *Prehospital Disaster Medicine, 28*(2), 127–131. doi:10.1017/S1049023X12001811

Uscher-Pines, L., Hausman, A., DeMara, P., Heake, G., & Hagen, M. G. (2009). Disaster preparedness of households with special needs in southeastern Pennsylvania. *American Journal of Preventive Medicine, 37*(3), 227–230. doi:10.1016/j.amepre.2009 .04.028

West, T. (2014, January 29). *Snowstorm leaves thousands stranded on roads, at offices and schools.* Retrieved February 2, 2014, from http://www.bizjournals.com/birmingham/news/2014/01/29/snowstorm-leaves-thousands-stranded-on.html

Yeager, V. A., Menachemi, N., McCormick, L., & Ginter, P. M. (2010). *The nature of public health emergency preparedness literature 2000–2008: A quantitative analysis. Journal of Public Health Management Practice, 16*(5), 441–449. doi:10.1097/PHH.0b013 e3181c33de4

CHAPTER

3

Crisis Intervention
and the Mental Health Response

CASE STUDY: The Responders

Marvin Rodriquez, a 34-year-old paramedic from Philadelphia, is concerned about his recent emotional health. He lives with his wife of 7 years and their twin daughters. The previous year he had been part of a team of first responders who supplemented New York City resources in response to the terrorist attacks on the World Trade Center (WTC) and surrounding area. Marvin worked at the site of the WTC at ground zero for 10 days beginning immediately after the event. He witnessed devastating loss of life and property and received little satisfaction by finding survivors. At the end of the 10 days, Marvin returned home and continued in his position in Philadelphia. He rarely spoke to his wife or other colleagues about his experience and felt that since he was not living close to the impact zone, he should not be affected. Now almost a year later, Marvin has started having recurring dreams about the attacks and is having difficulty sleeping and eating. In addition, he often finds himself becoming angry at slight provocations and is having difficulty concentrating at work.

Responding to the mental health needs of disaster victims takes a special skill set. The responder must have a strong understanding of crisis intervention theory and understand how those models apply in a disaster situation. While many people encounter traumatic circumstances equating to crisis in everyday life, disaster situations pose a distinct set of circumstances. Tremendous issues of loss, including loss of life, property, livelihood, routine, community, and independence, characterize disasters. These issues alone are multifaceted; however, they can become more complex when factoring in variables such as low socioeconomic status, prior level of functioning, capacity of support networks, and cultural and religious beliefs.

A capable responder integrates methods addressing all factors while providing the tools needed to help victims begin the process of healing and restoration.

With the expansion of disaster mental health services and increase in numbers of professional responders, there has been a subsequent upsurge in literature discussing disaster mental health response. Articles are surfacing that provide a narrative of the responder's perspective, response environments, and necessary personal characteristics. One example is a 2010 article by Dass-Brailsford discussing characteristics of an effective crisis responder. According to the literature, a competent responder thinks and acts quickly, processing large amounts of information and problem solving in different and creative ways. Since responders do not always have the available resources present in a clinical setting, they must be willing to frame issues and responses within the context of available, often limited, resources. They must recognize sometimes obscure opportunities to assist the victims in gaining control and mastery over immediate tasks necessary for stabilization and recovery, all the while portraying a sense of calm, demonstrating empathy, and maintaining healthy boundaries among those they serve as well as among other responders and organizations. Mental health responders are not always responsible solely for the mental health needs of victims, but frequently support other responders.

Shelby and Tredinnick (1995) state that it is important to implement interventions that empower clients and provide immediate supports improving client functioning. In contrast to service delivery in traditional settings, disaster response involves more physical interaction with the victims through hugging, hand-holding, and shoulder touching. These forms of physical interaction may be inappropriate with clients in a traditional clinical setting, but seem appropriate in the post-disaster setting (Shelby & Tredinnick, 1995). The mental health responder should be particularly aware that disaster response consists of long hours in suboptimal environments that are physically and emotionally demanding (Adams, 2007; Kaul, 2002). Responders should work well in a team context and independently, as there is often little access to direct supervision. As discussed in Chapter 1, persons interested in pursuing work as a disaster responder should seek the necessary training to be able to effectively respond in such situations (Bartley, 2007; Kaul, 2002).

In a perfect world, responders intervene with a small group of people, provide ongoing support and counseling, refer to appropriate follow-up resources, and track the progress of their intervention. However, disaster mental health and crisis response is unique. Responders are faced with providing "one-session" counseling in settings that include crowded shelters, makeshift clinics, and many times, simply door to door. Accommodating for these conditions and being aware of the limited time available to provide field interventions are essential. Instead of formal long-term counseling, mental health responders generally provide interventions collectively termed "psychological first aid" (PFA), a Band-Aid approach providing necessary primary services in a short amount of time.

This chapter reviews common techniques for providing post-disaster mental health services to victims in crisis. Covering common psychological effects of disasters from a general perspective, this chapter explores best practices for responding, including an overview of PFA.

COMMON REACTIONS TO STRESS AND TRAUMA

The definition of a crisis is similar to the definition of a disaster, namely, a situation where the current needs exceed the available resources. A crisis situation results in loss of life, property, and livelihood. Crises significantly alter the lives of individuals, families, and communities, creating conditions that exceed a person's ability to not only function, but also endure and succeed. While not all crisis situations occur because of a disaster, a disaster surely can cause crisis situations.

A crisis occurs when a given situation presents obstacles that are insurmountable, exceeding a person's internal and external resources. It is easy to focus on the danger aspects of a crisis, neglecting opportunities to exceed previous limits and expand capacity. Crisis intervention involves implementing interventions that support the victim, provide immediate assistance, and provide concrete resources necessary for stabilization. Lillibridge and Klukken (1978) discuss that crisis can bring about a sense of failure in traditional problem solving, which in turn can lead to panic, confusion, and a feeling of hopelessness. Effective interventions target those feelings to provide centering, clarity, and empowerment.

In order to normalize stress reactions for victims, the responder should have a working knowledge of signs of stress. Common effects of stress include physical, emotional, and behavioral responses (Halpern & Tramontin, 2007; Smith & Segal, 2013). Box 3.1 outlines common stress reactions; however, this list is not exhaustive. Stress responses can include any behavior that is atypical for the person, including a wide variety of physiological and psychological responses.

Stress reactions can occur at any point throughout the crisis and in the weeks and months following. These reactions may be isolated or concurrent with similar reactions. The U.S. Department of Veterans Affairs (2011) discusses three

BOX 3.1

Common Reactions to Stress and Disasters

Emotional responses	Physiological responses	Behavioral responses
Shock and disbelief	Trembling or shaking	Dietary changes
Sadness	Rapid breathing	Isolation
Guilt	Stomach tightening	Hyperarousal to stimuli
Feelings of helplessness	Insomnia	Use of drugs and alcohol
Shame	Racing thoughts	Dependence on others
Anger	Fatigue	Impulsivity
Distress	Nausea/diarrhea	Smoking
Irritability	Muscle tension	
Tearfulness	Headache	
Panic	Edginess	

phases of reactions during a disaster. As with all phased models, it is important to remember that persons do not always progress through the phases in a linear fashion, but often overlap phases or parts of phases as they progress. The three phases include the *impact* phase, the *immediate post-disaster* phase, and the *recovery* phase.

Impact Phase

The *impact phase* is the time period immediately connected to the event. During this phase, persons may react stunned, and thoughts and actions may be disorganized. Persons may not be able to respond to simple commands or coordinate thoughts in order to move toward appropriate actions. Some persons may appear to be "phased" or walking around in a fog. They may exhibit disassociation and have difficulty connecting with those around them. These reactions are brought about by feelings of helplessness, threat of loss of life or repeated trauma, separation from loved ones, and sometimes guilt for not being able to prevent the incident or help those in need.

Immediate Post-Disaster

In the *immediate post-disaster* phase, responders may be able to identify some initial acute mental health effects. Again, the reactions during this phase are varied and it is important to recognize variability as normal, especially when triaging for mental health services. It is not uncommon during this phase to witness persons exhibiting numbness and shock and appearing to be "going through the motion." During this phase, many victims display anger and frustration at their circumstances and at the steps needed for recovery. Flashbacks may also begin to surface. Although flashbacks may be indicative of symptoms of posttraumatic stress disorder (PTSD), it is important to view the flashbacks as what may be symptoms of a normal response. Reactions during this phase may mimic significant mental health disorders; however, they should diminish over time. Persons at this phase are generally overwhelmed and feel hopeless and helpless.

Recovery Phase

As persons move into the final phase, the *recovery phase*, they begin to adjust to the reality that the recovery period may indeed be a long period of adaptation and change. This is the phase where media coverage of the event usually wanes and temporary supports provided are deemed no longer necessary. It is during this phase that the reality of loss and magnitude of long-term needs becomes apparent.

Crisis situations create high levels of stress. Normalization of feelings is a critical component of crisis intervention, as stress is a normal reaction to an abnormal event. Of equal importance is the ability to recognize common triggers that transport the person back to the time and feeling of the original event, generating subsequent stress reactions. For example, the smell of smoke may take a person back to the moment that they experienced a house fire, the sound of an oncoming thunder storm may remind a person of the hours before a tornado touched down, and the sound of a car backfiring may remind a person of the sound of gunfire prior to a mass shooting. Triggers should be recognized and anticipated as a natural part of the recovery process and can be as stress producing as the actual event.

MENTAL HEALTH EFFECTS OF DISASTERS

The field of disaster mental health is relatively young, and literature on long-term effects has not benefitted from a comprehensive knowledge base as has other issues. It is agreed that mental health is an integral part of emergency and medical response (North & Pfefferbaum, 2013); however, what is the extent of mental health needs post-disaster?

In 2002, Norris and colleagues published an empirical review of data including 60,000 disaster victims representing 160 samples to determine psychological distress as well as mediating factors (Norris et al., 2002a). Mediating factors increase the likelihood that negative effects would be present after a precipitating event. As in most disaster literature on mental health effects, the results indicated that symptoms ranged from little effects or minimal effects lasting a short time period, to severe or more significant effects impacting functioning for longer time periods. Similar to literature on stress reactions, there is great variation in what constitutes a "normal" response. The authors found that for most persons symptoms peaked in the first year and tended to improve over time. Norris, Friedman, and Watson (2002b) found in one sample that 11% of the presenting population had minimal impairment, 51% had moderate impairment, and 39% had severe or very severe impairment within the first year post-disaster. These problems included anxiety, depression, PTSD, general psychological distress, acute stress disorder, and stress-related health problems.

However, not all studies reflect the same high levels of negative effects. Studies on populations exposed to the 9/11 WTC attacks find lower levels of severe effects. PTSD symptoms range from 5% to 35% in 1 year post-disaster (Boscarino & Adams, 2008; Yehuda, 2002). Some researchers report probable prevalence of PTSD at 11.2% in the short-term period after the attacks (1 to 2 months) with follow-up indicating that the longer term effects actually increased to 16% 2 to 3 years after the event (Ozbay, Auf der Heyde, Reissman, & Sharma, 2013). These results should be considered in comparison to general population estimates for PTSD, which range from 5% to 6% in men to 10% to 14% in women (Yehuda, 2002). The literature also provides insight into the mental health needs of first responders, who although may not have had a direct impact, have high levels of exposure to the trauma of others. Several studies discuss comorbidity of possible symptoms of PTSD and depression in first responders (Chiu et al., 2011; Fullerton, Ursano, & Wang, 2004) and the subsequent need for mental health support, but not necessarily long-term intervention.

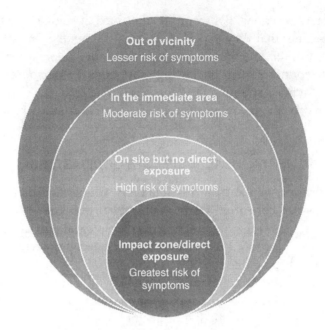

Out of vicinity
Lesser risk of symptoms

In the immediate area
Moderate risk of symptoms

On site but no direct exposure
High risk of symptoms

Impact zone/direct exposure
Greatest risk of symptoms

FIGURE 3.1 Psychological risk zones.

Proximity to the event impacts the risk of a person demonstrating negative effects. Figure 3.1 provides an overview of psychological risk zones, or a diagram of how proximity to the event can influence risk. Persons who are eyewitnesses or have direct exposure to an event are at higher risk to develop symptoms than persons who are in the immediate area but do not have direct exposure or are out of the vicinity entirely. Symptoms may manifest as increases in addictive behaviors or mental health issues. Boscarino and Adams (2008) found that persons with greater exposure to events demonstrated greater levels of alcohol consumption. The increase in alcohol consumption was also associated with concurrent mental health conditions that included anxiety, symptoms of PTSD, and poor overall health, although not all studies support significant increase in alcohol post-disaster (North, Adinoff, Pollio, Kinge, Downs, & Pfefferbaum, 2013).

It is also important to note that symptoms of PTSD are often confused with other disorders, and careful delineation must occur in order to provide accurate treatment. The *Diagnostic and Statistical Manual of Mental Disorders* (5th ed., *DSM-5*; American Psychiatric Association, 2013) clearly defines that in order for symptoms to be classified as PTSD there must be qualifying exposure to a traumatic event. This exposure includes directly experiencing the event with threat of danger, witnessing the event in person, or learning that the event occurred to a family member and included threatened or actual violent or accidental death. North and colleagues (2011) discuss that the presence of a qualifying event is equally as important as geographic proximity in their study of New York City employees affected by the 9/11 attacks on the WTC. Three years post-event PTSD symptoms were present in 35% of those with direct exposure. The authors caution that geographic distance alone is not sufficient to estimate prevalence rates, and that additional factors should be considered when planning for provision of mental health services.

In addition to the proximity of the person to the disaster (psychological risk zone), there are other variables to consider that influence risk for mental health issues post-disaster. For example, the type of disaster plays a role in how the event is viewed and integrated into a person's conceptualization. A disaster that is localized, with confined injuries, loss of life, and limited property damage may be easier to integrate than an event that produces widespread and catastrophic loss of life and property. Ongoing and widespread exposure to traumatic images and devastating circumstances are more difficult to integrate, resulting in psychological fatigue.

The source of the disaster is also significant. Natural disasters that offer warning and an opportunity to secure persons and property have a different effect than random man-made disasters that threaten the sense of personal safety. Disasters such as the WTC attacks and the Oklahoma City bombings result in scenarios where there is repeated exposure to media images of loss of life, suffering, and gruesome realities. Due to the nature of the disaster there is a loss of sense of safety and security, and uncertainty about continued and subsequent attacks. The resulting "hypervigilance" can exhaust coping skills in persons who already are dealing with the stress of the actual event.

In addition to the type of disaster, the location of the event may also be a factor when considering risk of negative outcomes. Osofsy and Osofsy (2013) reported symptoms of depression and PTSD in the 30% to 45% range in the 2 years following Hurricane Katrina. On the surface, those rates look alarmingly higher than the 5% to 14% general population estimates; however, there were precipitating variables. Hurricane Katrina impacted an area that already had high-risk factors for the development of mental health disorders. Multiple risk factors such as race, socioeconomic status, and poverty were present prior to Hurricane Katrina, resulting in a general population demonstrating pre-existing vulnerabilities to mental health issues.

What the limited research consistently shows, however, is that not all crises develop into personal traumas requiring professional intervention. The presence of human resilience and the capacity to adapt should not be discounted. In fact, most persons who experience a disaster will not develop psychological problems or require formal intervention (Bisson, Brayne, Ochberg, & Everly, 2007; Everly & Flynn, 2006). Boscarino and Adams (2008) found that only 10% of adults living in New York City received crisis intervention services in the year following the WTC attacks. Seven percent of the population sampled received those services through their employer, which may be a higher percentage than if the persons solicited services on their own.

Distinguishing between issues occurring as a result of the disaster and those pre-existing is a key task for the mental health responder. North and Pfefferbaum (2013) report that up to 40% of persons reporting to shelters post-disaster for mental health issues had pre-existing issues exacerbated by the event. Therefore, a general guideline to consider is that if a person has mental health issues prior to the disaster, he or she will most likely continue or get worse after the disaster. Consequently, a person without pre-existing mental health issues has a greater likelihood of not needing significant intervention post-disaster to return to his or her prior level of functioning.

Mediating Effects

A mediating effect is a condition or variable that impacts or influences the presence of another condition. Sometimes referred to as risk factors (a factor that increases the probability of an outcome), mediators increase the likelihood that a condition may be present after an event. While not clear predictors, mediators should be used as red flags to identify persons at high risk for mental health issues.

The research is clear that there is empirical support for some risk factors, including gender, age, socioeconomic status, family structure, pre-existing stressors, parental distress, level of exposure to the event, interpersonal conflict, and external locus of control (Adams & Boscarino, 2005; Boscarino & Adams, 2008; Halpern & Tramontin, 2007; Norris et al., 2002b). These factors may influence the presence of symptoms as well as duration and severity. For example, studies find that females have symptoms that are longer lasting and are more severe than males. Persons of low socioeconomic status may have a lower level of education, literacy, and restricted access to financial and personal resources. They are more likely to demonstrate greater levels of distress than those with higher socioeconomic status and access to resources.

Although racial diversity has been previously identified as a risk factor, it is not always supported by research. In some circumstances, minority groups tend to fare better than majority groups. Boscarino and Adams (2008) found no racial or ethnic differences for incidence of PTSD in persons 1 year after the WTC attacks. In fact, African Americans were found to exhibit less depression and did not demonstrate adverse health effects in a study of 2,368 persons 1 year after the WTC attacks (Boscarino & Adams, 2008). Even though race and ethnicity are not always found to be predictors of poor outcomes, the demographic makeup of the geographic location of the disaster may reflect a community that comprises minority populations who are in lower socioeconomic categories. In these instances it is not necessarily race, but socioeconomic status, that generates the risk.

Family factors may also contribute to risk. Boscarino, Adams, and Figley (2004) found that the victim who had a history of child abuse or some other form of previous trauma exhibited greater symptoms and mental health effects post-disaster. In contrast, families and individuals with strong social support networks fare better from a mental health perspective than those with limited or fragmented systems. Positive family dynamics can provide much-needed support after an event. Children will look to parents and older family members to provide clues on response. Children are highly sensitive to such external factors and seek guidance from others on appropriate reactions.

Mediating factors within an event can also pose risks, even though there is great variation in individual impact. The greater the level of exposure to the event, the greater the possibility of experiencing negative outcomes. Victims who experience a high level of loss or significant injury may have a more difficult time of recovery than those who did not suffer a loss or injury. Separation of family members is also a risk factor. Families who need to relocate or who are separated during evacuation efforts may have a more difficult recovery. Reunification of family members is a task that needs to be completed as soon as possible after the event in order to facilitate coping and recovery.

Some degree of stress and resulting mental health issues are always factors to be considered. Along with those reactions, however, come disorders associated with loss of life, namely grief and associated grief disorders. Since disasters often produce issues of loss on multiple levels, it is important to consider how to intervene with grief reactions as a part of any response.

Complicated Grief and Prolonged Grief Disorder

Bereavement and grief are mental health issues common in post-disaster work. There are many sources of grief and loss in a disaster. Loss of life, loss of property, loss of livelihood, and loss of security are just some of the sources. Wells (2006) highlights that temporary or permanent losses may include family members, friends, pets, homes, comfort, and predictability of life. Persons in a post-disaster situation are often not only grieving their own losses, but may also be witnessing death around them or viewing horrifying images. Persons may be interacting with others who have suffered loss and are in the midst of their own grieving process. From an intervention perspective, this section focuses on loss of life; however, responders should be aware that other losses may be present and complicate the grieving process.

Gray, Maguen, and Litz (2004) discuss that traumatic bereavement and complicated grief (or prolonged grief disorder) is one of the lesser-discussed issues post-disaster. Disaster-related grief, or grief that is the result of sudden or violent loss, can create greater psychological disturbance than grief resulting from an anticipated death. In the event of a sudden and violent loss, there is increased risk for subsequent mental health disorders and the recovery period may be longer than with anticipated loss (Kristensen, Weisaeth, & Heir, 2012).

When working with the bereaved, it is important to recognize wide variances in individual adaptation and recovery. In the instance of complicated grief, or grief due to sudden, violent, or multiple losses, persons may exhibit symptoms similar to PTSD. Symptoms may include intense longing for the person who has died and may be accompanied by intrusive thoughts.

Prolonged grief disorder, or profound grieving that exists past 12 months, has been identified in 14% to 76% of the population after disasters (Johannesson et al., 2009; Kristensen et al., 2012; Shear, Jackson, Essock, Donahue, & Felton, 2006). Even though prolonged grief disorder is present in the literature, it remains unrecognized as a diagnosis in *DSM-5* (Bryant, 2013). *DSM-5*, however, does list persistent complex bereavement disorder as a condition for further study, reflecting criteria similar to prolonged grief disorder such as persistent yearning and longing for the deceased, intense sorrow, emotional pain, and preoccupation with the circumstances of the death (*DSM-5*). These symptoms must have persisted for at least 12 months in order to be categorized as a grief disorder. This time frame suggests that there is a significant time window for grief symptoms to be present without indicating pathological signals.

The knowledge base for the treatment of grief shows promising results. Wittouck, Van Autreve, DeJaegere, Portzky, and van Heeringen (2011) conducted a meta-analysis of published interventions for the prevention and treatment of complicated grief. The authors concluded that interventions aimed at the *prevention* of grief were not effective. Healthy grieving is part of a healing process; therefore it may not be necessary to try to prevent the grief response. However, short- and long-term interventions aimed at the *treatment* of complicated grief show some success. Interventions aimed at alleviating bereavement symptoms include cognitive behavioral therapy, interpersonal therapy, and motivational interviewing (Simon, 2013). While the literature supports the use of such interventions, it is important to apply them in the context of a comprehensive assessment. Some studies indicate that in cases of nontraumatic grief such interventions are not significantly more effective than no treatment. However, these interventions may be more effective than no treatment in cases of traumatic grief (Lilienfeld, 2007). These findings suggest that care must be taken to distinguish the type of grief before a longer term intervention is initiated. Cognitive behavioral therapy, interpersonal therapy, and motivational interviewing are all interventions that function best within the context of a prolonged therapeutic relationship, which may not be feasible post-disaster.

In the case of disaster work, responders should implement immediate or early interventions with short-term effectiveness to initiate a health grieving process. Gray and colleagues (2004) provide such guiding principles for early intervention with persons who have experienced a traumatic grief. The principles include (a) refraining from providing formal intervention immediately after the trauma, (b) conducting an initial risk screening and delayed symptom-based screening, (c) utilizing empirically informed early interventions for disaster victims, and (d) assessing and treating traumatic grief. These principles are similar to principles outlined in PFA. In fact, Gray and colleagues (2004) discuss that PFA is an appropriate intervention in the period immediately following the trauma, and that more in-depth formal interventions should be avoided in the early periods. Of equal importance, however, is to screen persons for risk factors that may indicate the potential for a more difficult recovery. Symptoms such as anxiety, tearfulness, and emotional shock are anticipated; however, risk factors such as previous history of mental health issues and low social support network should be noted.

After the initial assessment, it is appropriate to begin to implement empirically informed early interventions that are not long term. These interventions may include psychoeducation and basic anxiety management. Normalization of symptoms is also appropriate at this stage. If a long-term therapeutic relationship is anticipated, the responder may also assess for traumatic grief and possible complications of the grieving process.

Supporting the bereaved in a disaster situation may be different from providing support in everyday clinical practice. In a disaster scenario, family members may be missing who are anticipated to be dead; however, information cannot be confirmed. The responder is often in the position of supporting persons as they await information about loved ones, and must be ready to respond with immediate support if the news of a death is delivered. This waiting time period can be extremely stressful and anxiety provoking. Once a death is confirmed, mental health responders may not only need to provide supportive comfort, but concrete services as well. This includes supportive assistance accepting and processing the information, as well as information about obtaining funeral services and burials. Mortuary and burial services may be complicated by the extent of the geographic damage and compromised community resources. At this point, it is critical to make sure that persons are connected with support systems and available networks capable of providing services. Keep in mind that some bereaved will require long-term interventions; however, this is difficult to assess during the impact and immediate post-disaster phases. Providing supportive and need-based concrete services will provide the initial foundation.

MODELS OF CRISIS INTERVENTION

Crisis scenarios develop in many different contexts, not just in disasters. While the research on disaster-specific response is still developing, research about crisis intervention offers a more established knowledge base. The point at which an individual is experiencing a crisis can be a highly productive time to offer services and support. In fact, some literature suggests that a time of crisis offers a "critical period," or a time when individuals are more receptive and able to receive help (Hoff, 2001). Responders need to be able to recognize these critical times and be able to respond appropriately to provide needed services.

Crisis intervention is a short-term process with specific goals. Different from long-term therapy, crisis intervention is specific and action-oriented. Some of the components of providing crisis intervention are to promote a sense of safety and security at both concrete and psychological levels. Crisis intervention involves exploring the person's experience through active listening, without probing too deeply or asking the person to re-experience the event through detailed dialogue. If the person is too traumatized to talk, the responder can simply provide reassurance and practical assistance. Crisis intervention focuses on identifying and prioritizing current needs, assessing functioning and coping skills, and then providing resources and solutions to address those needs. This may take the form of support, psychoeducation, or linkage to concrete services.

Models of phases of crisis intervention provide some parallel with crisis reactions. Phases in crisis reactions can be aligned with the *impact* phase, *immediate post-disaster* phase, and the *recovery* phases discussed earlier in the chapter.

Dass-Brailsford (2007) outlines a similar phase in crisis intervention including the *acute* phase, the *outward adjustment* phase, and the *integration* phase. During the acute phase, individuals may exhibit common stress reactions that include both physiological and psychological symptoms. It is not unusual to witness persons exhibiting outward grief and anxiety, panic, confusion, and psychological symptoms such as disorientation, shock, numbness, and disbelief. As individuals move through the *acute* phase, they begin to process the reality of the event and begin attempts at mastery and early stages of recovery. It is important to note, however, that this *outward adjustment* phase may begin to appear as early as 24 hours after the event, but varying reactions may indicate a stronger psychological state than is actually occurring. It is not until the *integration* phase that individuals truly begin to be successful at mastery of the situations. During this phase, individuals integrate the new reality and begin to fully make sense of the circumstances initiated by the crisis. They may begin to alter their assumptions of what works in their life and adapt to the new circumstances.

Crisis intervention aims to assist individuals in restoring a sense of equilibrium while restoring psychological functioning. It also aims to minimize the effects of continued trauma or harm while providing emergency and temporary care. Interventions that are applicable in the acute phase are often labeled as first-order interventions. These interventions consist of immediate and short-term intervention such as PFA aimed at stabilizing the situation, establishing safety, meeting immediate physical needs, and providing support. Second-order interventions are more applicable to the outward adjustment and integration phases and consist of providing crisis therapy or longer term therapeutic services once an individual has achieved stabilization (Wiger & Harowski, 2003). Shelby and Tredinnick (1995) discuss the importance of first meeting an individual's basic needs, such as food, shelter, and safety, in order to move the individual from a crisis state to one of strength and resiliency.

It is not uncommon for individuals to move throughout the phases in a nonlinear fashion as information and circumstances change. However, the overall goal is to reduce symptoms of distress and strengthen areas of problem solving and coping. Rosenthal-Gelman and Mirabito (2005) remark that practitioners providing crisis intervention services take on multiple roles, intervening at any system level. This is especially true in disaster work, where affected systems may include micro-, mezzo-, or macrolevels.

James and Gilliland (2005) provide a model of crisis intervention that involves three listening steps and three action steps. These steps are outlined below and provide a nice framework that simplifies the steps involved. Variance in application of the model is dependent on the individual's circumstances, responder expertise, and available resources.

Gilliland's six-step model:

1. Listening
   a. Defining the problem
   b. Ensuring client safety
   c. Providing support

2. Action
    a. Examining alternatives
    b. Making plans
    c. Obtaining commitment

Roberts (2002) and Roberts and Ottens (2005) discuss the use of the Assertive Community Treatment (ACT) intervention model for mental health response. In the Roberts model, the acronym ACT stands for *Assessment*, *Crisis Intervention*, and *Trauma Treatment*. Within the ACT model is a specific section devoted to crisis intervention. The embedded crisis intervention model delineates seven stages for intervening with persons in crisis. Similar to the model posed by Gilliland, the Roberts model focuses on providing a sense of safety and security, problem solving, and emotional support.

Stage 1: Assess Lethality/Conduct Assessment

During this immediate stage, the responder should assess the individual's mental status and assess for risk of suicide or harmful behavior. A biopsychosocial assessment provides a framework for prioritizing concrete medical and psychological needs.

Stage 2: Establish Rapport

Crisis intervention involves providing immediate services within a short time period. In spite of these conditions, the responder should immediately begin to establish a rapport with the person he or she is helping and work to establish a relationship of trust and security.

Stage 3: Identify Problems

Any given crisis can bring about problems on a multitude of levels. Crisis intervention aims to quickly identify problems and dimensions of those problems, and identify challenges present that may make the problems more difficult to solve.

Stage 4: Deal With Feelings

Persons experiencing a crisis should be provided the opportunity to express their feelings. Active listening, reflecting, and paraphrasing are all skills that are useful when working with persons in crisis. A responder should be prepared to deal with intense feelings and emotions and be able to use such skills to provide support and encouragement.

Stage 5: Explore Alternatives

Stage 5 in the crisis intervention stages allows responders to draw on the individual's strengths and resiliency in order to identify coping skills that have worked in the past. As responders help the individual explore alternatives, they are able to draw out resources that the individual brings to use for the next stage, developing a plan.

Stage 6: Develop Action Plan

An action plan provides the individual with a road map for acting on steps to achieve his or her needs. The action plan may identify support systems at an individual or community level as well as provide referrals to receive continued services.

Stage 7: Follow-Up

While follow-up is not always practical and available in a disaster scenario, an ideal component of crisis intervention would be to provide follow-up services and assess progress toward goals. Follow-up should be utilized whenever possible.

INTERVENTIONS FOR DISASTER MENTAL HEALTH

Disaster mental health involves providing needed psychosocial services necessary to help persons return to their pre-event level of functioning. Disaster mental health services can be short term or long term, and delivery concepts may vary depending on individual circumstances. While there are many models of long-term psychosocial intervention, this chapter will focus on early, brief interventions that can be delivered within the context and limitations of immediate disaster response. These interventions in fact may be the most effective in terms of alleviating stress and suffering, and facilitating recovery. Boscarino and Adams (2008) conclude that early, brief interventions that included information and social and spiritual support were very effective. Long-term therapy did not result in better outcomes, but often worse outcomes over time (Boscarino & Adams, 2008).

For decades, psychological debriefing, or critical incident stress debriefing (CISD), was presented as the gold standard for crisis intervention and post-disaster services. Like many crisis intervention models, the goal of this CISD intervention is to decrease stress reactions and facilitate recovery. The intervention is initiated 24 to 78 hours after the incident and utilizes a small-group approach that reviews the facts of the incident, personal thoughts and reactions, discussion of stress symptoms, and education (Mitchell, n.d.; Roberts, Kitchiner, Kenardy, & Bisson, 2010).

CISD, although common, has had mixed results when it comes to the evidence. Early studies that utilize this approach with first responders show some positive results (Chemtob, Tomas, Law, & Cremniter, 1997; Jenkins, 1996). Studies with positive outcomes utilized the method in its intended small-group format and focused on first responders (Mitchell, n.d.; Mitchell & Everly, 1997). However, studies that specifically examine future rates of PTSD find that psychological debriefing is not effective in preventing symptoms and in fact may even worsen symptoms of PTSD in disaster victims (Gray et al., 2004; Lilienfeld, 2007;

Norris et al., 2002b; Roberts et al., 2010; Rose, Bisson, Churchill, & Wessely, 2009). However, research on effective immediate intervention post-disaster is often difficult to conduct due to the nature of a disaster. The variance in delivery methods, difficulty in maintaining long-term contact with victims, and individuality of the disaster event make data collection, randomized controlled trials, and intervention integrity difficult to implement. Although psychological debriefing as a collective method demonstrates mixed results, Mitchell (n.d.) draws parallels with elements of the process to a type of PFA that is delivered in a group setting. Cognizant of the limitations of psychological debriefing, PFA is becoming the recognized preferred model of immediate mental health intervention among first responders.

Psychological First Aid

PFA was first introduced for use in disasters in 1954 by Drayer, Cameron, Woodward, and Glass. As one point on a continuum of care, PFA addresses immediate safety concerns and biopsychosocial needs without providing extensive psychotherapy (Everly & Flynn, 2006). Although the use of PFA does not have an extensive empirical base, it is recognized as an approach that is guided by evidence-based principles, and it is becoming a widely accepted treatment model (Chandra et al., 2014; Fox et al., 2012; Halpern & Tramontin, 2007; NIMH, 2002; Pandya, 2013; Vernberg et al., 2008). The use of PFA shows tremendous promise as an effective intervention; however, it must be stressed that there currently is insufficient evidence to make a definitive conclusion. PFA is currently being utilized as an immediate intervention by organizations such as the U.S. Department of Veterans Affairs, the International Federation of Red Cross and Red Crescent Societies, the American Psychological Association, and Community Emergency Response Teams. Most appropriate in the immediate or early stages of disaster response, PFA is guided by evidence-based principles.

Hobfoll and colleagues (2007) identified five elements of immediate intervention that are evidence-based, and are included in models of PFA. Immediate interventions post-disaster should ensure the following: (a) promote a sense of safety, (b) promote calming, (c) promote sense of self and collective efficacy, (d) promote connectedness, and (e) promote hope.

1. *Promote sense of safety*: Promoting a sense of safety is an important first step in any type of mental health intervention. Persons need to be assured that they will not be subjected to further risk of life or injury. Safety is a relative construct and may include physical and psychological components. Persons need physical safety that may include basic provisions such as food and shelter, but also need psychological safeguards such as control of the flood of information, identifying information about loved ones and their safety, and an interruption in posttraumatic stimulus.

2. *Promote calming*: Persons experiencing a disaster are often in a heightened state of arousal or hyperarousal. By reducing the symptoms of the stress response and promoting a sense of calm, responders are able to move persons to a state where they can better process information and options. It is important to recognize that efforts to decrease the stress response do not need to include lengthy dialogue about the persons' experience. CISD has received criticism for exacerbating the stress response by enhancing the state of arousal through the retelling of the experience. An important element in immediate interventions is to help the person normalize the stress reaction and help to put the reactions in the proper context. Persons who are assisted in viewing stress reactions as appropriate responses to an extraordinary stressor can reframe stress in a productive manner. Helping persons to solve problems and providing psychoeducation can facilitate a sense of control and mastery.

3. *Promote sense of self and collective efficacy*: Once calm, promoting a sense of self and collective efficacy establishes that the person is capable and competent to master the challenges ahead. It is important to provide the persons with a sense that they have the capability to cope with the new stressors. While not everyone may outwardly demonstrate positive coping skills, those skills may be nurtured and reinforced by responders. Self-efficacy should be reinforced with concrete supportive resources that are available and accessible to assist with recovery. True empowerment is only possible if resources are available, and persons should not be misled about availability of resources, especially in locations where community infrastructure may be compromised.

4. *Promote connectedness*: Social connections are particularly important post-disaster, and persons should be assisted in connecting with loved ones and those in their social support system. The process of connectedness helps prevent emotional detachment and facilitates the recovery process. Responders should be able to assess whether social support is positive, which can be healing, or negative, such as those minimizing and invalidating feelings. Negative support systems can be especially counterproductive and destructive at a point where persons are vulnerable.

   Connectedness should also be promoted in a culturally competent manner. Consideration should be made for how social support systems are viewed within cultures, and no connection should be made in a manner that goes against a person's cultural beliefs. Connectedness is also an element that may be facilitated by spiritual resources such as the use of rabbis, chaplains, priests, and other important spiritual leaders.

5. *Promote hope*: The final element integrates previous elements to help promote a sense of hope. It is critical to provide services that foster a sense of hope and help the persons focus on long-term recovery and future-oriented processes.

As one can perceive, the above evidence-guided elements are present in models of PFA. Halpern and Tramontin (2007) assert that there are broad goals of PFA that include such elements. The goals of PFA include:

1. Relieve suffering (physical and emotional)
2. Improve short-term functioning (including decision making)
3. Help survivor's course of recovery (encouraging and enhancing coping)
4. Provide linkage to critical resources

In order to meet those goals, the following actions should be initiated:

1. Attend to physiological needs
2. Attend to safety needs
3. Provide information and orientation to services (including information about loved ones; see Box 3.2)
4. Help clients access social support
5. Assist with traumatic grief

BOX 3.2

Information Overload: How Much Is Too Much?

Psychoeducation, or the provision of information considered a standard component of PFA, is present in additional interventions such as cognitive behavioral therapy and is recommended by the National Institute of Mental Health. Information can provide a sense of control and provide persons with a future reference if needed. However, some studies indicate that when it comes to information, more information is not always better (Brewin, Andrews, & Valentine, 2000; Rubin et al., 2007). In general, persons require basic information and information on how to best access available resources, but often turn to social networks to provide that information.

Information is also a cost-effective intervention, which can be delivered individually or through group settings via one-to-one interventions, media campaigns, community locations, Internet, and social media. Topics may include information on stress reactions, coping mechanisms, stages of loss and grief, and community resources. Delivering current and appropriate information can be a valuable and efficient intervention when utilized appropriately. Responders should be careful to monitor information delivery and look for situations of information overload or increasing stress due to unceasing information streams. Appropriate information may need to be delivered multiple times and in varying formats, including multiple languages, in order to be effective.

These principles are in keeping with recommendations by Yehuda (2002), who discussed that traumatized people need to feel a sense of safety and support, and receive normalization of feelings related to psychobiological reactions to stressors that can be overwhelming. Everly and Flynn (2006) describe these as the "ASACC Principles" of PFA (see Box 3.3).

McCabe and colleagues (2013) describe a model similar to Halpern and Tramontin (2007) and Everly and Flynn (2006) that is based on six PFA competency domains. Providers need to master the following competencies in order to deliver effective actions and meet the intended goals.

> *Competency area #1: Initial contact, rapport building, and stabilization.* Providers should be able to engage in active listening and provide empathy and support in order to provide a sense of comfort and support, and meet immediate psychological needs. They should be able to quickly build rapport and portray a sense of stability to the situation.
>
> *Competency area #2: Brief assessment and triage.* Providers should be able to conduct an initial screening and assessment in order to evaluate baseline functioning and distinguish between functional and dysfunctional behavior. At this point, it is critical to be able to assess for risk of harm to self or others, feelings of desperation and hopelessness, and potential for suicide.

BOX 3.3

"ASACC Principles" of PFA

A—Assessment of need for intervention
S—Stabilize
    Establish rapport
    Identify medical needs
    Meet basic needs
    Assess functional impairment
    Reduce situational stressors
    Provide safety and security
A—Assess and triage
C—Communicate
    Establish supportive presence
    Provide empathic listening and reassurance
    Offer stress management skills
C—Connect
    Refer and connect with support systems

Source: Everly and Flynn (2006).

Competency area #3: Intervention. Providers should utilize available skills
  to help mitigate symptoms of acute distress and fostering, and access
  coping mechanisms.
Competency area #4: Triage. This competency area involves the ability to
  triage persons and distinguish between those who require immediate
  care and those whose care is able to be deferred or referred to another
  professional. Keep in mind that not all persons who present may require
  ongoing care or referral.
Competency area #5: Referral, liaison, and advocacy. In the case of persons
  who require referral services, the provider should be skilled in liaison
  and advocacy services. In post-disaster scenarios, providers must be
  aware of available resources and be prepared to connect persons with
  more intensive services when required. These services may take the
  form of concrete or psychological services and may include long-term
  counseling or immediate intensive counseling for urgent scenarios. This
  competency area also includes the provision of information that may be
  of benefit. Good regulation of information delivery involves assessment
  of the needs of individuals as well as their capacity to process and
  integrate the information for a health outcome.
Competency area #6: Self-awareness and self-care. The disaster responder is often
  the last to recognize his or her limits. Responders are often exposed to
  prolonged images of grief and suffering, difficult living and working
  conditions, and limited resources. As such, it is easy for the responder
  to neglect his or her own needs while he or she is helping others.
  Competency area #6 encourages providers to recognize signs of burnout
  and recognize the effects of vicarious trauma and stress. Whenever
  possible, providers should utilize good self-care principles and recognize
  their limits and necessity to take care of their own needs. It is only through
  good self-awareness and that they will be able to competently serve others.

While the models for PFA discuss similar actions, competencies, and tasks, Gard
and Ruzek (2006) assert that there are specific tasks that coincide with the phases
of recovery. For example, the immediate response phase includes tasks such as
outreach and survivor engagement, facilitating social support and providing
education. The secondary response (recovery) phase also includes facilitating
social support, but adds normalizing responses, problem solving, connecting
with resources, assessment, and follow-up. Gard and Ruzek (2006) also reiterate
that the early days and weeks are best used to identify *risk* of long-term problems, instead of searching for diagnoses.

   Perhaps the most comprehensive model of PFA can be found in the
Psychological First Aid Field Operations Guide (2006) developed by the National
Child Traumatic Stress Network and the National Center for PTSD. The *PFA Field
Guide* provides detailed outlines of the goals, tasks, and actions and was developed as a definitive guide for responders. Table 3.1 summarizes the content of the
guide and presents an outline for delivery that is inclusive of previous models
and competencies discussed.

TABLE 3.1 Overview of PFA

CONTACT AND ENGAGEMENT	
Goal	*To respond to contacts initiated by survivors, or to initiate contacts in a nonintrusive, compassionate, and helpful manner*
Tasks	• Introduce yourself/ask about immediate needs • Maintain highest level of confidentiality as possible
SAFETY AND COMFORT	
Goal	*To enhance immediate and ongoing safety, and provide physical and emotional comfort*
Tasks	• Ensure immediate physical safety • Provide information about disaster response activities and services • Attend to physical comfort • Promote social engagement • Protect from additional traumatic experiences • Help separated family members • Attend to grief and spiritual issues • Provide information about mortuary services • Support survivors involved in body identification
STABILIZATION	
Goal	*To calm and orient emotionally overwhelmed or disoriented survivors*
Tasks	• Stabilize emotionally overwhelmed survivors • Orient emotionally overwhelmed survivors • Assess need for medical referral
INFORMATION GATHERING: CURRENT NEEDS AND CONCERNS	
Goal	*To identify immediate needs and concerns, gather additional information, and tailor PFA interventions*
Tasks	May include: • Nature and severity of experiences during the disaster • Death of a loved one • Concerns about post-disaster circumstances and ongoing threats • Separation from or safety of loved ones • Physical illness, mental health concerns, and medication needs • Losses (home, school, property, pets) • Feelings of guilt or shame • Thoughts of harm to self or others • Availability of social support • Prior alcohol or drug use, or trauma exposure • Specific family concerns
PRACTICAL ASSISTANCE	
Goal	*To offer practical help to survivors in addressing immediate needs and concerns*
Tasks	• Offer practical assistance to children and adolescents • Identify most immediate needs • Clarify the need • Discuss an action plan • Act to address the need

(continued)

TABLE 3.1 Overview of PFA (*continued*)

CONNECTION WITH SOCIAL SUPPORTS	
Goal	*To help establish brief or ongoing contacts with primary support persons and other sources of support, including family members, friends, and community helping resources*
Tasks	• Enhance access to primary support persons • Encourage use of immediately available support persons • Discuss support seeking and giving • Consider special needs of children and adolescents • Model support
INFORMATION ON COPING	
Goal	*To provide information about stress reactions and coping to reduce distress and promote adaptive functioning*
Tasks	• Provide basic information on stress and coping • Review common psychological reactions to trauma and loss • Talk with children about physical and emotional reactions • Provide information on ways of coping • Teach simple relaxation skills • Assist with developmental issues • Address anger and highly negative emotions • Help with sleeping problems • Address alcohol and substance use
LINKAGE WITH COLLABORATIVE SERVICES	
Goal	*To link survivors with available services needed at the time or in the future*
Tasks	• Provide direct link to additional services • Make appropriate referrals for older adults, adolescents, children • Promote continuity in helping relationships

Adapted and included (with permission) from Brymer (2006).

SUMMARY AND CONCLUSIONS

The provision of mental health services post-disaster is a skill that is embraced by responders in varying disciplines. PFA is an accepted model that combines evidence-based principles integrating the concepts of stabilization, assessment, and referral. While there is currently not a strong evidence base to support the specific interventions, it is a cost-effective intervention that is theoretically supported. The concepts are adaptable to different populations and should be sensitive to such differences (Wessely et al., 2008).

In a crisis scenario, cultural competence can often appear to be less important than quick provision of services, but it is known to be an integral part of the acceptance of services and care providers (Ulezi & Jackson, 2010). Rosen, Greene, Young, and Norris (2010) in their review of disaster mental health service projects remind readers that services that are adapted to the unique needs and cultures of the communities have a greater chance of gaining a presence. The authors reiterate that cultural competence includes recognizing and respecting local cultures and customs, being aware of help-seeking behaviors and how those may be addressed through interventions, and involving community leaders and organizations whenever possible to ensure that services are culturally and linguistically competent.

Mental health interventions are most effective when they emphasize that persons are most likely experiencing normal reactions to an abnormal situation. Responders should be careful to avoid mental health terminology and labels, and be cognizant that not all persons experiencing a disaster will require services. Responders should not underestimate the impact of practical assistance and the provisions of basic concrete and psychological services. Responders should work from an assumption of individual competences and resilience, focusing on strengths, personal resources, and potential. The use of established support networks can be utilized in a post-disaster scenario to strengthen individual response and assist in recovery.

Although it is difficult to fully assess the potential for negative outcomes in the immediate and early periods, there are some instances where referrals for ongoing long-term counseling are appropriate. When individuals report severely deteriorated functioning since the event, including inability to feed themselves, care for dependents, or perform simple tasks, a referral for ongoing treatment may be necessary. Individuals who begin abusing illegal substances or who exhibit severe anxiety, outbursts of anger, threats of harm, hearing voices, or uncontrollable crying may require more intensive interventions than are provided immediately. And finally, persons with a pre-existing mental illness, developmental disability, or severe physical illness will require additional resources and connections past the immediate intervention period. As always, it is important that mental health services, including those services provided through PFA, are not forced on a person, and are delivered in a way that respects cultural differences and demonstrates cultural competency.

The literature base on disaster mental health is clearly one of the more developed of disaster topics. However, it is imperative that work continue to strengthen the knowledge and validate interventions. Future research should include empirically designed studies on specific immediate interventions, assessment, and mental health triage in the field, and long-term interventions and follow-up. Each disaster is different, providing more opportunity to learn about effectiveness.

REFERENCES

Adams, L. M. (2007). Mental health needs of disaster volunteers: A plea for awareness. *Perspectives in Psychiatric Care, 43*(1), 52–54.

Adams, R. E., & Boscarino, J. A. (2005). Differences in mental health outcomes among Whites, African Americans, and Hispanics following the September 11 attacks. *Psychiatry, 68*, 250–265.

American Psychiatric Association. (2013). *Diagnostic and statistical manual of mental disorders* (5th ed.). Arlington, VA: American Psychiatric Association.

Bartley, A. G. (2007). Confronting the realities of volunteering for a national disaster. *Journal of Mental Health Counseling, 29*(1), 4–16.

Bisson, J. I., Brayne, M., Ochberg, F. M., & Everly, G. S. (2007). Early psychosocial intervention following traumatic events. *American Journal of Psychiatry, 164*(7), 1016–1019. doi:10.1176/appi.ajp.164.7.1016

Boscarino, J. A., & Adams, R. E. (2008). Overview of findings from the World Trade Center Disaster Outcome Study: Recommendations for future research after exposure to psychological trauma. *International Journal of Emergency Mental Health, 20*(4), 275–290.

Boscarino, J. A, Adams, R. E., & Figley, C. R. (2004). Mental health service use 1-year after the World Trade Center disaster: Implications for intervention and research. *Psychiatry Research, 26,* 346–358. doi:10.1097/NMD.0b013e3182043b39

Brewin, C. R., Andrews, B., & Valentine, J. D. (2000). Meta-analysis of risk factors for PTSD in trauma-exposed adults. *Journal of Consulting and Clinical Psychology, 68,* 748–766. doi:10.1037/0022-006X.68.5.748

Bryant, R. A. (2013). Prolonged grief: Where to after diagnostic and statistical manual of mental disorders, 5th edition? *Current Opinions in Psychiatry.* doi:10.1097/YCO .0000000000000031

Brymer, M., Jacobs, A., Layne, C., Pynoos, R., Ruzek, J., Steinberg, A., . . . Watson, P. (2006). Psychological first aid: Field operations guide (2nd ed.). National Child Traumatic Stress Network and National Center for PTSD. Retrieved November 28, 2013, from http://www.nctsn.org

Chandra, A., Kim, J., Pieters, H. C., Tang, J., McCreary, M., Schreiber, M., & Wells, K. (2014). Implementing psychological first-aid training for medical reserve corps volunteers. *Disaster Medicine and Public Health Preparedness, 27,* 1–6.

Chemtob, C., Tomas, S., Law, W., & Cremniter, D. (1997). Postdisaster psychosocial intervention. *American Journal of Psychiatry, 134,* 415–417.

Chiu, S., Niles, J. K., Webber, M. P., Zeig-Owens, R., Gustave, J., Lee, R., . . . Prezant, D. J. (2011). Evaluating risk factors and possible mediation effects in posttraumatic depression and posttraumatic stress disaster comorbidity. *Public Health Reports, 126,* 201–209.

Dass-Brailsford, P. (2007). *A practical approach to trauma: Empowering interventions* (pp. 93–115). Thousand Oaks, CA: Sage.

Drayer, C. S., Cameron, D. C., Woodward, W. D., & Glass, A. J. (1954). Psychological first aid in community disaster. *Journal of the American Medical Association, 156*(1), 36–41.

Everly, G. S., & Flynn, B. W. (2006). Principles and practice procedures for acute psychological first aid training for personnel without mental health experience. *International Journal of Emergency Mental Health, 8*(20), 1–8.

Fox, J. H., Burkle, F. M., Bass, J., Pia, F. A., Epstein, J. L., & Markenson, D. (2012). The effectiveness of psychological first aid as a disaster intervention tool: Research analysis of peer-reviewed literature from 1990–2010. *Disaster Medicine and Public Health Preparedness, 6*(3), 247–252. doi:10.1001/dmp.2012.39

Fullerton, C. S., Ursano, R. J., & Wang, L. (2004). Acute stress disorder, posttraumatic stress disorder, and depression in disaster or rescue workers. *American Journal of Psychiatry, 161,* 1370–1376.

Gard, B. A., & Ruzek, J. I. (2006). Community mental health response to crisis. *Journal of Clinical Psychology, 62*(8), 1029–1041. doi:10.1002/jclp.20287

Gray, M. J., Maguen, S., & Litz, B. T. (2004). Acute psychological impact of disaster and large-scale trauma: Limitations of traditional interventions and future practice recommendations. *Prehospital and Disaster Medicine, 19*(1), 64–72. doi:10.1017 /S1049023X00001497

Halpern, J., & Tramontin, M. (2007). *Disaster mental health theory and practice.* Belmont, CA: Brooks/Cole.

Hobfoll, S. E., Watson, P., Bell, C. C., Bryant, R. A., Brymer, M. J., Friedman, M. J, . . . Ursano, R. J. (2007). Five essential elements of immediate and mid-term mass trauma intervention: Empirical evidence. *Psychiatry, 70*(4), 283–315. doi:10.1521/psyc.2007 .70.4.283

Hoff, L. A. (2001). *People in crisis: Clinical and public health perspectives* (5th ed.). San Francisco, CA: Jossey-Bass.

James, R. K., & Gilliland, B. E. (2005). *Crisis intervention strategies.* Belmont, CA: Thomson.

Jenkins, S. R. (1996). Social support and debriefing efficacy among emergency medical workers after a mass shooting incident. *Journal of Social Behavior and Personality, 11,* 447–492.

Johannesson, K. B., Lundin, T., Hultman, C. M., Lindam, A., Dyster-Aas, J., Arneberg, P., & Michel, P. O. (2009). The effect of traumatic bereavement on tsunami-exposed survivors. *Journal of Traumatic Stress, 22,* 497–504. doi:10.1002/jts.20467

Kaul, R. E. (2002). A social worker's account of 31 days responding to the Pentagon disaster: Crisis intervention training and self-care practices. *Brief Treatment and Crisis Intervention, 2*(1), 33–37.

Kristensen, P., Weisaeth, L., & Heir, T. (2012). Bereavement and mental health after sudden and violent losses: A review. *Psychiatry, 75*(1), 76–97. doi:10.1521/psyc.2012. 75.1.76

Lilienfeld, S. O. (2007). Psychological treatments that cause harm. *Perspectives on Psychological Science, 2*(1), 53–70. doi:10.1111/j.1745-6916.2007.00029.x

Lillibridge, E. M., & Klukken, P. G. (1978). *Crisis intervention training.* Tulsa, OK: Affective House.

McCabe, O. L., Everly, G. S., Brown, L. M., Wendelboe, A. M., Abd Hamid, N. H., & Tallchief, V. L. (2013). Psychological first aid: A consensus-derived, empirically supported, competency-based training model. *American Journal of Public Health.* Retrieved November 17, 2013, from http://ajph.aphapublications.org/doi/pdf/10.2105 /AJPH.2013.301219

Mitchell, J. T. (n.d.). Critical Incident Stress Debriefing (CISD). Retrieved November 17, 2013, from http://www.info-trauma.org/flash/media-e/mitchellCriticalIncident StressDebriefing.pdf

Mitchell, J. T., & Everly, G. S. (1997). The scientific evidence for Critical Incident Stress Management. *Journal of Emergency Medical Service, 22,* 86–93.

National Institute of Mental Health (NIMH). (2002). *Mental health and mass violence: Evidence-based early psychological intervention for victims/survivors of mass violence.* (NIH Publication No. 02-5138). Washington, DC: Government Printing Office.

Norris, F. H., Friedman. M. J., Watson, P. J., Byrne, C. M., Diaz, E., & Kaniasty, K. (2002a). 60,000 disaster victims speak: Part I. An empirical review of the empirical literature, 1981–2001. *Psychiatry, 65*(3), 207–239. doi:10.1521/psyc.65.3.207.20173

Norris, F. H., Friedman, M. J., & Watson, P. J. (2002b). 60,000 disaster victims speak: Part II. Summary and implications of the disaster mental health research. *Psychiatry, 65*(3), 240–260. doi:10.1521/psyc.65.3.240.20169

North, C. S., Adinoff, B., Pollio, D. E., Kinge, S., Downs, D. L., & Pfefferbaum, B. (2013). Alcohol use disorders and drinking among survivors of the 9/11 attacks on the World Trade Center in New Your City. *Comprehensive Psychiatry, 54*(7), 962–969. doi:10.1016/j.comppsych.2013.03.027

North, C. S., & Pfefferbaum, B. (2013). Mental health response to community disasters: A systematic review. *Journal of the American Medical Association, 310*(5), 507–518. doi:10.1001/jama.2013.107799

North, C. S., Pollio, D. E., Smith, R. P., King, R. V., Pandya, A., Suris, A. M., . . . Pfefferbaum, B. (2011). Trauma exposure and Posttraumatic Stress Disorder among employees of New York City companies affected by the September 11, 2001 attacks on the World Trade Center. *Disaster Medicine and Public Health Preparedness, 5*(2), S205–S213.

Osofsky, H. J, & Osofsky, J. D. (2013). Disaster mental health: Around the world and across time, Hurricane Katrina and the Gulf Oil Spill. *Psychiatric Clinics of North America, 36*(3), 371–383.

Ozbay, F., Auf der Heyde, T., Reissman, D., & Sharma, V. (2013). The enduring mental health impact of the September 11th terrorist attacks: Challenges and lessons learned. *Psychiatric Clinics of North America, 36*(3), 417–429.

Pandya, A. (2013). A review and retrospective analysis of mental health services provided after the September 11 attacks. *Canadian Journal of Psychiatry, 58*(3), 128–134.

Roberts, A. R. (2000). An overview of crisis theory and crisis intervention. In A. R. Roberts (Ed.), *Crisis intervention handbook: Assessment, treatment and research* (2nd ed., pp. 3–30). New York, NY: Oxford University Press.

Roberts, A. R. (2002). Assessment, crisis intervention and trauma treatment: The integrative ACT intervention model. *Brief Treatment and Crisis Intervention, 2*(1), 1–21.

Roberts, A. R., & Ottens, A. J. (2005). The seven-stage crisis intervention model: A road map to goal attainment, problem solving and crisis resolution. *Brief Treatment and Crisis Intervention, 5*(4), 329–339. doi:10.1093/brief-treatment/mni030

Roberts, N. P., Kitchiner, N. J., Kenardy, J., & Bisson, J. I. (2010). Multiple session early psychological interventions for the prevention of post-traumatic stress disorder (Review). *Cochrane Database of Systematic Reviews.* Retrieved November 17, 2013, from http://www.thecochranelibrary.com

Rose, S. C., Bisson, J., Churchill, R., & Wessely, S. (2009). Psychological debriefing for preventing post traumatic stress disorder (PTSD) (Review). *Cochrane Database of Systematic Reviews.* Retrieved November 17, 2013, from http://www.thecochranelibrary.com

Rosen, C. S., Greene, C. J., Young, H. E., & Norris, F. H. (2010). Tailoring disaster mental health services to diverse needs: An analysis of 36 crisis counseling projects. *Health and Social Work, 35*(3), 211–220.

Rosenthal-Gelman, C., & Mirabito, D. M. (2005). Practicing what we teach: Using case studies from 9/11 to teach crisis intervention from a generalist perspective. *Journal of Social Work Education, 41*(3), 479–493.

Rubin, G. J., Brewin, C. R., Greenberg, N., Hacker-Hughes. J. G., Simpron, J., & Wessely, S. (2007). Enduring consequences of terrorism: A seven month follow-up survey of reactions to the bombings in London on July 7 2005. *British Journal of Psychiatry, 190*, 350–356. doi:10.1192/bjp.bp.106.029785

Shear, K. M., Jackson, C. T., Essock, S. M., Donahue, S. A., & Felton, C. J. (2006). Screening for complicated grief among Project Liberty service recipients 18 months after September 11, 2001. *Psychiatric Services, 57*, 1291–1297. doi:10.1176/appi.ps.57.9.1291

Shelby, J. S., & Tredinnick, M. G. (1995). Crisis intervention with survivors of natural disaster: Lessons from Hurricane Andrew. *Journal of Counseling and Development, 73*, 491–497. doi:10.1002/j.1556-6676.1995.tb01784.x

Simon, N. M. (2013). Treating complicated grief. *Journal of the American Medical Association, 310*(4), 416–423. doi:10.1001/jama.2013.8614

Smith, M., & Segal, J. (2013, June). Traumatic stress: How to recover from disasters and other traumatic events. Retrieved November 17, 2013, from www.helpguide.org/mental/disaster_recovery_trauma_stress_coping.htm

Simon, N. M. (2013). Treating complicated grief. *JAMA, 310*(4), 416–423.

Ulezi, N. C., & Jackson, A. (2010). Cultural competence in crisis intervention. Retrieved November 18, 2013, from www.crisisprevention.com/Resources/Article-Library /Nonviolent-Crisis-Intervention-Training-Articles/Cultural-Competence-in -Crisis-Intervention

U.S. Department of Veterans Affairs. (2011, December). Phases of traumatic stress reactions in a disaster. Retrieved November 18, 2013, from www.ptsd.va.gov/professinal /pages/phases-trauma-reactions.asp

Vernberg, E. M., Steinberg, A. M., Jacobs, A. K., Brymer, M. J., Watson, P. J., Osofsky, J. D., . . . Ruzek, J. I. (2008). Innovations in disaster mental health: Psychological first aid. *Professional Psychology: Research and Practice, 39*(4), 381–388.

Wells, M. E. (2006). Psychotherapy for families in the aftermath of a disaster. *Journal of Clinical Psychology, 62*(8), 1017–1027. doi:10.1002/jclp.20286

Wessely, S., Bryant, R. A., Greenberg, N., Earnshaw, M., Sharpley, J., & Hacker-Hughes, J. (2008). Does psycho-education help prevent post traumatic psychological distress? *Psychiatry, 71*(4), 287–302. doi:10.1521/psyc.2008.71.4.287

Wiger, D. E., & Harowski, K. J. (2003). *Essentials of crisis counseling and intervention.* Hoboken, NJ: John Wiley & Sons.

Wittouck, C., Van Autreve, S., DeJaegere, E., Portzky, G., & van Heeringen, K. (2011). The prevention and treatment of complicated grief: A meta-analysis. *Clinical Psychology Review, 31*, 69–78. doi:10.1016/j.cpr.2010.09.005

Yehuda, R. (2002). Post-traumatic stress disorder. *New England Journal of Medicine, 346*, 108–114. doi:10.1056/NEJMra012941

Vulnerable Populations

Pregnant Women, Infants, and Children and Disasters

CASE STUDY: Parenting the Special Needs Child

The hotel provided a safe space where the Smith family could make the first attempt at re-establishing their routine. Carla, a 10-year-old girl with autism, was having a difficult time adjusting since her family was evacuated from their home after the hurricane. The shelter provided in the local community was the only option to wait out the storm; however, it soon became evident that Carla's family would not be able to stay there for long. Carla's mother spent much of the first 24 hours talking to Carla about the storm, explaining why they needed to be at the shelter. Carla had difficulty sleeping and ate very little due to her diet restrictions. The noisy environment of the shelter, and the steady activity, made it impossible for Carla to remain calm. Carla constantly asked when she would be able to return to the classroom she goes to daily and see her friends. While the transfer to the hotel was not an ideal situation, it provided the structure and routine that Carla needed for her family to begin the road to recovery.

Certain populations are especially vulnerable during a disaster, including persons at the beginning and end points of the life cycle. As such, pregnant women, infants, and children are especially susceptible and at risk post-disaster, comprising a significant proportion of those requiring services. Hurricane Katrina alone impacted over 56,000 pregnant women and 75,000 infants, and the needs were substantial (Callaghan et al., 2007). Of primary concern was disruption in access to a clean water supply, limited or no access to safe food, exposure to environmental toxins, and crowded shelter conditions. Additionally, disruption in the public health and medical–clinical infrastructure led to interruption in access to preventive and primary medical care (Callaghan et al., 2007). Routine medical care is critical during the prenatal and the postpartum periods, and continuity of care is important.

A common concern throughout other chapters in this book is the difficulty in obtaining evidentiary support for how disasters affect vulnerable populations and what interventions may offset those effects. The Cochrane database (www .thecochranelibrary.com), a primary source for rigorous systematic reviews of evidence, provides empirical evidence for common interventions and is considered a "gold standard" source for literature reviews. Turner, Barnes, Reid, and Garrubba (2010) conducted a review of the Cochrane database to determine whether or not current guidelines on perinatal and child health delivery in crisis situations were grounded in evidence. The researchers found no explicit evidence support for common guidelines; however, they identified some reviews that contribute to the evidence base and provide support. While these reviews are helpful, many of the existing studies evaluated interventions delivered in underdeveloped countries. Differing complexities of resource delivery and overall response composition in underdeveloped countries sometimes makes it difficult to draw a direct application in a developing country; however, extrapolation of guiding principles is possible.

The absence of an extensive literature base should not be surprising. The fields of perinatal and pediatric health care are among the most developed across the board; however, gathering evidence on implementing similar interventions within the post-disaster setting is fraught with dilemmas. In reality, conducting research on children in nondisaster settings presents special ethical considerations, in spite of controlled environments and available caregivers. The post-disaster setting poses additional barriers, including separation of child and caregiver, lack of opportunity for consent or assent, and logistical issues. From a methodological perspective, difficulties include lack of post-disaster assessment tools and restrictions of utilizing convenience-only and nonrepresentative samples (Masten & Osofsky, 2010). Along with the relative infrequency and randomness of disasters, it is easy to comprehend why the post-disaster literature base is limited.

Even though there is a scarcity of studies on post-disaster *interventions*, there is a growing body of literature on the *effects* of disasters on the perinatal and pediatric populations. Information on the consequences of disasters on these populations is on the rise, and guidelines are evolving that draw from current knowledge in these areas, as well as interventions in comparative (not identical) situations.

PREGNANT WOMEN AND INFANTS

Health Effects

It is well documented that exposure to environmental toxins, poor or interrupted access to health care, and psychological stress can lead to negative health outcomes for pregnant women and infants. Torche and Kleinhaus (2012) researched a population of women exposed to earthquakes during their pregnancy and found that exposure at different points in gestation increases incidence of preterm birth when compared to women with no earthquake exposure. Larger earthquakes can have devastating effects in underdeveloped countries, such as the 2010 earth-quake in Haiti that took the lives of over 300,000 and displaced 1.5 million (CNN Library, 2014); however, smaller earthquakes can also be destructive and fatal, such as the 1971 earthquake in San Fernando, California, and the 1964 earth-quake in Prince William Sound, Alaska (U.S. Department of the Interior, 2012). Preterm birth appears to be a phenomenon related specifically to earthquakes that is not consistently supported throughout other types of natural disasters. Preterm birth may lead to significant health and developmental outcomes for the infant, including long-term intellectual and developmental disabilities, communication delays, behavior problems such as attention deficit hyperactivity disorder, cerebral palsy, autism, asthma, bronchopulmonary dysplasia, hearing and vision problems, and frequent infections (March of Dimes, 2013).

Harville, Xiong, and Buekens (2010) also found influences on physical and mental health among women directly exposed to a disaster. Perinatal effects were primarily related to decreased fetal growth and infant birth weight, lead-ing to subsequent health consequences. Currie and Rossin-Slater (2013) found somewhat differing results than Torche and Kleinhaus (2012) in their examina-tion of over four million birth records from 1996 to 2008. They found that mater-nal exposure to hurricanes in the third trimester did not influence birth weight, but rather increased the likelihood of delivery complications and compromised infant health. Researchers delineated that such exposure resulted in higher inci-dence of infant need for mechanical ventilation and meconium aspiration syn-drome, a condition occurring when the infant is deemed under stress (Currie & Rossin-Slater, 2013; Lee, 2011).

Along with pregnancy and delivery effects, researchers found increased incidence of unplanned pregnancy and sexually transmitted diseases (STDs) post-disaster (Harville, Xiong, & Buekens, 2010). While not associated with provision of *primary* medical care, such outcomes speak to the disruption in secondary ser-vices provided by public clinics, such as *preventative* care. An important compo-nent of health service delivery in shelters is the provision of contraceptive care, not only to prevent unplanned pregnancy but also to prevent the spread of disease.

Infant Feeding Post-Disaster

Infant feeding post-disaster influences both health and mental health outcomes for mother and infant. The literature base on infant feeding is more developed than others, resulting in evidence-based intervention guidelines as well as policy rec-ommendations. Changes in infant feeding practices are disruptive to both mother and infant, leading to higher mortality and morbidity from infectious disease. Breastfeeding, the preferred post-disaster method, offers significant health and mental health benefits and should be encouraged whenever possible (California Department of Public Health [CDPH], 2012; Eidelman, 2013; Gribble, McGrath, MacLaine, & Lhotska, 2011; Lawrence, 2011; Office on Women's Health, 2013).

From a health perspective, breastfeeding provides nutrition, protection from infections, reduction in the risk of sudden infant death syndrome (SIDS), reduction in the risk of respiratory infections and asthma, and protection against diarrhea (Infant and Young Child Feeding in Emergencies [IFE] Core Group, 2007; Lawrence, 2011; Office on Women's Health, 2013). Breast milk is nutritionally optimal and always at the correct temperature, providing not only nourishment and hydration but also warmth. In areas where a contaminated water supply is suspected, breast milk guards against the use of questionable water sources. Breastfeeding also suppresses fertility, an important consideration for women in the absence of available contraceptive alternatives (Eidelman, 2013; Gribble, McGrath, MacLaine, & Lhotska, 2011; Lawrence, 2011; Office on Women's Health, 2013).

From an emotional perspective, breastfeeding additionally provides benefits to both mother and infant. Breastfeeding reduces women's physiological responses to physical and emotional stress resulting from the release of oxytocin, the "feel good" hormone. The mechanics of breastfeeding, close skin-to-skin contact between mother and infant, provides comfort, warmth, and security, lessening feelings of anxiety and depression (Lawrence, 2011; Office on Women's Health, 2013). Initiation of breastfeeding is possible even if the mother was not breastfeeding prior to the disaster. Women supplementing breast milk or exclusively formula feeding can be encouraged to initiate frequent skin-to-skin contact and nonnutritive sucking. Once the breast-milk supply is established, it will gradually increase over subsequent days and weeks, decreasing the need for formula supplements (AAP, 2007). It is important during this process that women receive a great deal of guidance and encouragement, with care given to not increase emotional stress in circumstances where the mother is unable to breastfeed. Common barriers to breastfeeding include the absence of professional and personal support systems, family displacement or relocation of the dyad, accessibility to areas providing privacy, and provision of safety to breastfeed, many of which can be controlled for in a family-centered setting (Gribble, McGrath, MacLaine, & Lhotska, 2011; Lawrence, 2011; Office on Women's Health, 2013).

Special care should be given when introducing formula for infant feeding, when breastfeeding is not an option. Donations and distributions of formula to relief agencies should be carefully monitored and controlled (Eidelman, 2013; Gribble, McGrath, MacLaine, & Lhotska, 2011). Water supplies should be determined safe prior to the use of powdered or concentrated formula and clean bottles and nipples made available. Professional support should be provided whenever possible to assist in changes in feeding practices and monitor for infant intolerance.

Mental Health Effects

In addition to health effects, disasters also have mental health consequences. Research indicates that disasters exacerbate and cause anxiety, depression, and grief responses within the perinatal population (ACOG, 2010). Prenatal maternal stress and depression, common during disasters, is a recognized factor leading to negative outcomes for mothers and infants, impacting infant behavioral, cognitive, and psychomotor development (Kingston, Tough, & Whitfield, 2012; McGrath, Records, & Rice, 2008; Zhu et al., 2014). Tees and colleagues (2010) explored this phenomenon when they studied maternal stress and infant temperament in dyads exposed to Hurricane Katrina. Investigators found that exposure itself did not increase the risk of difficult infant temperament; however, mothers who reported high stress levels also reported difficult temperament in their infants, whether or not such difficulties were evident through other observations. These findings are consistent with literature suggesting that maternal mental health is a stronger indicator of infant temperament than infant characteristics. Similar research denotes that infants of mothers with a history of posttraumatic stress disorder, a possible occurrence post-disaster, may have difficulties with emotional regulation, a necessary skill to help infants recover from distress (Enlow, Kitts, & Blood, 2011).

Women in general are at increased risk to suffer from mental health effects post-disaster (Corrarino, 2008; Halpern & Tramontin, 2007; Norris, Friedman, & Watson, 2002) and are additionally at risk for safety concerns. Literature suggests that pregnant women especially are at high risk for intimate partner violence and sexual assault post-disaster (ACOG, 2010; Clemens & Hietala, 1999; Thornton & Voigt, 2007), a topic that has been minimally covered in the U.S. literature on disasters. While there is some international literature that discusses domestic violence and sexual assault during times of crisis, especially in refugee settings, there is even less on information on potential interventions (Chew & Ramdas, 2005; Delaney & Shrader, 2000; Thornton & Voigt, 2007). The increase in violence is due to a multitude of factors, including increased stress and psychological strain in personal relationships, overcrowded conditions in shelters, male assertion of power and control, substance abuse and misuse, and disruption in community-based police and security services (Thornton & Voigt, 2007; New York City Alliance Against Sexual Assault, 2006). Providing safe environments for pregnant women and their infants should be a priority; however, this is frequently unattainable post-disaster when public safety resources are stretched incredibly thin.

Given the wide range of potential health and mental health issues possible in a post-disaster scenario, it is particularly important that preparedness planning be made available to pregnant and postpartum women. Preparedness education should be specific to the perinatal population, going beyond what is provided generally through mass-media messaging. Emerging literature supports the use of one-to-one education interventions to increase preparedness levels in high-risk populations (Baker & Baker, 2010; Baker & Cormier, 2013; Baker, Baker, & Flagg, 2012), and opportunities to provide such education should be sought after. Giarratano and colleagues (2010) identified such an opportunity via childbirth education classes, especially in geographic areas that are considered high risk. The author suggests that preparedness education components should be based on an all-hazards model, providing recommendations for both evacuation and sheltering in place. Evacuation is the option that provides the greatest reduction in hazard risk and exposure; however, this is not always viable. In both cases, preparedness is critical to ensure safety for mother and infant. Giarratano and colleagues (2010) identified the components for preparedness education within childbirth classes that include the following:

- Identification of community risk and potential hazards
- Identification of local disaster plans and community alerts
- Resource identification for evacuation routes, and plans and locations of a public shelter plan
- Information about maintaining pregnancy health throughout the crisis
- Labor support preparation and identification of signs of early labor
- Compilation of a home birth emergency kit
- Instructions in infant care during emergency situations, including first aid and cardiopulmonary resuscitation (CPR)
- Preparedness for breastfeeding and guidelines on alternative feeding if necessary
- Skill development for coping with stress
- Resources for additional support and information

Inclusion of this type of preparedness information utilizes an available opportunity accessing established childbirth education classes to build on foundation knowledge of preparedness.

CHILDREN

While the needs of pregnant women and infants are unique, so are the needs of children. Children are markedly vulnerable in a disaster, with vulnerability varying significantly depending on the degree of exposure to the event, parental response to the event, age of the child, presence of pre-existing mental health issues, and separation from parents or caregivers. Younger children may be preverbal, unable to express their concerns, or provide self and caregiver information. Children may have difficulty seeking safety, escaping dangerous situations, or making decisions at critical times during disasters. Accommodating these special considerations requires specific planning sensitive to children's needs (Cornette & Pu-Kai So, 2011; National Commission on Children and Disasters, 2010).

From a medical perspective, children are more than simply "little adults," requiring age-appropriate treatment, equipment, and supplies. They are susceptible to greater health consequences from disasters in general than adults, but even more so to chemical, biological, and radiological exposure due to their proximity to the ground, body size, and composition (Branson, 2011; Conway & Pike, 2010). This vulnerability is demonstrated through the victim population. Infants and younger children are over-represented as victims, especially during public health emergencies that involve outbreaks of disease (Barfield et al., 2011; CDC, 2009).

As minors, children require the care of parents and caregivers. Separation from caregivers is a mitigating factor in disaster response. After Hurricane Katrina, more than 5,000 children were reported missing as people were dispersed and evacuated to other states (Broughton, Allen, Hannemann, & Petrikin, 2006). Separation of child and caregiver adds to the complexity of meeting the needs of children, inhibiting information gathering, presenting safety and security issues in sheltering, and adding additional stress and anxiety to the child. Their inherent dependency results in significant issues related to sheltering, care, and reunification with family members to ensure child safety.

Along with separation, relocation impacts children differently from adults. Relocation of the family home post-disaster can cause significant distress and disruption in the child's life. Hansel, Osofsky, Osofsky, and Friedrich (2013) conducted a study on school-age students who relocated to other geographic areas after Hurricane Katrina instead of returning to their homes in New Orleans and surrounding areas. The authors found that relocation was a significant factor in child distress; however, findings were influenced by child age. Older children who were relocated after the hurricane exhibited more symptoms of trauma; however, younger children who were temporarily relocated and then returned home had more trauma symptoms. Development across the child life span contributes to the shifting of dependency from parents to peers, and on to independence. Disasters disrupt social networks that are pivotal to child and adolescent adjustment.

Across the age spectrum, children are vulnerable to mental health effects post-disaster such as depression, anxiety, grief, and behavioral problems. Children and adolescents in general are psychologically vulnerable to such effects, although not always to the point of requiring long-term intervention (Beaton et al., 2009; Norris, Friedman, & Watson, 2002; Stuber, Galea, Pfefferbaum, Vandivere, Moore, & Fairbrother, 2005). Younger children, while more vulnerable, may have a lower exposure risk due to the protection of caregivers. Older children, capable of more developed coping capacities, generally access a wider range of social support. However, older children may have higher exposure to disaster elements as a result of their independence (Green et al., 1991; Masten & Osofsky, 2010). It is not unusual for adolescents to exhibit behavioral problems such as delinquency and substance use, and they should be carefully monitored for significant behavior changes. Younger children may exhibit difficulties such as regression, acting out, clinginess, or extra dependence on adults. Box 4.1 outlines some common reactions of children to stress at varying ages.

Emotional disturbance in children post-disaster is higher than general population estimates. Mclaughlin and colleagues (2009) in their study of children impacted by Hurricane Katrina reported a rate of 9.3% in the study population in the 2 years following the disaster as opposed to the general population estimate of 4% to 7%. As with general issues of pediatric psychological reaction, there are considerable mediating factors that come into play. Children experiencing a significant disaster-related stressor (such as death of a family member) are at greater risk of developing problems than those experiencing more benign stressors such as power outages and minimal household damage. In addition, family factors such as low-income level, poverty, and history of family psychopathology influence reactions, increasing the risk for emotional disturbance (Masten & Osofsky, 2010; Mclaughlin et al., 2009). These are not unlike variables that are significant with mental health issues among adults; however, children do not always possess the emotional maturity to control for such factors.

BOX 4.1

Parenting After Disaster

Stress reactions by age—common responses after disasters

Preschool	School Age	Pre-Teen/Adolescent
Regression	Regression	Withdrawal
Eating disorders	Nightmares	Acting out
Bed-wetting	Violent play	Sleeping/eating disturbances
Whining/crying	Acting out	Depression
Neediness	Fear	Anger
Fear	Irritability	Role confusion
Anxiety	Sibling competition	Headaches/physical complaints
Sleeping disorders	Preoccupation with event	Risk-taking behaviors
		Overwhelmed by emotions but unable to share feelings

Children With Special Needs

A subpopulation of children, specifically children with special health care needs, requires extra consideration during disasters. Approximately 20%, or one in five households, have a child with special health care needs, equating to over eleven million children nationwide, and their needs are extensive. Special health care needs include physical and psychological concerns ranging from chronic issues such as asthma and diabetes to highly complex issues such as cerebral palsy and severe developmental delay (American College of Emergency Physicians, 2008; NS-CSHCN, 2009/2010). Impairments include autism, cognitive limitations, vision, hearing and physical limitations, learning disabilities, severe emotional disturbances, and behavior disorders. Attending to the uniqueness of such impairments requires very different and specialized adaptation and response considerations. The 2009/2010 National Survey of Children with Special Health Care Needs reported that nationwide almost 50% require at least five or more specific health care services or have specialized equipment needs. Coordination of services is complex, relying on multiple care providers and plans. Breakdown in the care network post-disaster leads to disruption of health care, exacerbating symptoms.

Rescue and recovery issues for children with special health care needs present difficulties for responders by complicating triage, stressing resources, and generating unique reunification needs (Chung & Shannon, 2007). Reunification needs of nonmedically needy children can stress an already taxed shelter and relocation system; however, children with special needs add to the complexity of the response. The numbers of children requiring special care post-disaster are significant. Medical teams in Houston evaluated over 3,500 displaced pediatric patients in a span of 13 days following Hurricane Katrina, after families had been relocated from the New Orleans area. Disaster Medical Assistance Teams (DMATs), a part of the Federal response system, report that approximately 30% of patients treated post-disaster are children, commenting that children are usually triaged at a higher severity level than adults, requiring specialized care providers, supplies, and services (Gausche-Hill, 2009; Gnauck et al., 2007). In April 2011, a Tuscaloosa, Alabama hospital provided care to over 100 pediatric patients in one night, including one site care and transport to a regional children's hospital (Kanter, 2012). As in the Tuscaloosa response, many pediatric patients arrive at health care facilities unaccompanied, without a caregiver or reunification plan (McBride, 2011). Past medical histories and reports on current medical conditions are unavailable, and the child's primary source of comfort is absent. Most general medical facilities are unprepared to handle such a surge in pediatric patients post-disaster. Barfield and colleagues (2011) recommend that pediatric critical care resources have the capacity to triple the number of functioning beds for a period of at least 10 days to accommodate patient surge from an influx of infants and children.

Medical concerns post-disaster are not only acute, but can also be long term. Immediate impacts of disasters such as flooding and destruction on physical structures like homes and community buildings can lead to long-term exposure to environmental toxins. Hurricane Katrina saw an extensive recovery and rebuilding effort that continues today. Damaged homes are sometimes vacant for weeks and months before persons return home and initiate the rebuilding process. Returning persons suffer long-term exposure to environmental conditions such as mold, roof and structure damage, and contaminated dust, dirt, and debris. Such exposure leads to an increase in lower and upper respiratory symptoms, which can trigger asthma and other pre-existing conditions (Rath et al., 2011).

Families of children with disabilities, a further subset of children with special needs, may be better prepared to effectively cope with stressors due to their special circumstances, but have greater dependency on community resources than typical children (Masten & Osofsky, 2010). Families accustomed to protecting children who are sensitive to external environmental factors often do so within a network of established care providers. Children with developmental disabilities may possess a higher tolerance for emergency situations due to past accommodation and are keenly capable of adapting with parental guidance. In responding to children with disabilities, parents are encouraged to trust in the child's abilities, communicate the child's strengths and abilities to those around him or her, and recognize that children have the natural ability to adapt post-disaster (Inagaki & Hayashi, 2013).

As with all children, but particularly children with disabilities, preparedness is critical. In spite of multiple needs, it is clear that children with special health care needs are no more prepared than the general population (Baker & Baker, 2010; Baker & Cormier, 2013). Families of children with disabilities find that general preparedness guidelines are insufficient to establish a plan meeting all necessities. Children with disabilities may have difficulty initiating preparedness behaviors due to limited mobility or cognitive issues. For example, it may be difficult to explain the need to take protective actions to a child who has cognitive issues, or it may be physically difficult to evacuate a child who has mobility and equipment needs. Families are less likely to evacuate children with special needs due to their physical vulnerabilities and psychological stress (Peek & Stough, 2010).

Disaster preparedness planning is also critical for families of children dependent on electrical devices such as home ventilators, feeding pumps, nebulizers, suction machines, and pulse oximeters. Families should be families with options to evacuate to a hospital or other medical facility if advance notice is provided. Alternative methods for powering devices in the event of a power failure, such as having a battery backup, household generator, or automobile inverter to provide power in case of emergency (ICE), are vital (Sakashita, Matthews, & Yamamoto, 2013). However, preparedness for electrical failure is not always apparent. A survey of 50 families with technology-dependent children found that only 44% had a plan for long-term power failure and that many families could not confirm whether or not the device had an available battery backup (Sakashita, Matthews, & Yamamoto, 2013). Since many power emergencies are unexpected and can occur in the middle of the night, making sure that electrical devices have an alarm is essential.

REUNIFICATION OF CHILDREN

Family reunification is a primary concern in preparedness and response, and should be a key component of all pediatric disaster planning (Cornette & Pui-Ka So, 2011). Reunification is not as simple as simply reuniting children with caregivers, but also ensuring that the identified caregivers are legitimate and providing a safe environment. Reunification is important to not only provide comfort and security to the child, but also to lower the risk of secondary injuries that may occur when a child is separated from his or her parent or legal guardian. Unfortunately, secondary injuries include intentional injuries such as violence, abuse, neglect, abduction, and exploitation, as well as unintentional injuries such as falls, injuries, and accidental poisoning (Brandenburg, Watkins, Brandenburg, & Schieche, 2007).

Reunification is an issue that needs to be tackled via preparedness and response efforts. Systems need to be standardized and utilize mutually compatible networks to share and synthesize available data. Information obtained is confidential and should only be released among agencies that are mandated to provide tracing, tracking, and reunification services. These agencies include health care facilities, state human resource offices, and local law enforcement. Once caregivers are identified, relationships must be verified and reunions coordinated only if there is mutual agreement and willingness on the part of the caregiver and the child. Alternative arrangements must be available in the event that reunification is not possible (Blake & Stevenson, 2009). From a prevention aspect, facilities that anticipate an influx of families and children should be prepared to offer services across ages to avoid separation of families and caregivers.

There is already some progress being made in the area of reunification. As a result of efforts from Hurricanes Katrina and Rita, as well as recovery efforts from the 2010 earthquake in Haiti, the National Center for Missing and Exploited Children (NCMEC) developed a nationwide system for identifying and reuniting children separated from their families or caregivers. Working with local and federal agencies, the NCMEC developed the Unaccompanied Minors Registry and the National Emergency Child Locator Center. The Unaccompanied Minors Registry allows the general public, emergency management agencies, law enforcement, disaster responders, and shelter workers to report and register minors who have been separated from their parents, guardians, and caregivers for the purpose of reunification. The National Emergency Child Locator Center provides a centralized call center that is activated in the event of an emergency, providing information about location and reunification of missing children (National Center for Missing and Exploited Children, 2014). The American Red Cross (ARC) also has an available website to assist families in staying connected. The ARC "Safe and Well" registry allows families to register their location and search for missing members in order to facilitate reunification (American Red Cross, 2013b). Both systems begin to answer the need for standardized national evacuee tracking and family reunification systems that ensure child safety (Branson, 2011).

SCHOOLS AND PRESCHOOLS

Intended to be a source of safety, schools and preschools are areas where children may be at risk if facilities do not have comprehensive disasters plans, or, if parents are not aware of plans. Literature highlights family reunification as a major issue in disaster response, and schools are sometimes limited in the extent to which they can assure appropriate reunification. However, the likelihood that children may be at school away from parents is a real concern, especially when dealing with man-made or unanticipated disasters (Cornette & Pui-Ka So, 2011). Furthermore, the same technology that can be beneficial immediately after a disaster can hinder response in school-related disasters. For example, parents are often first notified of an emergency by students using personal cell phones instead of the school alert network. In a crisis situation, parents are more likely to send unauthorized people, who may be geographically closer, to pick up their children from school without following established check-out protocols. What seems to be a logical solution for expediting family reunification has unintended consequences, leaving the school system unable to keep an accurate account of which children remain and which children are with parents (Kubicek, Ramirez, Limbos, & Iverson, 2008).

Schools are key stakeholders in preparedness planning for mass casualty events; however, they do not always participate in table top planning and execution of drills. One school survey on preparedness found that 95.6% of schools had an evacuation plan, but 30% had never conducted a drill or exercise to test the plan, and many had not coordinated the plan with local emergency officials. Additionally concerning was that 22.1% made no provisions for children with special health care needs (Graham, Shirm, Liggin, Aitken, & Dick, 2006). Schools should prepare to provide both physical and psychological safety services, including mental health services for all children in their care (Cowan & Rossen, 2014). Collaborating with local emergency managers and planning committees, following the National Incident Command System, and including provisions for dealing with children with special needs are vital components.

Commonly utilized as sheltering facilities, schools should establish an infra-structure including supplies of food, water, health care services, and enough human resources to adequately supervise and care for sheltering children, espe-cially in the case of acute weather emergencies. Once developed, plans should be tested through exercises including all stakeholders (AAP Council on School Health, 2008). Implementing guidelines by all agencies that care for children, including child care providers, often called upon to provide emergency child care services post-disaster, ensures unified response. Unfortunately there is still much work to be completed in this area. A recent report by Save the Children highlights that the gaps in preparedness are striking, as over 50% of states in the United States fail to meet the minimum standards for schools and child care centers set forth by the National Commission on Children and Disasters for protecting children (Save the Children, 2013b). Preparedness programs established at the school, state, and district levels ensure collaboration and coordinated efforts (Branson, 2011).

PERSONAL PREPAREDNESS

Although we know that the preparedness level of the general population is inadequate, as a rule homes that have children are more likely to engage in pre-paredness planning (Diekman, Kearney, O'Neil, & Mack, 2007; Eisenman et al., 2009; Murphy, Cody, Frank, Glik, & Ang, 2009). A study of women in Arkansas found that 48% of postpartum women surveyed had an emergency plan, and having a plan is an emerging predictor of behavior (Zilversmit, Sappenfield, Zotti, & McGehee, 2014). A similar study exploring the effects of preparedness on behavior reports that persons who have an emergency plan are very likely to seek shelter prior to a storm as opposed to those without a plan (Cong, Liang, & Luo, 2014). Future research should yield subsequent studies evaluating the effectiveness of such plans.

If preparedness is a predictor of protective behavior, we can cautiously make the assumption that preparedness in turn has the capacity to decrease negative effects of disasters. In fact, emerging research appears to tentatively support that theory. Evidence from the April 2011 Alabama tornado outbreak reviewing 60 patient records from patients seen in emergency departments (EDs) found that three children who used personal protection devices sustained only minor injuries (Campbell, Baker, & Monroe, 2012). Although anecdotal in nature, this study is one of the first of its kind, implying that behaviors that implement the use of protective devices, such as bike helmets and infant car seats, may in fact prevent injuries.

Developing preparedness plans should be a family affair, with children of all ages actively involved according to their level of development (see Tables 4.1 and 4.2). Many websites include resources that make it fun for children to

TABLE 4.1 Disaster Guidelines for Pregnant Women and Infants

BE INFORMED
<ul><li>Be aware of the types of disasters that occur in your area</li><li>Be aware of county warning procedures, evacuation plans, and shelters before disaster strikes</li><li>Be aware of evacuation procedures in your workplace; know the location of fire extinguishers and emergency alarms</li><li>Monitor television, radio, Internet, and social media news reports as able for information from authorities on local conditions and official instructions</li><li>Know your community's response and evacuation plans</li></ul>
MAKE A PLAN
General<ul><li>Be familiar with signs of early labor</li><li>Talk about potential emergencies and how to respond with your family</li><li>Make sure to review the emergency plan with all family members</li><li>Make a fire escape plan with two ways out of every room</li><li>Practice your fire and emergency drills twice a year</li><li>Identify a family meet-up place if family members are separated</li><li>Choose someone outside your home to be an emergency "check-in" contact</li></ul>
Sheltering in Place and Evacuation<ul><li>Develop a plan to shelter in place in the event that you are unable to evacuate or are advised by officials to stay where you are<ul><li>○ Locate a safe room in the house</li><li>○ Know the location of protective gear such as bike helmets and child car seats</li><li>○ List "last-minute" items to take to safe locations (if time permits)<ul><li>■ Purse or wallet</li><li>■ Cell phone and charger</li><li>■ Shoes and protective clothing</li><li>■ Car keys</li></ul></li></ul></li><li>Make a backup plan to get to the hospital or health center</li><li>Let your health care provider's office know where you will be</li><li>Register with the American Red Cross "Safe and Well" registry</li><li>If you have a case manager or participate in a program such as *Healthy Start*, let your case manager know where you will be</li><li>If your baby is in the neonatal intensive care unit or hospitalized, find out the hospital's plan for sheltering and evacuation</li><li>Develop a plan to evacuate</li><li>Plan two ways out of every room</li><li>Always evacuate if you are told by medical or other official personnel to evacuate or seek treatment</li><li>Know how and when to turn off water meters, gas, and electricity at the main switches; keep needed tools available; provide these instructions to members of your personal support network</li><li>Follow recommendations for mitigating potential impairments for evacuating: bolt bookshelves to walls; anchor outdoor items that can be projectiles in high winds and hurricanes; install hurricane shutters (if appropriate to area); trim trees that overhang roofs; repair cracks in ceilings and foundations; store flammable materials away from heat sources</li></ul>
Communication—Family, Friend, and Neighbor Communication Plan<ul><li>Select someone outside the house to be an emergency "check-in" person</li><li>Choose a meeting place outside of your home and in your community in case you cannot get home</li><li>Make sure that all cell phones have an in case of emergency (ICE) number</li><li>Ensure everyone in the house has a copy of the emergency communication plan</li></ul>

(continued)

TABLE 4.1 Disaster Guidelines for Pregnant Women and Infants (*continued*)

BUILD A KIT

- Basic supplies: a 3-day supply of food, water, first aid, and tools; prepare a kit for sheltering in place and a smaller, lightweight version if you need to evacuate
- Medical supplies: at least a week's supply of any medicine or medical supplies that you use (or as much as you can afford to keep on hand)
- Medical documents: include copies of important documents in a waterproof container in your emergency kit, including a list of all medications, prescriptions, doctor's orders, medical records, description of medical equipment used and needed and operating instructions (include style and serial number), medical insurance cards and/or Medicare/Medicaid cards, physician contact information, list of allergies, and health history
- Make copies of important health records, including immunization records for mom and baby—place on flash drive and have it updated at prenatal visits
- Have a list of phone numbers and locations of other obstetricians, midwives, and birth locations; copy of your prenatal record and medications
- Include supplies necessary in case of labor and home delivery: clean towels; waterproof pads for the bed or car; medium-sized bowl (for the placenta); disposable gloves
  ○ Supplies for cutting the umbilical cord: boiled shoelaces or string to be used as cord clamps; sharp, clean scissors or single-sided razor blade (note: no need to use wipes on umbilical area)
  ○ Supplies for mother after birth: cold packs; ibuprofen or acetaminophen; sanitary pads; antibacterial wipes
  ○ Supplies for newborn baby: newborn hat or cap (can use adult sock); case of diapers (roughly 70 per week); suction bulb; large blanket; receiving blankets; long cloth or towel to keep mom and baby together; bowl for collecting expressed milk; syringes or small cup for feeding expressed milk or formula
- Baby carrier—there may not be a crib available at your destination
- Hand sanitizer
- Extra infant clothes
- Multiple pacifiers and blankets
- Other documents: consider including records such as social security number, guardianship papers, charge and bank account information, tax records, will, etc.
- Other supplies: portable, battery-powered radio with extra batteries; battery-operated television if you have hearing impairment; flashlight and extra batteries; sanitation items (hand sanitizer, moist towelettes, and toilet paper); matches in a waterproof container; whistle to call for help; extra cash or traveler's checks if possible

Sources: American Red Cross (2013a); Centers for Disease Control and Prevention (CDC, 2012); Federal Emergency Management Agency (2013); March of Dimes (2006).

participate in disaster planning and be involved in all aspects (see Appendix). Children should be engaged in age-appropriate tasks developing communication plans, reviewing household safety, and participating in the building of disaster kits. Such activities help build the child's comfort level, ensuring awareness of responsibilities during a disaster.

PARENTING AFTER DISASTERS

Disasters place persons into a state of uncertainty and, oftentimes, crisis. For families with children, that state extends beyond the needs of the adults to the children in the household. Children's needs are complex, from emotional comfort

TABLE 4.2 Disaster Guidelines for Families With Children

BE INFORMED
• Be aware of the types of disasters that occur in your area • Be aware of county warning procedures, evacuation plans, and shelters before disaster strikes • Be aware of evacuation procedures in your workplace; know the location of fire extinguishers and emergency alarms • Monitor television, radio, Internet, and social media news reports as able for information from authorities on local conditions and official instructions • Know your community's response and evacuation plans
MAKE A PLAN
General • Create a fire escape plan with two ways out of every room • Practice your fire and emergency drills twice a year • Identify a family meet-up place if family members are separated • Pregnant women: make a backup plan for getting to the hospital or health care center • Choose someone outside your home to be an emergency "check-in" contact

Sheltering in Place and Evacuation
• Develop a plan to shelter in place in the event that you are unable to evacuate or are advised by officials to stay where you are
  ○ Locate a safe room in the house
  ○ Know location of protective gear such as bike helmets and child car seats
  ○ List "last minute" items to take to safe locations (if time permits)
    ▪ Purse or wallet
    ▪ Cell phone and charger
    ▪ Shoes and protective clothing
    ▪ Car keys
• Develop a plan to evacuate
  ○ Plan two ways out of every room
  ○ Always evacuate if you are told by medical or other official personnel to evacuate or seek treatment
• Make a backup plan to get to hospital or health center for members with special health care needs
• Register with the American Red Cross "Safe and Well" registry
• If you have a case manager or participate in a program such as *Healthy Start*, let your case manager know where you will be
• Know how and when to turn off water meters, gas, and electricity at the main switches; keep needed tools available; provide these instructions to members of your personal support network
• Follow recommendations for mitigating potential impairments for evacuating: bolt bookshelves to walls; anchor outdoor items that can be projectiles in high winds and hurricanes; install hurricane shutters (if appropriate to area); trim trees that overhang roofs; repair cracks in ceilings and foundations; store flammable materials away from heat sources
• Review locations of communication plan and emergency kit (or "go" kit) in case of evacuation
• Present a calm demeanor to allay fears of children in the event of disaster, providing age-appropriate honest and realistic information

Communication—Family, Friend, and Neighbor Communication Plan
• Before an emergency happens, sit down with family members and decide how you will get in contact with each other, where you will go, and what you will do in an emergency. Each family member should keep a copy of the plan
  ○ card for wallet
  ○ child backpack
  ○ taped to school notebook
  ○ in cell phone
• Establish a friend or family member outside the disaster area as an emergency contact

(continued)

TABLE 4.2 Disaster Guidelines for Families With Children (*continued*)

• Make sure your child's school of day care knows what your child is supposed to do in the event of an emergency • Include Emergency Information Form for Children with Special Needs (APP) (if applicable) • Make sure there is an in case of emergency (ICE) contact in all cell phones
BUILD A KIT

• Basic supplies: a 3-day supply of food, water, and clothes; prepare a kit for sheltering in place and a smaller, lightweight version ("go" kit) if you need to evacuate
• Other supplies for emergency kit: first aid kit; extra batteries; matches in a waterproof container; toothbrush, toothpaste, soap; paper plates, plastic cups and utensils, paper towels; battery-powered or hand-crank radio; sleeping bag or warm blanket for each person; flashlights; whistle to signal for help; manual can opener; local maps; prescription medication and glasses
• Comfort items and/or toys, age appropriate such as dolls, stuffed animals, pacifier, blanket, books, puzzles, games
• Baby supplies
  ○ General supplies: case of diapers; medications; antibacterial and baby wipes; blanket or fabric to help carry baby; nonperishable baby and table food if over 6 months; comfort items (toy, blanket, etc.); sealable plastic bags for soiled diapers; diaper rash ointment
  ○ If breastfeeding: breastfeeding mothers should continue if possible
  ○ If formula feeding: 3 days' worth of pre-washed bottles and formula or disposable cups; ready-made formula or sterile water to mix formula
• Medical supplies: at least a week's supply of any medicine or medical supplies that you use (or as much as you can afford to keep on hand), an extra pair of prescription glasses if used, backup supplies for any visual aids you use, extra batteries for hearing aids and extra hearing aids if available, charger for motorized wheelchairs or other battery-operated medical/assistive devices
• Medical documents: include copies of important documents in a waterproof container in your emergency kit, including a list of all medications, prescriptions, doctor's orders, medical records, description of medical equipment used and needed and operating instructions (include style and serial number), medical insurance cards and/or Medicaid cards, physician contact information, list of allergies and health history, and a list of nonprofit or community-based organizations that may be able to assist with your disability needs
• Make copies of important health records—place on flash drive and have it updated at medical visits
• Medical alert tags or written descriptions of your disability and support needs; if you have a communication disability, include information for responders on the best way to communicate, and laminated communication board if you need assistance understanding others or being understood
• Copy of Emergency Health Information Form for Children
• Other supplies: portable, battery-powered radio with extra batteries; battery-operated television if you have hearing impairment; flashlight and extra batteries; sanitation items (hand sanitizer, moist towelettes, and toilet paper); matches in a waterproof container; whistle to call for help; extra cash or traveler's checks if possible

Sources: American Red Cross (2013a); Federal Emergency Management Agency (2013); March of Dimes (2006).

and physical security to basic food and shelter. Supplying these needs varies according to the individual child and his or her developmental stage.

The role of a parent post-disaster is to effectively balance the needs of the child against resources, family circumstances, and additional stressors. This is not always an easy task, especially when there has been significant damage, family relocation, or loss of resources. However, the recovery of the child is very dependent on the recovery of the parent, as children look to parents and other adults for cues on how to manage those stressors and guide behavior.

It is known that family factors have a significant effect on child functioning and coping after stressful events (Gorman-Smith, Henry, & Tolan, 2004). Emerging research indicates an association between altered parenting post-disaster and child risk for future symptoms of PTSD. Cobham and McDermott (2014) found that while the majority of parents do not report significant changes in parenting behavior post-disaster, they report significant increases in anxiety and protective behaviors. This in turn may contribute to an increase in risk of symptoms of PTSD in their children. Parents who have difficulty utilizing positive coping mechanisms are also more likely to use corporal punishment, a risk factor in PTSD (Kelley, Self-Brown, Le, Vigna Bosson, Hernandez, & Gordon, 2010). Conversely, maternal acceptance in parenting (allowing the child to ask questions, providing support and comfort) has been deemed a protective factor in post-disaster populations (Wilson, Lengua, Meltzoff, & Smith, 2010). Parenting behaviors that support children include limiting television time and exposure, providing emotional support, and providing factual information.

Research consistently supports that children do better in a safe environment with a set routine. Parents relying on their knowledge of the child determine their child's needs, identify behavior that is different from normal, and distinguish stress responses within developmental guidelines. Primary goals of parenting post-disaster include establishing a sense of trust, security, and safety within the child; providing care and comfort to the child; and being aware of the specific needs based on the individual temperament of the child (Gaffney, 2006). Safeguarding children post-disaster through monitoring exposure to information, especially media information that may contain images that are confusing or frightening to younger children, is a common role of parenting (Masten & Osofsky, 2010).

Modeling adaptive coping skills for children is recommended for teaching appropriate methods to deal with feelings. Parents should make time to be available to listen to their children's concerns and answer questions honestly with age-appropriate information. Engaging children in both preparedness and recovery behaviors is a positive way to equip children with the skills they need to feel empowered to adapt to uncertain situations. Establishing a routine such as getting children back in school as soon as possible helps to relay to children that life will continue and recovery will be achieved. Not neglecting their own needs, parents should strive to take care of themselves, especially when feeling overwhelmed and unable to control their own emotions. Parents who feel like they are unable to cope with the stressors should seek help from family, friends, professionals, and other community resources (Hilt, 2013; Masten & Osofsky, 2010).

Children should be encouraged to utilize their own resources to work through emotions. For example, play is very important to younger children, providing a way to process information and work out issues. Older children and adolescents may seek more support from peers; however, they rely on parents to provide factual information. Parenting guidelines from Save the Children (2013), and the Federal Emergency Management Agency and ARC (2004) provide recommendations suitable for all ages and are categorized below:

1. Information
2. Limit children's exposure to television and constant inflow of information
3. Provide factual, age-appropriate information
4. Comfort and support
5. Listen to your child's concerns
6. Provide physical and emotional comfort as a top priority
7. Encourage children and model positive coping skills
8. Routines
9. Establish or re-establish a routine as soon as possible
10. Connections
11. Utilize available support networks
12. Recognize the need for help and reach out to friends, family, and community supports
13. Involvement
14. Involve children of all ages in disaster preparedness and planning
15. Assign children specific tasks to help with recovery

Children and adolescents can be especially vulnerable after disasters; however, parents can be proactive to help their children cope with the aftereffects and prepare for future events. Building resiliency is possible through open communication, family support, and providing structure and routine.

RESPONDER GUIDELINES FOR INFANTS AND CHILDREN

First responders come from a wide variety of backgrounds and clinical settings. While it is not expected that all responders will be experts on all types of populations, there are certain characteristics of children that require special consideration. Guidelines for children, while they are considered a vulnerable population, cannot be combined with guidelines for general vulnerable populations. Preparedness planning for children is unique as their needs are distinct (Cornette & Pui-Ka So, 2011). Branson (2011) delineates that children have physiological and psychological differences that place them at greater risk during a disaster than adults. Physiological differences include having a higher center of gravity and larger head in comparison to body size, making them more likely to suffer from falls and head injuries. Children have a great skin surface for their body weight, making them at greater risk for hypothermia and dehydration. Because children have less bony protection of internal organs, they have a greater risk of sustaining multiorgan injuries in a disaster. Additional characteristics such as rapid heart and respiratory rate and shorter height make children at risk for higher exposure to environmental toxins, including chemical and biological toxins resulting from faster intake of airborne agents and close proximity to the ground, where agents are more likely to be concentrated (Conway & Pike, 2010).

Psychologically, children do not always possess the developmental maturity to cope well during a disaster. Their immature cognitive and coping skills make them less likely to be able to process information quickly and flee from danger, or take other self-protective measures. Underdeveloped verbal ability may hinder their capacity to identify needs, or provide information that assists with treatment or reunification with family members. Younger children are more dependent on caregivers and may have difficulty coping in their absence.

General Training and Planning

It is well documented that all-hazards preparedness planning needs to consider issues and scenarios involving children, and actively include children in drills (Barfield et al., 2011; Mace et al., 2012; Mason et al., 2011). Strategies need to be able to address immediate as well as long-term physical, mental health, education, housing, and other recovery needs (Branson, 2011).

Training and planning should occur for any medical facility or service provider across the perinatal and pediatric spectrum. Callaghan et al. (2007) provides specific guidelines for those taking care of pregnant and postpartum women. Recommendations include ascertaining pregnancy status as a part of intake in medical facilities and shelters, recognizing the effects of exposure of toxins on the mother and infant, and being aware of vaccination risks and benefits for pregnant women. Postpartum issues include being able to educate and assist mothers with breastfeeding and alternative feeding, and providing contraceptive care.

DMATs as well as other first responders should be trained and equipped to handle emergency deliveries and postpartum needs of mother and infant (see Table 4.3). Field teams in particular should ensure that they include obstetrics and gynecology professionals with advanced training. Pinkert and colleagues (2013) studied responses after the 2010 Haiti earthquake and the 2011 Japanese tsunami, reporting that 50% of obstetric cases handled by the field team involved complicated deliveries. Authors recommended that outreach teams also include an obstetrics and gynecologic medical provider as well as a team midwife, and that expectations include being able to perform cesarean sections in austere conditions. Outreach teams should also consider including a midwife from the local area, who may be accustomed to local cultures and taboos. Responders from outside the geographic area should be mindful that many cultures have specific customs and rituals surrounding the birth experience that should be accommodated for whenever possible. Responders should also recognize that ethical concerns may often come into play in emergency situations with limited availability of resources (Pinkert et al., 2013).

TABLE 4.3 Responder Guidelines for Pregnant Women, Infants, and Children

GENERAL TRAINING

• Include all stakeholders in disaster planning
  ○ Medical and mental health networks
  ○ Parents and caregivers
  ○ Children
• Specialized training for pregnant women, infants, and children should be included in all response content
• Be aware of developmental stages that influence children's coping and response capacities
• Medical facilities, schools, and daycare centers should plan and execute disaster-specific drills

COMMUNICATION STRATEGIES
General • Present a calm demeanor with age-appropriate honest and realistic information about the situation when communicating with children • Be equipped with alternative communication forms (such as picture charts) for nonverbal children • Recognize communication needs unique to varying health and mental health disorders • Involve children in treatment plans and information at an age-appropriate level • Ask children directly about their experience in a compassionate, age-appropriate manner
HEALTH AND MENTAL HEALTH ISSUES
• Expand capabilities of response teams to include pediatric-specific training, guidance, supplies, and staffing • Emergency medical services should be capable of transporting and providing pre-hospital pediatric care • Support breastfeeding by mothers of infant children • Control distribution of breast-milk substitutes and ensure medical supervision • Immediate attention should be given for the nutritional care and needs of orphans and unaccompanied infants and young children • Ensure access to health care providers with lactation experience • Create safe locations for breastfeeding women • Provide access to prenatal vitamins and contraceptive care • Provide access to pregnancy testing • Ensure health care centers are willing to accept pregnant evacuees • Ask parents and caregivers about Emergency Health Information Forms • Utilize evidence-guided interventions such as psychological first aid • Provide opportunity for mental health assessment • Be familiar with referral networks and available resources • Initiate family-center care practices whenever possible
EVACUATION AND RESCUE
• Limit separation of family whenever possible • Be aware of availability of community resources that accept pregnant women, children, and families • Facilitate reunification with known, safe caregivers • Provide opportunity for children to bring comfort items with them during evacuation

Sources: AAP (2013); Centers for Disease Control and Prevention (CDC, 2007); March of Dimes (2013); Pfefferbaum and Shaw (2013).

Ethical decisions such as when to provide care are complex in a modern medical facility; however, the complexities increase when the provider is faced with providing high-risk care in mass casualty situations.

Disaster planning is also critical for neonatal intensive care units (NICUs), which must be prepared to not only provide inpatient services but also to evacuate medically fragile infants if necessary (Phillips, Niedergesaess, Powers, & Brandt, 2012). Femino, Young, and Smith (2013) discuss findings from a simulated NICU evacuation, identifying priority areas. Preparedness and evacuation plans need to be developed, including the use of all resources, staff, and response partners. Planning should also involve parents, who may be responsible for assisting in evacuations. Family communication and care plans are essential in the NICU environment, outlining family roles, responsibilities, and logistics.

Planning for patient surge in general and pediatric medical centers is imperative. Practice exercises should anticipate providing services for at least 10 days after an event. Resourcing for the initial surge in local pediatric emergency mass critical care should include regional resources and criteria for dispersing patients as necessary. Practice exercises should include pediatric components at all levels (Barfield et al., 2011). Providers should be encouraged to be aware of potential pediatric issues at triage, including requesting copies of the Emergency Information Form for Children with Special Needs (AAP) from families if they have a copy, and screening for mental health problems (AAP, 1999; Pfefferbaum & North, 2013).

Hospital EDs should also participate in mass casualty drills involving pediatric patients and their families as a way to evaluate policies and procedures. Family-center care practices should be implemented and be a component in disaster planning. Such practices include allowing the parent to remain with the child during triage and stabilization, recognizing the parent as an important part of the care plan, and appreciating that the child may be accompanied by a larger family system than typical due to disaster scenarios. Families accompanying children post-disaster may require additional space to accommodate extended family members, and alternative systems of support may be sought after. Family reunification should be a top priority and novel methods, such as the use of digital photography, may be necessary to facilitate the intake process (Mason et al., 2011).

Recognizing complexities and situation variability is also an integral part of disaster planning. While an all-hazards approach is the general recommendation, some disasters present unique effects for children. For example, training for radiological and nuclear emergencies that impact children should be standardized, taking into account differences between children and adults in terms of physical and psychosocial vulnerabilities (Conway & Pike, 2010). But training for all hazards should not be limited to health care facilities alone. Schools and child care facilities should also be trained in responding to mental and behavioral health issues, especially post-disaster when the school becomes the facility most visited during recovery (Beaton et al., 2009).

Psychosocial Issues

In addition to health concerns, responders need to be aware of the psychosocial issues affecting children. Communication is one such area where responders can meet the special needs of pediatric patients. In emergency medical situations, it is important to maintain communication with caregivers about the child status during triage and treatment. Older children should also be aware of treatment plans and be given age-appropriate information. It may be necessary to utilize alternative methods such as picture charts to communicate with nonverbal children, and such resources should be available to responders (Blake & Stevenson, 2009). Although logistically difficult, special attempts should be made to maintain lines of communication when children are separated from caregivers. Many times local Volunteer Organizations Active in Disaster (VOADs) can help facilitate such communication when working with separated families. Responders should also be prepared to support linguistic and cultural differences that may be present among populations and communities (Mason et al., 2011). Aligning with local and community care providers whenever possible can help responders identify cultural issues and provide guidelines for providing culturally competent care. Keeping families together post-disaster should be a priority for all responders. Being familiar with shelters that can accommodate children and following safety protocols on reunification are a pivotal component of providing children with needed support (Blake & Stevenson, 2009).

Providing education and outreach on mental and behavioral health issues post-disaster can be a useful tool for children, families, and caregivers. Information provided should be developmentally appropriate and include expected psychological reactions (Beaton at al., 2009). Multiple modes of information transmission can be considered, including print materials (helpful for distribution in clinics and shelters), web-based information, and television and radio public service announcements. Persons who have been impacted by a disaster may need to receive information multiple times in differing formats; however, information overload can occur, so providers should look for signs that persons are becoming overwhelmed with information. Some information, with guidance on where to locate more in-depth information, appears to be the ideal balance.

Pfefferbaum and North (2013) recommend initial screening at intake for heightened risk for mental health issues; however, it is important to remember that development of long-term issues such as PTSD is the exception rather than the norm. Training in mental and behavioral health for children should be integrated as a part of general training of responders in public health and medical response. Responders should receive enhanced mental health training including psychological first aid and interventions providing social support. Recognizing signs of grief reactions and being able to provide supportive interventions and referral to grief counseling are also important (Branson, 2011).

Not unlike psychological interventions for adults, the pediatric literature on post-disaster mental health effects has a limited knowledge base. However, there are some promising interventions from both a preparedness and response perspective. Favorable preparedness interventions include involving children in disaster awareness programs and building resilience through school-based classroom interventions. Cognitive behavioral therapy for children demonstrating persisting mental health effects is also showing promise, as are traumatic grief interventions and the use of psychological first aid for acute symptoms (Pfefferbaum, Newman, & Nelson, 2014).

The existing trajectory of disaster response denotes an acute and chronic phase for intervention. Initial responders may be limited by time and resources to provide more than cursory interventions, however initiating the road to recovery. When long-term intervention is indicated, responders should facilitate referral to treatment and other services in shelter facilities, clinics, schools, churches, and community centers (wherever people may go to seek services; Beaton et al., 2009). It is frequently discussed that a child's dependence on a routine can be used to facilitate the path to recovery. Establishing a sense of normalcy and routine as soon as possible is especially effective when working with children. This does not necessarily mean immediately returning to a pre-event level of functioning; however, returning to school or predictable, supportive environments and routines can help the child self-regulate and participate in recovery (Beaton et al., 2009).

Pfefferbaum and Shaw (2013) discuss practice parameters and best practices for working with children and adolescents. They state that it is important to expand the circle of identifying children with special needs beyond just medical and mental health issues. Special needs may also encompass children exposed to maltreatment or poverty, children residing in foster care, halfway houses, domestic violence shelters, or homeless youth. Recommendations include:

- Utilizing evidence-guided interventions such as psychological first aid
- Utilizing psychoeducation and providing information on stress-reduction techniques
- Monitoring access to media coverage and exposure to disaster-related content
- Asking children directly about their experiences and reactions and being able to provide realistic, age-appropriate responses
- Evaluating the use of familiar settings such as schools and community centers to provide assessment and longer term treatment
- Encouraging family intervention and involving family members in the recovery process

SUMMARY AND CONCLUSIONS

Pregnant women, infants, and children are especially vulnerable post-disaster due to their unique health and mental health needs, comprising a significant percentage of the population requiring services. Families, caregivers, and responders should all recognize those vulnerabilities and engage in preparedness and response behaviors accommodating those risks. Populations involving pregnant women, children, and families should be involved in all levels of planning in order to ensure that their needs are met in a disaster scenario. Including content specific to such populations in responder training will help alleviate outcome differences and the risk of higher morbidity. Expanding the evidence base on intervening and health and mental health issues post-disaster is imperative to equip responders with available best evidence and promote culturally competent care.

REFERENCES

Academy for Breastfeeding Medicine. (2005). Support for breastfeeding is crucial for infant health in the aftermath of natural disasters. Retrieved September 17, 2013, from http://www.ennonline.net/pool/files/ife/web-abm-disasters-2005-pr-usa.doc

Adelman, H. S., & Taylor, L. (2006). Mental health in schools and public health. *Public Health Reports, 121*(3), 294–298.

American Academy of Pediatrics (AAP). (2007). Infant nutrition during a disaster: Breastfeeding and other options. Retrieved September 18, 2013, from http://www2 .aap.org/breastfeeding/files/pdf/InfantNutritionDisaster.pdf

American Academy of Pediatrics Committee of Pediatric Emergency Medicine (AAP). (1999). Emergency preparedness for children with special health care needs. *Pediatrics, 104*(4). Retrieved February 1, 2014, from http://pediatrics.aappublications .org/content/104/4/e53.full

American Academy of Pediatrics Council on School Health. (2008). Disaster planning for schools. *Pediatrics, 122*(4), 895–901. doi:10.1542/peds.2008-2170

American College of Emergency Physicians. (2008). *Children with special health care needs.* Retrieved March 13, 2013, from http://www.acep.org/patients.aspx?id=26128

American College of Obstetricians and Gynecologists (ACOG). (2010). *Obstetrics & Gynecology, 115*(6), 1339–1342.

American Red Cross. (2013a). *Children.* Retrieved September 19, 2013, from http://www .redcross.org/prepare/location/home- family/children

American Red Cross. (2013b). *Safe and well.* Retrieved March 1, 2014, from https://safeand well.communityos.org/cms/index.php

Baker, L., & Baker, M. (2010). Disaster preparedness among families of children with special healthcare needs. *Disaster Medicine and Public Health Preparedness, 4*(3), 240–245. doi:10.1001/dmp.2010.28

Baker, L., & Cormier, L. (2013). Disaster preparedness and families of children with special needs: A geographic comparison. *Journal of Community Health, 38*(1), 106–112. doi:10.1007/s10900-012-9587-3

Baker, M. D., Baker, L. R., & Flagg, L. E. (2012). Preparing families of children with special healthcare needs for disasters: An education intervention. *Social Work in Health Care, 51*(5), 417–429. doi:10.1080/00981389.2012.659837

Barfield, W. D., Krug, S. E., Kanter, R. K., Gausche-Hill, M., Brantley, M. D., Chung, S., Kissoon, N.; the Task Force for Pediatric Emergency Mass Critical Care. (2011). Neonatal and pediatric regionalized systems in pediatric emergency mass critical care. *Pediatric Critical Care Medicine, 12*(6), s128–s134. doi:10.1097/PCC.0b013 e318234a723

Beaton, R. D., Murphy, S. A., Houston, J. B., Reyes, G., Bramwell, S., McDaniel, M., . . . Pfefferbaum, B. (2009). The role of public health in mental and behavioral health in children and families following disasters. *Journal of Public Health Management Practice, 15*(6), E1–E11.

Blake, N., & Stevenson, K. (2009). Reunification: Keeping families together in crisis. The *Journal of Trauma, Injury, Infection and Critical Care, 67*(2), s147–s151.

Brandenburg, M. A., Watckins, S. M., Brandenburg, K. L., & Schieche, C. (2007). Operation child-ID: Reunifying children with their legal guardians after Hurricane Katrina. *Disasters, 31*(3), 277–287. doi:10.1111/j.0361-3666.2007.01009.x

Branson, R. D. (2011). Disaster planning for pediatrics. *Respiratory Care, 56*(9), 1457–1465. doi:10.4187/respcare.01405

Broughton, D. D., Allen, E. E., Hanneman, R. E., & Petrikin, J. E. (2006). Getting 5,000 families back together: Reuniting fractured families after a disaster: The role of the National Center for Missing and Exploited Children. *Pediatrics, 117*, s442–s445. doi:10.1542/peds.2006-0099S

California Department of Public Health (CDPH). (2012). Child and infant feeding emergency information. Retrieved September 17, 2013, from http://www.cdph .ca.gov/HealthInfo/healthyliving/childfamily/Documents/MO-BFP-Emergency Supplies-2012-12-11.pdf

Callaghan, W. M., Rasmussen, S. A., Jamieson, D. J., Ventura, S. J., Farr, S. L., Sutton, P. D., . . . Posner, S. F. (2007). Health concerns of women and infants in times of natural disasters: Lessons learned from Hurricane Katrina. *Maternal and Child Health Journal, 11*(4), 307–311.

Campbell, C. M, Baker, M. D., & Monroe, K. W. (2012). Prevention of child injuries during tornadoes: Cases from the 2011 tornado outbreak in Alabama. *Pediatric Emergency Care, 28*(12), 1389–1390. doi:10.1097/PED.0b013e318276c8a3

Centers for Disease Control and Prevention (CDC). (2007). Critical needs in caring for pregnant women during times of disaster for non-obstetric health care providers. Retrieved February 18, 2014, from www.emergency.cdc.gov/disasters/pregnantdi sasterhcp.asp

Centers for Disease Control and Prevention (CDC). (2009). Surveillance for pediatric deaths associated with 2009 Pandemic Influenza A (H1N1) virus infection—United States, April–August 2009. *Morbidity and Mortality Weekly, 58*(34), 941–947.

Centers for Disease Control and Prevention (CDC). (2012). *Information for pregnant women—Fact sheet.* Retrieved February 18, 2014, from http://emergency.cdc.gov /disasters/pregnantfactsheet.asp

Chew, L., & Ramdas, K. (2005). *Caught in the storm: The impact of natural disasters on women.* San Francisco, CA: Global Fund for Women. Retrieved March 11, 2014, from http:// www.globalfundforwomen.org/impact/publications/impact-reports/239-impact -natural-disasters

Chung, S., & Shannon, M. (2007). Reuniting children with their families during disasters: A proposed plan for greater success. *American Journal of Disaster Medicine, 2*, 113–117.

Clemens, P., & Hietala, J. (1999). Risk of domestic violence after flood impact: Effects of social support, age, and history of domestic violence. *Applied Behavioral Science Review, 7*(2), 199–208. doi:10.1016/S1068-8595(00)80020-3

CNN Library (updated February 2014). Haiti earthquake fast facts. Retrieved March 1, 2014, from http://www.cnn.com/2013/12/12/world/haiti-earthquake-fast-facts/

Cobham, V. E., & McDermott, B. (2014). Perceived parenting change and child posttraumatic stress following a natural disaster. *Journal of Child and Adolescent Psychopharmacology, 24*(1), 18–23. doi:10.1089/cap.2013.0051

Cong, Z., Liang, D., & Luo, J. (2014). Family emergency preparedness plans in severe tornados. *American Journal of Preventive Medicine, 46*(1), 89–93. doi:10.1016/j.amepre .2013.08.020

Conway, B., & Pike, J. (2010). Hospital response for children as a vulnerable population in radiological/nuclear incidents. *Radiation Protection Dosimetry, 142*(1), 58–62. doi:10.1093/rpd/ncq281

Cornette, E. C., & Pui-Ka So, A. (2011). Children and disaster planning: The National Commission on Children and Disasters' findings and recommendations. *Journal of Emergency Management, 9*(2), 11–16. doi:10.5055/jem.2011.0049

Corrarino, J. E. (2008). Disaster-related mental health needs of women and children. *MCN: The American Journal of Maternal and Child Health Nursing, 33*(4), 242–248. doi:10.1097/01.NMC.0000326079.26870.e3

Cowan, K. C., & Rossen, E. (2014). Responding to the unthinkable: School crisis response and recovery. *Kappan, 95*(4), 8–12.

Currie, J., & Rossin-Slater, M. (2013). Weathering the storm: Hurricanes and birth outcomes. *Journal of Health Economics, 32*, 487–503. doi:10.1016/j.jhealeco.2013.01.004

Delaney, P. I., & Shrader, E. (2000). Gender and post-disaster reconstruction: The case of Hurricane Mitch in Honduras and Nicaragua. Retrieved March 10, 2014, from www.gdnonline.org/resources/reviewdraft.doc

Diekman, S. T., Kearney, S. P., O'Neil, M. E., & Mack, K. A. (2007). Qualitative study of homeowners' emergency preparedness: Experiences, perceptions and practices. *Prehospital and Disaster Medicine, 22*(6), 494–501. doi:10.1017/S1049023X00005318

Eidelman, A. I. (2013). Breastfeeding mitigates a disaster. *Breastfeeding Medicine, 8*(3), 344–345. doi:10.1089/bfm.2013.9989

Eisenman, D. P., Glik, D., Gonzalez, L., Maranon, R., Zhou, Q., Tseng, C., & Asch, S. (2009). Improving Latino disaster preparedness using social networks. *American Journal of Preventive Medicine, 37*, 512–517. doi:10.1016/j.amepre.2009.07.022

Enlow, M. B., Kitts, R. L., & Blood, E. (2011). Maternal posttraumatic stress symptoms and infant emotional reactivity and emotion regulation. *Infant Behavior and Development, 34*(4), 487–503. doi:10.1016/j.infbeh.2011.07.007

Federal Emergency Management Agency (FEMA). (2013). *Make a plan, infants and young children.* Retrieved September 17, 2013, from http://www.ready.gov/infants-young-children, http://www.ready.gov/kids

Federal Emergency Management Agency (FEMA) & American Red Cross (ARC). (2004). *Helping children cope with disaster* (Publication FEMA478, A4499). Jessup, MD: Federal Emergency Management Agency.

Femino, M., Young, S., & Smith, V. C. (2013) Hospital-based emergency preparedness: Evacuation of the Neonatal Intensive Care Unit—the smallest and most vulnerable population. *Pediatric Emergency Care, 29*(1), 107–113. doi:10.1097/PEC.0b013e31827b8bc5

Gausche-Hill, M. (2009). Pediatric disaster preparedness: Are we really prepared? *The Journal of Trauma, Injury, Infection and Critical Care, 67*, s73–s76. doi:10.1097/TA.0b013e3181af2fff

Giarratano, G., Sterling, Y. M., Matthews, P., Deeves, G., Bernard, M. L., & Danna, D. (2010). Targeting prenatal emergency preparedness through childbirth education. *Journal of Obstetric, Gynecologic and Neonatal Nursing, 39*(4), 480–488. doi:10.1111/j.1552-6909.2010.01159.x

Gnauck, K. A., Nufer, K. E., Lavalley, J. M., Crandall, C. S., Craig, F. W., & Wilson-Ramirez, G. B. (2007). Do pediatrics and adult victims differ? A descriptive analysis of clinical encounters from four natural disaster DMAT deployments. *Prehospital Disaster Medicine, 22*, 67–73.

Gorman-Smith, D., Henry, D. B., & Tolan, P. H. (2004). Exposure to community violence perpetration: The protective effects of family functioning. *Journal of Clinical Child and Adolescent Psychology, 33*, 439–449.

Graham, J., Shirm, S., Liggin, R., Aitken, M. E., & Dick, R. (2006). Mass-casualty events at schools: A National Preparedness Survey. *Pediatrics, 117*(1), e8–e15. doi:10.1542/peds.2005-0927

Green, B. L., Korol, M., Grace, M. C., Vary, M. G., Leonard, A. C., Gleser, G. C., & Smitson-Cohen, S. (1991). Children and disaster: Age, gender and parental effects on PTSD. *Journal of the Academy of Child and Adolescent Psychiatry, 30*(6), 945–951.

Gribble, K. D., McGrath, M., MacLaine, A., & Lhotska, L. (2011). Supporting breastfeeding in emergencies: Protecting women's reproductive rights and maternal and infant health. *Disasters, 35*(4), 720–738. doi:10.111/j.1467-7717.2011.01239.x

Halpern, J., & Tramontin, M. (2007). *Disaster mental health theory and practice.* Belmont, CA: Brooks/Cole.

Hansel, T. C., Osofsky, J. D., Osofsky, H. J., & Friedrich, P. (2013). The effect of long-term relocation on child and adolescent survivors of Hurricane Katrina. *Journal of Traumatic Stress, 26,* 613–620. doi:10.1002/jts.21837k

Harville, E. W., Xiong, X., & Buekens, P. (2010). Disasters and perinatal health: A systematic review. *Obstetrical and Gynecological Survey, 65(11),* 713–728. doi:10.1097/OGX.0b013e31820eddbe

Hilt, R. (2013). Terrorism and disasters in the news: How to help kids cope. *Pediatric Annals, 2*(6), 226. doi:10.3928/00904481-20130522-03

Inagaki, M., & Hayashi, T. (2013). An important message for parents of children with developmental disabilities who have encountered an unprecedented disaster. *Brain and Development, 35,* 193–194. doi:10.1016/j.braindev.2012.08.009

Infant and Young Child Feeding in Emergencies (IFE) Core Group. (2007). Infant and young child feeding in emergencies: Operational guidance for emergency relief staff and program managers. Retrieved September 17, 2013, from http://www.ennonline.net/pool/files/ife/ops-guidance-2-1-english-010307-with-addendum.pdf

Kanter, R. K. (2012). The 2011 Tuscaloosa tornado: Integration of pediatric disaster services into regional systems of care. *Journal of Pediatrics, 161*(3), 526–530. doi:10.1016/j.jpeds.2012.02.016

Kelley, M. L., Self-Brown, B. L., Bosson, J. V., Hernandez, B. C., & Gordon, A. T. (2010). Predicting posttraumatic stress symptoms in children following Hurricane Katrina: A prospective analysis of the effect of parental distress and parenting practices. *Journal of Traumatic Stress, 23*(5), 582–590.

Kingston, D., Tough, S., & Whitfield, H. (2012). Prenatal and postpartum maternal psychological distress and infant development: A systematic review. *Child Psychiatry and Human Development, 43,* 683–714. doi:10.1007/s10578-012-0291-4

Kubicek, K., Ramirez, M., Limbos, M. A., & Iverson, E. (2008). Knowledge and behaviors of parents in planning for and dealing with emergencies. *Journal of Community Health, 33,*158–168. doi:10.1007/s10900-007-9078-0

Lawrence, R. A. (2011). Disasters at home and abroad. *Breastfeeding Medicine, 6*(2), 53–54. doi:10.1089/bfm/2011.9993

Lee, K. G. (updated November 14, 2011). Meconium aspiration syndrome. Retrieved March 3, 2014, from http://www.nlm.nih.gov/medlineplus/ency/article/001596.htm

Mace, S. E., Doyle, C., Fuchs, S., Gausche-Hill, M., Koenig, K. L., Sorrentino, A., & Johnson, R. W. (2012). Pediatric patients in a disaster: Part of the all-hazard, comprehensive approach to disaster management. *American Journal of Disaster Medicine, 7*(2), 111–125.

March of Dimes. (2006). Prepare for a disaster: Information for anyone caring for a newborn. Retrieved January 15, 2014, from http://www.marchofdimes.com/baby/prepare-for-a-disaster-information-for-anyone-caring-for-a-newborn.aspx

March of Dimes (2013). Long-term health effects of premature birth. Retrieved March 12, 2014, from http://www.marchofdimes.com/baby/long-term-health-effects-of -premature-birth.aspx#

Mason, K. E., Urbansky, H., Crocker, L., Connor, M., Anderson, M. R., & Kisson, N. (2011). Pediatric emergency mass critical care: Focus on family-centered care. *Pediatric Critical Care Medicine, 12*(6), s157–s162. doi:10.1097/PCC.0b013e318234a812

Masten, A. S., & Osofsky, J. D. (2010). Disasters and their impact on child development: Introduction to the special section. *Child Development, 81*(4), 1029–1039. doi:10.1111 /j.1467-8624.2010.01452.x

McBride, D. L. (2011). Children and disaster planning: National Commission Findings. *Journal of Pediatric Nursing, 26*(6), 593–594. doi:10.1016/j.pedn.2011.05.002

McGrath, J. M., Records, K., & Rice, M. (2008). Maternal depression and infant temperament characteristics. *Infant Behavior and Development, 31*(1), 71–80.

Mclaughlin, K. A., Fairbank, J. A, Gruber. M. J., Jones, R. T., Lakoma, M. D., Pfefferbaum, B., . . . Kessler, R. C. (2009). Serious emotional disturbance among youth exposed to Hurricane Katrina 2 years post-disaster. *Journal of the American Academy of Child and Adolescent Psychiatry, 48*(11), 1069–1178.

Murphy, S. T., Cody, M. C., Frank, L. B., Glik, D., & Ang, A. (2009). Predictors of emergency preparedness and compliance. *Disaster Medicine and Public Health Preparedness, 3*, S1–S9.

National Center for Missing and Exploited Children. (2014). *Disaster response.* Retrieved March 1, 2014, from http://www.missingkids.com/DisasterResponse

National Commission on Children and Disasters. (2010). *2010 Report to the President and Congress.* Retrieved March 1, 2014, from http://www.ahrq.gov/prep/nccdreport

National Survey of Children with Special Health Care Needs (NS-CSHCN). (2009/2010). Data query from the Child and Adolescent Health Measurement Initiative. Retrieved February 12, 2014, from Data Resource Center for Child and Adolescent Health website: www.childhealthdata.org

New York City Alliance Against Sexual Assault. (2006). *Katrina, natural disasters and sexual violence.* Retrieved March 10, 2014, from http://www.svfreenyc.org/research_fact sheet_111.html

Norris, F. H., Friedman, M. J., & Watson, P. J. (2002). 60,000 disaster victims speak, II: Summary and implications of the disaster mental health research. *Psychiatry, 65*(3), 240–260.

Office on Women's Health, U.S. Department of Health & Human Services. (2013, September 24). Why breastfeeding is important. Retrieved March 10, 2014, from http://www.womenshealth.gov/breastfeeding/why-breastfeeding-is-important/

Peek, L., & Stough, L. M. (2010). Children with disabilities in the context of disaster: A social vulnerability perspective. *Child Development, 81*(4), 1260–1270. doi:10.1111 /j.1467-8624.2010.01466.x

Pfefferbaum, B., & North, C. S. (2013). Assessing children's disaster reactions and mental health needs: Screening and clinical evaluation. *Canadian Journal of Psychiatry, 58*(3), 135–142.

Pfefferbaum, B., & Shaw, J. A.; the American Academy of Child and Adolescent Psychiatry Committee of Quality Issues. (2013). Practice parameter on disaster preparedness. *Journal of the American Academy of Child & Adolescent Psychiatry, 52*(11), 1224–1238. doi:10.1016/j.jaac.2013.08.014

Pfefferbaum, B., Newman, E., & Nelson, S. D. (2014). Mental health interventions for children exposed to disasters and terrorism. *Journal of Child and Adolescent Psychopharmacology, 24*(1), 24–31. doi:10.1089/cap.2013.0061

Phillips, P., Niedergesaess, Y., Powers, R., & Brandt, R. (2012). Disaster preparedness: Emergency planning in the NICU. *Neonatal Network, 31*(1), 5–15. doi:10.1891/0730 -0832.31.1.5

Pinkert, M., Dar, S., Goldberg, D., Abargel, A., Cohen-Marom, O., Kreiss, Y., & Merin, O. (2013). Lessons learned from an obstetrics and gynecology field hospital response to natural disasters. *Obstetrics and Gynecology, 122*(3), 532–536. doi:10.1097/AOG .0b013e31829b5938

Rath, B., Young, E. A., Harris, A., Perrin, K., Bronfin, D. R., Ratard, R., . . . Magnus, M. (2011). Adverse respiratory symptoms and environmental exposures among children and adolescents following Hurricane Katrina. *Public Health Reports, 129*, 853–860.

Sakashita, K., Matthews, W. J., & Yamamoto, L. G. (2013). Disaster preparedness for technology and electricity-dependent children and youth with special healthcare needs. *Clinical Pediatrics, 52*(6), 549–556. doi:10.1177/0009922813482762

Save the Children. (2013a). Disaster preparedness tips for parents. Retrieved September 18, 2013, from http://www.savethechildren.org/site/c.8rKLIXMGIPI4E/b.7522429 /k.2474/Disaster_Preparedness_Tips_for_Parents.htm

Save the Children. (2013b). A national report card on protecting children in disasters. Retrieved March 1, 2014, from http://www.savethechildren.org/site/c.8rKLIXM GIpI4E/b.8777053/k.F31D/Get_Ready_Get_Safe_Disaster_Report_Card.htm

Stuber, J., Galea, S., Pfefferbaum, B., Vandivere, S., Moore, K., & Fairbrother, G. (2005). Behavior problems in the New York City's children after the September 11, 2001 terrorist attacks. *American Journal of Orthopsychiatry, 75*(2), 190–200. doi:10.1037 /0002-9432.75.2.190

Tees, M. T., Harville, E. W., Xiong, X., Buekens, P., Pridjian, G., & Elkind-Hirsch. (2010). Hurricane Katrina-related maternal stress, maternal mental health and early infant temperament. *Maternal and Child Health Journal, 14*(4), 511–518. doi:10.1007 /s10995-009-0486-x

Thornton, W. E., & Voigt, L. (2007). Disaster rape: Vulnerability of women to sexual assaults during Hurricane Katrina. *Journal of Public Management and Social Policy, 13*(2), 23–49.

Torche, F., & Kleinhaus, K. (2012). Prenatal stress, gestational age and secondary sex ration: The sex-specific effects of exposure to a natural disaster in early pregnancy. *Human Reproduction, 27*(2), 558–567. doi:10.1093/humrep/der390

Turner, T. J., Barnes, H., Reid, J., & Garrubba, M. (2010). Evidence for perinatal and child health care guidelines in crisis settings: Can Cochrane help? *BMC Public Health, 10*(170). doi:10.1186 /1471-2458-10-170

United States Department of the Interior. (2012, November). Deaths from U.S. earthquakes. Retrieved February 18, 2014, from http://earthquake.usgs.gov/earthquakes /states/us_deaths.php

Wilson, A. C., Lengua, L. J., Meltzoff, A. N., & Smith, K. A. (2010). Parenting and temperament prior to September 11, 2001, and parenting specific to 9/11 as predictors of children's posttraumatic stress symptoms following 9/11. *Journal of Clinical Child and Adolescent Psychology, 39*(4), 445–459. doi:10.1080/15374416.2010.486317.

Zhu, P., Sun, M. S., Hao, J. H., Chen, Y. J., Jiang, X. M., Tao, R. X. . . Tao, F. B. (2014). Does prenatal maternal stress impair cognitive development and alter temperament characteristics in toddlers with health birth outcomes? *Developmental Medicine and Child Neurology, 56*(3), 283–289. doi:10.1111/dmcn.12378

Zilversmit, L., Sappenfield, O., Zotti, M., & McGehee, M. A. (2014). Preparedness planning for emergencies among postpartum women in Arkansas during 2009. *Women's Health Issues, 24*(10), e83–e88. doi:10.1016/j.whi.2013.10.006

Persons With Disabilities and Disasters

A significant proportion of the American population is affected by disabilities. According to the Federal Emergency Management Agency (FEMA) Office of Disability Integration and Coordination, 56.4 million Americans (20% of the population) have at least one disability, including 12% of all children, 10% of adults aged 18 to 64, and 38% of seniors over age 65 (FEMA, 2011). FEMA further breaks down these statistics by type of disability and indicates: 30 million with a hearing disability, 14 million with a mobility disability, 10 million with a vision disability, 2 million with a speech disability, and 16.1 million with a cognitive, intellectual, or mental health issue. In addition, one in three Americans takes prescription drugs to treat chronic disease. Others may suffer a temporary disability from illness, accident, or surgery.

Among the populations that are vulnerable in disasters, such as frail older adults, infants and children, and people with mental illnesses, the research literature is perhaps most extensive for those with physical disabilities. In part, this is due to federal regulations, such as the Americans with Disabilities Act (ADA) and lessons learned from the problems encountered by the disabled in recent U.S. disasters including the 9/11 World Trade Center (WTC) bombings and Hurricane Katrina.

Nonetheless, a clear need exists for much more empirical research on disaster preparedness and recovery. Much of the research literature on individual preparedness takes the form of survey data to assess perceptions of preparedness and self-report of preparedness activities. For first responder intervention in disaster with the disabled, much of the literature also involves survey data, but far less has been published on evidence of effectiveness of measures than in individual planning.

THE VULNERABILITY OF PERSONS WITH DISABILITIES IN DISASTERS

CASE STUDY: Snowstorm, Oregon

In 2008, a rare winter storm buried Portland, Oregon under more than a foot of snow. The city was gridlocked. Nickole Chevron was stuck in her home for 8 days. Many people would consider that an inconvenience. For Nickole, whose muscles are too weak to support her body, those 8 days were potentially life-threatening. Born with spinal muscular atrophy, a genetic disease that progressively weakens the body's muscles, Nickole is fully reliant on a wheelchair and full-time caregivers for most routine tasks. Being alone for 8 days was not an option. So Nickole signed up for "Ready Now!," an emergency preparedness training program developed through the Oregon Office of Disability and Health.

"The most important thing I learned from 'Ready Now!' was to have a back-up plan in case of an emergency situation," she said. "When I heard the storm was coming, I emailed all my caregivers to find out who lived close by and who would be available. I made sure I had a generator, batteries for my wheelchair, and at least a week's supply of food, water and prescription medication" (CDC, 2012).

While all disasters create new physical barriers and disrupt services, for people with disabilities, unexpected disaster may prevent them from doing tasks they are accustomed to being able to accomplish independently; disasters may also prevent those with disabilities from responding to disasters in the way that others do (CIDNY, 2004). A number of researchers have identified individuals with disabilities as one of the most vulnerable populations in a wide range of disasters (e.g., Chou et al., 2004; Hogaboom, Oyster, Riggins, & Boninger, 2013; Hogan et al., 2011; Lemyre, Gibson, Zlepnig, Meyer-Macleod, & Boutette, 2009; Peek & Stough,

2010; Renne, Sanchez, & Litman, 2011). Logistically, difficulties exist in responding to the disabled in a disaster because emergency personnel may be already
spread thin, with little extra resources to assist individuals with special disability needs (NCD, 2009). Rural areas may be overwhelmed due to isolation, lack
of resources, and lack of personnel. Urban areas may be overwhelmed due to
the sheer number of people involved in a disaster. Many of the guidelines for
disaster evacuation for the general population involve moving (walking or run-
ning) or communicating in ways that may not be possible for some persons with
disabilities. The National Council on Disability (NCD, 2009) has identified three
main types of disability and described key concerns affecting them in a disaster:
mobility, sensory, and developmental/cognitive.

The Vulnerability of Persons With Mobility Impairments/Chronic Health Conditions in Disasters

Approximately 5.5% of adults aged 21 to 64, 16% of adults aged 65 to 75, and
33.4% of adults aged 75 and older in the United States report a mobility disability
(Erikson, Lee, & von Schrader, 2012). According to the NCD (2009), individuals
with a mobility disability have little to no use of their legs or arms and often rely
on wheelchairs, walkers, or other devices to maintain movement. Key concerns
during a disaster include the ability to quickly shelter for a rapid-onset event,
losing durable medical equipment during an evacuation, transportation in debris
covered roads, and reoccupying a home that may be damaged.

Individuals with mobility impairments or chronic health conditions may be
at increased personal risk during a disaster. One simulation experiment assessed
the potential problems that individuals with mobility disabilities might face in
a disaster (Rahima, 1994). A living room was set up with 72 participants going
through the earthquake simulation. Of these, 24 had powered wheelchairs,
24 had manual wheelchairs, and 24 were able-bodied as a comparison group.
Those in wheelchairs had much more difficulty navigating the room than the able-
bodied, and among wheelchair users, those in manual wheelchairs performed
instructed tasks significantly faster than the ones with powered wheelchairs. Real-
life accounts of the WTC attack revealed difficulties among the disabled in evacuating. Some workers with disabilities were helped by colleagues without disabilities,
but some relying on wheelchairs and walkers were left behind to wait for rescuers
who were never able to reach them (NIST, 2005; Sullivan, & Häkkinen, 2006).

Difficulties such as lack of accessibility to food and clean water, extremes of
heat or cold, physical and mental stress, possible injury, or exposure to infection may
exacerbate existing problems for persons with disabilities (Mokdad et al., 2005). For
those who require some assistance for completing activities of daily living, a disaster
may separate a person with a disability from access to health care workers and/or
treatment facilities. The losses in a disaster may affect those with mobility disabilities differentially than the general population due to loss of mobility aids, medicines,
and durable equipment (Kett, Stubbs, & Yeo, 2005). After Hurricane Katrina, a telephone survey indicated that 20.6% of survivors with one or more chronic conditions

either cut back or terminated their treatment due to the disaster (HKCAG & Kessler, 2007). During the 1998 ice storm of Eastern Canada, many patients dependent on power or home health care had to be transported to hospitals (Riddex & Dellgar, 2001). Such loss of independence was also described in a qualitative study involving focus groups with 56 survivors of Hurricane Katrina who had disabilities or worked with individuals with disabilities (Fox, White, Rooney, & Rowland, 2010). While families were an important source of support, many reported stress associated with having to live with family members after the storm and having to be dependent on them to take care of basic needs. In addition, disruptions in access to transportation, health care, employment, and communications made it difficult to return to the level of independence experienced before the storm.

The Vulnerability of Persons With Sensory Limitations or Cognitive/Developmental Disorders in Disasters

The two main types of sensory disabilities involve either hearing or visual limitations. According to the NCD (2009), the key concerns for individuals with sensory disabilities during a disaster are being able to read the educational and training materials for preparing for a disaster, hearing warning messages or seeing the area of concern on televised weather maps, understanding the meteorologist if closed captioning is not offered or if they turn away from the camera, and navigating to shelters.

Approximately 2.2% of adults aged 21 to 64, 9.1% of adults aged 65 to 74, and 22.7% of adults aged 75 or older report a hearing disability (Erikson et al., 2012). Rates are higher for report of hearing loss. According to the National Institute on Deafness and Other Communication Disorders (NIDCD, 2010), approximately 30% of adults aged 65 to 75 and 47% of adults aged 75 or older have experienced some degree of hearing loss. In addition, the NIDCD reports that only one in five people who could benefit from a hearing aid actually uses one. The use of the term "disability" in association with deafness is also problematic. Individuals who are deaf do not always view themselves as disabled, but as part of a deaf culture, whose members are part of a linguistic minority group centered on the use of sign language (Engelman et al., 2013).

A recent review of the peer-reviewed literature found that there was almost no information about emergency preparedness and training for individuals who are deaf or hard of hearing (Engelman et al., 2013). Many members of the deaf community rely on sign language in order to communicate and English may be best considered a second language (Calgaro et al., 2013). The problem is exemplified by the conditions for the deaf community during Hurricane Katrina (Sullivan & Häkkinen, 2006). Deaf individuals were isolated to an area designated as the "Deaf Area" without adequate signing translators and unable to hear the public address announcements. Today, problems still exist with preparedness and response information not being available in accessible forms and limited options for contacting emergency services during a disaster (Calgaro, 2013).

Approximately 1.8% of adults aged 21 to 64, 4.1% of adults aged 65 to 74, and 10.3% of adults aged 75 or older report a visual disability (Erikson et al., 2012). Overall, approximately 1 million Americans are legally blind and 12 million are visually impaired (AAO, 2011; CDC, 2011). While disaster and disability research and sources often identify the visually impaired as a vulnerable population, peer-reviewed literature on any aspect of disasters and visual impairments is lacking. One account described two cases during the WTC attack of guide dogs assisting owners to safety, with one dog descending 71 floors (Sullivan & Häkkinen, 2006). Chapter 9 provides information on disasters and animals, which includes attention to service animals that are vital to assisting the blind during disasters.

Very little information was identified in the literature involving disasters and persons with cognitive and developmental limitations in disasters. Some face communication issues that are similar to those with hearing difficulties; others face similar problems to those with mobility impairments in reliance on caretakers to meet their activities of daily living. Approximately 4.3 % of adults aged 21 to 64, 5.5% of adults aged 65 to 74, and 14.5% of adults aged 75 or older report a hearing disability (Erikson et al., 2012). According to the NCD (2005), individuals with a developmental/cognitive disability have conditions that may affect the ability to listen, think, speak, read, write, do math, or follow instructions. Key concerns during a disaster are difficulty in understanding instructions, fear of responders, and isolation in a shelter, from friends, family members, or caretakers.

Willingness of Health Care Workers to Respond in Disasters

One of the challenges in mounting a successful response to a disaster with any vulnerable population involves accounting for the extent to which a disaster affects those who are called to respond. In some cases, the conditions of the disaster may prevent health care workers from being able to reach vulnerable populations, such as those with disabilities. In other cases, health care workers may be unwilling to respond due to the need to take care of their own families or due to fears of becoming injured or infected.

Over seven million people rely on home health care services due to disability or age, representing nearly three times the number of hospitalized patients (Gershon et al., 2007; Knebel & Phillips, 2008). In the United States, there are approximately 17,700 public and private home health care agencies that employ nurses, home health aides, social workers, physical therapists, respiratory therapists, durable medical equipment providers, and personal caregivers (Knebel & Phillips, 2008). A disaster may create a major disruption in services for these individuals. One meta-analysis reviewed 25 quantitative and 2 qualitative studies to determine the willingness of health care workers to respond to a disaster situation (Chaffee, 2009). It was found that the three primary factors determining willingness to respond were the type of disaster, concern for family, and concern about personal safety.

A particular concern of home health care workers is disasters that involve the outbreak of an infectious disease. One study surveyed 1,025 home health aides, home attendants, and personal care workers who were asked whether or not they would care for a client who was in quarantine due to exposure to an infectious agent such as avian influenza or anthrax (Gershon et al., 2007). The majority (51%) said that they would not provide care, 38% were "not sure," and 11% indicated that they would provide care. The study also surveyed 217 registered nurses, asking them if they would be willing to provide care for a patient with avian influenza if personal protective equipment were provided. Of the nurses, 37% said that they would, 27% said they would not, and 37% said that they were not sure.

A number of logistical issues also arise with pandemics for those who receive home care or reside in a health care facility. Infectious disease may spread more rapidly in these populations due to potential introduction of the virus by health care workers in contact with multiple people or due to general compromised health (Campbell, Gilyard, Sinclair, Sternberg, & Kailes, 2009). During a pandemic, hospitalized patients may be discharged as soon as feasible to make way for those who are more acutely ill, putting further strain on home health care resources (Knebel & Phillips, 2008). In pandemics, it can be anticipated that the availability of home care workers may be decreased significantly, while the need for their services increases significantly.

THE DISASTER FRAMEWORK AND PERSONS WITH DISABILITIES

CASE STUDY: World Trade Center, 9/11/2001

One man's final image as he left the 80th floor (of the WTC on September 11, 2001) and made it to safety was that of a room full of people using wheelchairs and walkers waiting to be rescued by the firefighters who were coming up the stairs. They all perished as the building collapsed shortly after. . . . After the [earlier] 1993 bombing, many tenants of the WTC and the building management for the complex were aware that evacuation plans for people with disabilities were needed. Unfortunately, the evacuation plan for people with disabilities was lethal to them: it consisted simply of requiring them to go to predetermined meeting sites within the building and wait for evacuation assistance (CIDNY, 2004, citing Melledy, 2001).

For individuals with disabilities, the three core components of personal preparedness are basically the same for individuals without disabilities: to develop an emergency plan, to prepare an emergency supply kit, and to develop a communication plan. For all three, preparedness should include plans both to shelter in place and to evacuate. However, for people with disabilities, making these arrangements can be more complex due to potential needs for specialized equipment, medications, and treatments, and for some, communication difficulties during a disaster. Table 5.1 provides disaster guidelines for persons with disabilities, Table 5.2 provides responder guidelines for persons with disabilities, and Table 5.3 provides employer guidelines for persons with disabilities.

TABLE 5.1 Personal Preparedness for Persons With Disabilities

BE INFORMED
• Be aware of the types of disasters that occur in your area and county warning procedures, evacuation plans, and shelters before disaster strikes • Be aware of evacuation procedures in your workplace; know the location of fire extinguishers and emergency alarms • Monitor television, radio, Internet, and social media news reports as able for information from authorities on local conditions and official instructions • Know your community's response and evacuation plans

MAKE A PLAN

General
• Keep by your bedside a charged phone, a flashlight, and prescription glasses
• Make an assessment of any limitations you may have that will require assistance in an emergency evacuation, including: mobility issues; fatigue or reduced stamina; respiratory conditions; emotional, cognitive, thinking, or learning difficulties; vision loss; hearing loss; temporary limitations such as recent surgery or accident; reliance on technology or medication that may not work in an emergency, such as hearing aids, wheelchair, gas mask, elevator, lighting, sounds
• Register with the local emergency services organization if special warning procedures, evacuation assistance, and/or special shelter facilities are needed; some fire departments also have registries for people who may need extra assistance
• Check the accessibility of local shelters and hotels and the availability of support services in those areas
• People living in nursing homes, assisted living facilities, or similar supervised settings should be aware of the disaster plans in place and how relatives will be notified if evacuation is necessary
• Perform routine mock drills and revise plan as necessary
• Complete an Emergency Health Information Card and keep it with you at all times
• Fire Safety:
  ○ Keep batteries charged in smoke alarms
  ○ Know where fire extinguishers are and how to operate them
  ○ Test smoke alarms once a month
  ○ For added safety, interconnect all the smoke alarms so that when one sounds, they all sound
  ○ If possible, purchase alarms with nonreplaceable (life-long) batteries designed to be effective for up to 10 years; these can be helpful for people who have difficulty changing batteries
  ○ If you are deaf, use strobe light smoke alarm alert devices; pillow and bed shakers can also be used
  ○ If you are hard of hearing, but not deaf, a smoke alarm accessory that produces a loud, mixed low-pitch sound is most effective; pillow and bed shakers can also be used
  ○ If possible, choose an apartment with a sprinkler system or install the system in home

Sheltering in Place and Evacuation
• Develop a plan to shelter in place
  ○ Be prepared to shelter in place in the event that you are unable to evacuate or are advised by local officials to stay where you are, including an emergency kit (see below)
  ○ If you use medical equipment at home that requires electricity, develop a backup plan for its use during a power outage
• Develop a plan to evacuate
  ○ Plan two ways out of every room
  ○ Know your community's response and evacuation plans and plan an evacuation route from your home
  ○ Plan for transportation if you need to evacuate to a shelter
  ○ Always evacuate if you are told by medical or other official personnel to evacuate or seek treatment
  ○ Keep equipment with you in an evacuation; if you use a wheelchair and cannot take it, bring the cushion

(continued)

TABLE 5.1 Personal Preparedness for Persons With Disabilities (*continued*)

○ If there is sufficient time, shut off valves for household utilities (gas, electricity, water)
○ Recommendations for mitigating potential impairments for evacuating: bolt bookshelves to walls; anchor outdoor items that can be projectiles in high winds and hurricanes; install hurricane shutters (if appropriate to area); trim trees that overhang roofs; repair cracks in ceilings and foundations; store flammable materials away from heat sources

Communication—Family, Friend, and Neighbor Communication Plan

- Make a list of family, friends, and others who will be part of your personal support network and communication plan
- Include a friend or relative from another area who would not be affected by the same emergency and can help if needed
- Decide where to meet your household members if you should become separated
- Notify members of your personal support network if you plan to go out of town
- Inform your personal support network how you plan to evacuate your home, school, or workplace and where you will go in the event of a disaster
- Make sure someone in your personal network has an extra key to your home and knows where you keep your emergency supplies
- If you use medical devices such as a wheelchair, oxygen, or other medical equipment, make sure several people in your personal support network know how to operate these devices
- If you receive support services such as meals, transportation, and home health care, talk with service providers about potential backup service providers in the area to which you will evacuate
- Make sure a trusted friend or relative has copies of important medical and any other important documents

BUILD A KIT

- Basic supplies:
  - ○ A 3-day supply of food and water
  - ○ Flashlight and batteries
  - ○ Hand-crank or battery-operated radio
  - ○ Cell phone with charger, inverter, or solar charger
- Basic first aid kit (American Red Cross for a family of four):
  - ○ Bandages and dressings: 2 absorbent compress dressings (5.9 inches); 25 adhesive bandages (assorted sizes); 1 adhesive cloth tape (10 yards × 1 inch);1 roller bandage (3 inches wide); 1 roller bandage (4 inches wide); 5 sterile gauze pads (3 × 3 inches); 5 sterile gauze pads (4 × 4 inches); 2 triangular bandages
  - ○ Medications/wound care: 2 packets of aspirin (for adults only); 5 antibiotic ointment packets (approximately 1 gram); 5 antiseptic wipe packets; 2 hydrocortisone packets
  - ○ Other supplies and equipment: blanket; breathing barrier (with one-way valve); instant cold compress; 2 pairs of nonlatex gloves (large); scissors; oral thermometer; tweezers
  - ○ First aid instruction booklet
- Medical supplies
  - ○ Medications: a 3- to 7-day supply of prescription medications if possible
  - ○ Equipment: as applicable, an extra pair of prescription glasses; hearing aid batteries and spare hearing aids (if available); incontinence supplies; battery charger for motorized wheelchairs or other battery-operated medical/assistive devices; list of style, serial number, and operating instructions for medical devices
  - ○ Documentation: copies of important documents in a waterproof container, including a list of all medications, prescriptions, doctor's orders, medical records and history, insurance cards and/or Medicare/Medicaid cards, physician contact information, list of allergies, list of nonprofit or community-based organizations that may be able to assist you with health needs
  - ○ Other medical Information: medical alert tags or written descriptions of your health/disability needs; if you have a communication disability, include information for responders on the best way to communicate, pen and paper or a laminated communication board

(*continued*)

TABLE 5.1 Personal Preparedness for Persons With Disabilities (*continued*)

- Other supplies for home emergency kit: whistle to signal for help; dust mask to help filter contaminated air and plastic sheeting and duct tape to shelter in place; sanitation items (moist towelettes, toilet paper, garbage bags); local maps; wrench or pliers to turn off utilities; manual can opener; extra cash or traveler's checks if possible; extra batteries; extra blankets
- Finances: Federal Emergency Management Association (FEMA) suggests making arrangements for direct deposit of paycheck and federal benefits and use of the Direct Express® prepaid credit card
- Other documents: consider including records such as social security number, charge and bank account information, tax records, will, etc. A portable thumb drive is an option for storing important information
- Pets and service animals: food, water, first aid, and other supplies if you have a pet or service animal (see Chapter 9)
- Prepare a kit for sheltering in place and a smaller, lightweight kit if you need to evacuate

Sources: ARC (2004, 2014); CDC (2014); CDR (1997); Kailes (2002); CIDNY (2004); FEMA (2012, 2014); ITTF (2004); Markenson et al. (2007); NCD (2005); NFPA (2013); NOD (2009b); OODH (2009); White et al. (2007).

Preparedness, Prevention, and Mitigation for Persons With Disabilities

Evidence of Development of an Individualized Emergency Plan Among Persons With Disabilities

The development of an emergency plan before a disaster strikes is essential across populations. Several studies have indicated that although persons with disabilities are more vulnerable than the general population in disasters, they tend to be no less likely to be prepared for a disaster. Some studies have found that individuals with disabilities are less likely to have developed an emergency plan.

In a random-digit-dial telephone survey of the noninstitutionalized population in Los Angeles County, significant differences were found in having a prior emergency plan among those who rated their health as fair/poor (34.8%) compared with those who rated their health as excellent (44.8%; Eisenman et al., 2009). Similar findings were found in a six-state analysis (Delaware, Louisiana, Montana, Nevada, New Hampshire, and Tennessee) of Behavioral Risk Factor Surveillance System (BRFSS) from 2006 to 2007. Researchers found that persons in these states with disabilities were significantly more likely to state that they were not prepared at all for an emergency (Smith & Notaro, 2009). Another BRFSS survey conducted in six states from 2006 to 2008 indicated that those with a physical disability, three or more chronic diseases, or perceived fair/poor health were less likely to have developed an emergency evacuation plan than their healthier counterparts (Bethel et al., 2011). The states in this survey were the same as the previous BRFSS, except that Georgia was used instead of New Hampshire. Surprisingly, in a survey of evacuees *after* Hurricane Katrina, persons with disabilities were found to be less likely to have developed a prior evacuation plan than those without disabilities (Spence, Lachlan, Burke, & Seeger, 2007).

Currently, little research is available that addresses differences in preparedness among individuals with different types of disabilities. In another multistate survey

TABLE 5.2 Responder Guidelines for Persons With Disabilities in Disasters

GENERAL TRAINING
• Disability sensitivity training to raise awareness of the diversity of the disability community, limiting effects of a disability, how to assist persons with disabilities, appropriate use of language, and disability-specific training

COMMUNICATION STRATEGIES

• General
  ○ Include on medical forms any special communication needs the person may have
• Hearing impaired
  ○ Have a communication board or notepads, pens, and pencils available
  ○ Learn emergency sign language and finger spelling
  ○ Face the individual directly and speak clearly
  ○ Make sure the individual evacuates with hearing aids, if applicable
• Visually impaired
  ○ Learn how to guide persons with visual impairments
  ○ Make sure the individual evacuates with eyeglasses, if applicable
• Intellectually impaired/developmentally disabled
  ○ Present information slowly, use simple language, and speak in short sentences; repeat if needed
  ○ Be aware that individuals with learning or cognitive disabilities may have difficulty in remembering or responding to disaster instructions
  ○ Limit unnecessary conversation if the person becomes confused or disoriented; the primary focus should be on the need to evacuate

HEALTH ISSUES
• Inquire about any medical conditions they may have • Inquire if medication is taken and if individuals have medications on hand • Ask if any assistance is needed with walking, eating, bathing, dressing, toileting, or medication administration • Assist evacuees in gathering necessary medications, assistive equipment (glasses, walkers, hearing aids, etc.) and other medical supplies or equipment • Learn how to move individuals who use a breathing apparatus or other life-sustaining equipment before evacuating • Learn to differentiate between persons with disabilities and individuals in need of medical treatment • Be aware that medical conditions may worsen in a disaster situation

EVACUATION AND RESCUE
• Ask persons with disabilities to explain the best way for transporting, transferring, and assisting them • Ask persons with disabilities if they need assistance to find family and friends • Ask persons with disabilities if they have a plan for where they will go when they leave the residence • Learn the use of wheelchairs and other specialized mobility equipment • Learn how to move and transfer the bedridden and frail older adults • Learn how to rescue persons from paratransit vans and buses • If individuals must be separated from assistive devices or service animals, make plan for return

Sources: CDR (1997); CIDNY (2004); Dyer, Regev, Burnett, Festa, and Cloyd (2008); FEMA (2010); Markenson, Fuller, and Redlener (2007); SILC (2004); White et al. (2007).

(California, Florida, Louisiana, Missouri, North Carolina, West Virginia, and Texas), differences in preparedness were assessed among those with medical impairments, mobility impairments, hearing impairments, cognitive impairments, visual impairments, and other impairments. The results from this telephone and mail-in survey (n = 1,162) found that persons with cognitive disabilities were the most likely to have

TABLE 5.3 Employer Guidelines for Persons With Disabilities in Disasters

ASSESS ACCOMMODATION NEEDS OF EMPLOYEES
<ul><li>After making a job offer, but before employment begins, an employer may ask all individuals whether they will need assistance during an emergency</li><li>An employer may periodically survey current employees to determine if they will require assistance in an emergency as long as the employer makes it clear that self-identification is voluntary and conveys the purpose of requesting information</li><li>An employer may ask individuals with known disabilities if they will need assistance during an evacuation</li></ul>*Note*: The American Disabilities Act requires employers to keep all medical information confidential; however, first aid and safety personnel may be informed

CREATE AN EMERGENCY EVACUATION PLAN
<ul><li>The plan should be written and distributed to all employees</li><li>Mock evacuation drills should be performed periodically</li><li>Evaluation plans should be periodically revised and updated</li><li>All accommodation equipment used in emergency evacuation should be inspected and maintained in proper working order</li></ul>

PROVISION OF GENERAL ACCOMMODATIONS
<ul><li>Emergency alarms and signs showing the emergency exit routes</li><li>Implement a "buddy system" for employees, involving employees working in teams so that they can locate one another</li><li>Designate areas of rescue assistance. If these areas do not have escape routes, they should have the following:<ul><li>Communication equipment (operating phone, cell phone, text telephone [TTY], and a two-way radio)</li><li>Closing door</li><li>Supplies that enable individuals to block smoke from entering the room from under the door</li><li>A window and something to write (marker, lipstick) or a "help" sign to alert rescuers</li><li>Respirator masks</li></ul></li></ul>

ACCOMMODATIONS FOR THOSE WITH MOTOR IMPAIRMENTS
<ul><li>Employers can purchase evacuation devices to move people with motor impairments down the stairs or across rough terrain. If used, personnel should be trained to use and maintain them.</li><li>Employers should remove physical barriers (boxes, supplies, furniture) to ensure a barrier-free route of travel out of the building</li><li>Employers may want to provide heavy gloves to protect assister's hands from debris when pushing a manual wheelchair, a patch kit to repair flat tires, and extra batteries for those who use motorized wheelchairs or scooters</li></ul>

ACCOMMODATIONS FOR THOSE WITH SENSORY IMPAIRMENTS
<ul><li>Employers should install lighted fire strobes or other visual or vibrating alerting devices to supplement audible alarms (strobe lights should not exceed five flashes per second due to risk of seizures)</li><li>Employers may want to provide alerting devices, vibrating paging devices, wireless communicators, or two-way paging systems to alert individuals with hearing impairments of the need to evacuate</li><li>Employers should install tactile signage and maps for employees with vision impairments such as Braille signage, audible directional signage, and pedestrian systems</li><li>Employers may want to provide alpha-numeric pagers or other communication devices to individuals with speech impairments so that they can communicate with personnel in an emergency</li></ul>

(continued)

TABLE 5.3 Employer Guidelines for Persons With Disabilities in Disasters (*continued*)

ACCOMMODATIONS FOR THOSE WITH COGNITIVE OR PSYCHOLOGICAL IMPAIRMENTS
• Employers should consider ways of communicating with people who have cognitive impairments such as picture of buddies, color coding of escape doors and areas of rescue assistance, and information on tape or CD-ROM • Employers should consider that those with psychiatric impairment may benefit from mock drills, or it could trigger anxiety. Those individuals should be notified ahead of time and given the opportunity to opt out

Sources: Kailes (2002); CIDNY (2004); DOL-ODEP-JAN (2013).

steps in place for household preparedness while those who were hearing impaired were the least likely (Gerber, Norwood, & Zakour, 2010). Further research in this area will be important to elucidate potential reasons why the hearing impaired may be less likely to prepare and to develop appropriate interventions.

One of the limitations of surveys of levels of preparedness is that in many cases they assess individuals' perceptions of preparedness rather than determining whether actual steps have been taken to make a plan for an emergency. One study that addressed the potential problem was a convenience sample of 487 individuals with spinal cord injuries who use a wheelchair more than 40 hours a week (McClure, Boninger, Oyster, Roach, & Nagy, 2011). Significant differences were found among those who felt they could evacuate in the event of an emergency and those who actually had a plan in place.

Preparation of an Emergency Kit Among Persons With Disabilities

The preparation of an emergency kit is also an essential step for preparedness during a disaster. For the general population, this minimally includes a 3-day supply of food and water, along with useful items such as a flashlight and battery-operated radio. However, for those with disabilities, the minimum level of preparation for survival may also include a supply of needed medications or specialized equipment. Since power outages are common in many types of disasters, it is important to make preparations for medical equipment that may be electrically operated or medications that may need refrigeration. Findings similar to emergency planning have been found with even minimal emergency supplies for the disabled: they are typically at least no more likely and often less likely to have prepared an emergency kit.

One example that illustrates the problem comes from a report of the particular difficulties faced in Southern California by the October 2003 wildfire disaster. At the time, it was the worst wildfire to date in Southern California, burning 730,000 acres, injuring over 200 people, and killing 22 (State Independent Living Council [SILC], 2004). The report indicates that among those with medical or physical disabilities, many had not prepared supplies of medications, durable medical equipment, or other supplies. The problem was compounded because many were located in isolated regions in the mountains that were difficult to access. In addition, due to the isolation, many people relied on wells that were operated by electricity, so they were left without access to potable water.

Several local studies have found that persons with physical disabilities were no more likely to have prepared an emergency kit than those without a disability. A random-digit-dial survey in Jefferson County, Alabama, conducted after a recent series of devastating tornados in the area found that those with diabetes, cardiovascular disease, poor perceived health status, and a mental or emotional activity limitation disability were no more likely than the general population to have prepared an emergency kit (McCormick, 2013). Another random-digit-dial survey of the noninstitutionalized population in Los Angeles County found significant differences in prior preparation of an emergency kit between those who rated their health as fair/poor (40.7%) and those who rated their health as excellent (53.1%; Eisenman et al., 2009). In addition, a survey of Katrina evacuees found that persons with physical disabilities were less likely to have prepared an emergency kit than those without disabilities (Spence, Lachlan, Burke, & Seeger, 2007).

Two of the multistate studies described previously for individual planning for disaster also found a lack of preparation of an emergency kit. Smith and Notaro's (2009) BRFSS data indicated that persons with disabilities were significantly more likely to state that they were not prepared at all for an emergency and were less likely to have a 3-day supply of water or a battery-operated radio. Disabled persons were found to be 1.2 times as likely to be unprepared. In this study, for those with a disability, being female, non-White, less educated, low income, single, and living in an urban area increased the likelihood of being unprepared. In the BRFSS survey, Bethel and colleagues (2011) found that those with fair/poor perceived health, a physical disability, or three or more chronic diseases were less likely to have basic preparedness items (food, water, flashlight, radio) than their healthier counterparts. Interesting though, those with disabilities were more likely to have a 3-day supply of medicine in this study. Although data is limited, these patterns may hold true cross-culturally. Following the 2006 flash floods that affected over 3,000 households in South West Japan, a cross-sectional study by questionnaire found that among 553 patients with rheumatoid arthritis in Japan, only half had taken medical preparedness measures and only one quarter had taken general preparedness measures (Tomio et al., 2012).

Contrasting with these studies, another BRFSS analysis found that individuals with disabilities were slightly more likely to make emergency preparations than those without disabilities (Ablah, Konda, & Kelley, 2009). The five states included in the study were those that use the preparedness modules developed by the Centers for Disease Control and Prevention (CDC): Arizona, Connecticut, Montana, Nevada, and Tennessee. Respondents were defined as prepared if they were deficient in no more than one of six actionable preparedness measures: evacuation planning, water supply, food supply, medication supply, radio, and flashlight. The prepared were more slightly likely than the unprepared to report a disability or health condition requiring special equipment, have diabetes, or have cardiovascular disease.

Another study that may be more telling surveyed 499 evacuees at American Red Cross shelters in Louisiana 2 weeks after Hurricane Katrina (Greenough et al., 2008). Here, rather than relying on respondents' reports of preparedness, they assessed whether or not evacuees had brought needed medication with them to the shelter. Among evacuees with chronic health conditions who arrived without their medications, 47.3% had hypertension, 42.2% had high cholesterol, and 43.6% had diabetes. Overall, among those with any major medical problem, which accounted for 55.6% of the evacuees, 48.4% arrived without medication.

One additional preparedness measure that merits some discussion is fire safety for individuals with hearing disability. Smoke detection devices include tactile bed and pillow shakers, visual strobe lights, and auditory beeping alarms. An important question that has arisen is determining the best device for those who are not deaf, but have mild to moderate hearing loss, particularly while asleep. To differing degrees, age-related hearing loss also affects older adults as well. A study involving 38 subjects with mild to moderately severe hearing loss (25–70 dB) in both ears during sleep tested the relative effectiveness of these devices in successfully waking them up from sleep (Bruck & Thomas, 2009). The research demonstrated that strobe lights awoke 27%, a high-pitched alarm (75 dB) awoke 56%, bed and pillow shakers awoke 80% to 84%, and a 520 Hz square wave T-3 sound alarm (75 dB) awoke 92%. The data suggested that a low-frequency square wave signal was most effective. One reason why this study is important is that it makes clear that the type of smoke alarm best for the hearing impaired differs according to the degree of hearing impairment. An additional finding is the importance of sprinkler systems. Hall (2013) found that sprinklers operated in 91% of structure fires large enough to activate a sprinkler and were effective 96% of the time. Although this study was geared toward preparedness in the workplace, individuals with mobility, hearing, or vision disabilities would particularly benefit from such devices in their homes.

Communication Planning Among Persons With Disabilities

Developing a communication plan is important across all populations facing a disaster. In many disasters, normal channels of communication such as phone and Internet service may be interrupted and it may not be possible to communicate with friends and family members during the event and perhaps for some time afterwards. For anyone, it is important to let members of your social network know where you will evacuate from home, work, or school so that you can be located. The importance of a personal support network is even more important for those with disabilities. For the issues involved may not just be locating friends and family, but having a support network available to help with special needs during a crisis. For those who use medical devices such as wheelchair, oxygen, or other medical equipment, one's support network should include several people who know how to operate these devices. For those who use support services such as home health care or meals, backup plans need to be made in case those services are interrupted. It is also important for those with disabilities to make sure that a friend or neighbor has a house key and that someone in your support network has a copy of important health information in case it is needed after an emergency evacuation.

Little empirical evidence is available on this topic, but the few studies and reports that have been done suggest that individuals with disabilities have a greater need for a support network, but may be less likely to have developed such a network as a safeguard in disaster. In a report from the 2003 Southern California wildfires, it was found that in many cases neighbors did not know where individuals with disabilities lived who needed transportation, nor did they have any way to contact family members (SILC, 2004). According to a broad National Organization on Disability (NOD)/Harris survey, 56% of people with disabilities did not know whom to contact about emergency plans in their community (NOD, 2004). In addition, the survey found that 61% had made no plans for how to quickly and safely evacuate their homes. Further, for those with disabilities who were employed, 32% indicated that no plans had been made for how to evacuate safely from their place of work.

Some evidence exists indicating that social networks improve disaster response for the disabled. In the previously described multistate study by Gerber and colleagues (2010), they found that respondents with multiple volunteer organization memberships have a better capacity to care for themselves in the event of a disaster and to effectively evacuate. Outside of the United States, interviews and questionnaires administered to 315 blind and visually impaired Dutch adolescents and young adults (aged 14–24) indicated that they had fewer extended family members, neighbors, and friends, resulting in a smaller social network compared to a previous study with those who did not have a disability (Kef, Hox, & Habekothé, 2000). Although more research is needed, these studies suggest that individuals with disabilities may have weaker social networks despite their greater need for such networks in order to improve their response and recovery in disasters.

Response and Recovery for Persons With Disabilities

A number of researchers have commented that there is a paucity of studies that address the effectiveness of current emergency preparedness policies and practices to assist persons with disabilities (e.g., Bloodworth, Kevorkian, Rumbaut, & Chiou-Tan, 2007; DOH, 2005; Fox, White, Rooney, & Rowland, 2007; Gerber et al., 2010; Rowland, White, Fox, & Rooney, 2007). A report from the NCD stated that there is a "clear lack of research validating best practices," and a "lack of evidence-based knowledge about how best to organize preparedness, response, and recovery efforts," for persons with disabilities (NOD, 2009a, p. 14).

Given that individuals with a disability constitute nearly one in five members of the population, addressing their needs is critical, not only to ensure the safety of persons with disabilities, but also to ensure that time and resources during a disaster are not taxed for the general population by inadequate and inefficient preparation for dealing with vulnerable populations. A study using data from the BRFSS from the New Orleans–Metairie–Kenner of Louisiana was analyzed to produce estimates from the number of community-dwelling people aged 65 or older with a disability requiring special equipment (McGuire, Ford, & Okoro, 2007). The research demonstrated that approximately 31.6% of older adults with a disability requiring special equipment might require assistance to evacuate. One study suggests that the need has not been adequately addressed by training. A survey of 30 randomly selected FEMA disaster sites between 1998 and 2003 to assess best practices found that people with disabilities were poorly represented in disaster planning (Fox et al., 2007). The study found that although federal training for meeting the needs of the disabled was available, only 27% of emergency managers had completed the train-ing. In addition, only 20% had emergency disability guidelines in place. Following Hurricane Katrina, an NOD study involving interviews with 26 individuals from shelters, community-based organizations, and emergency operations centers found that only 50% of those interviewed had policies, plans, and guidelines in place to accommodate persons with disabilities prior to the hurricane (NOD, 2005).

While few empirical studies are available on the effectiveness of responder practices and policies for persons with the disabled, several post-disaster reports do serve to highlight some of the problems. A report after the 2003 Southern California wildfires found a number of problems with responder rescue efforts (SILC, 2004). Many persons with disabilities who required mobility aids to walk or move were evacuated without those aids. Complicating that issue was a prob-lem that many local independent living centers and paratransit providers were not included in the emergency planning process. Evacuees who were hearing impaired lacked interpreters, were not able to understand public address sys-tems, and televisions were not captioned. In addition, local Red Cross shelters initially did not allow service animals into the shelters.

Similar problems for responder and recovery workers were found in a report on persons with disabilities in New York following the 9/11 terrorist attacks (CIDNY, 2004). Warnings and instructions were not being routinely communicated in ways that could be seen, heard, and understood by people with disabilities. Transportation and access to resources was also a problem. People with disabilities were not always able to travel to sites providing relief services and supplies and delivery of food, medication, oxygen, paratransit services, and home care were unavailable for a pro-longed period of time for those in the "frozen zone," a high-security area where pedestrian and vehicular traffic was restricted. This became a serious issue not only due to lack of basic supplies of food and water, but it also created difficulties in getting prescription medicines and other medical supplies and treatments.

Disparities may also exist between existence of plans and the ability to implement the plans that are in place. In one study, five agencies providing home health care to indigent populations in New Orleans were evaluated in terms of emergency planning and implantation (Kirkpatrick & Bryan, 2007). It was found that although the State Department of Health had provided leadership in making emergency plans, it had not provided such leadership in terms of implementa-tion. The problem was compounded by local departments of health having little responsibility in emergency planning. Further, there was a lack of coordination and effective communication at all government levels.

Kirkpatrick and Bryan (2007) have outlined four recommendations that can lead to more successful evacuations among home health care providers caring for the disabled and others in need of these services:

1. *Early evacuation*—Evacuating before local government announces a mandatory evacuation order was the most important attribute of a successful evacuation. Those agencies that evacuated patients 72 hours ahead of the storm were able to avoid evacuation traffic and found accommodations for their clients with greater success.

2. *Shelter identification outside the high-risk areas*—Being able to i special needs shelters early proves crucial for evacuation su hesitation meant the number of shelters available would d along with the ability to provide care to people with speci

3. *Implement a volunteer communication system*—One agency recruitea volunteers to find transportation assistance for its clients, which greatly improved evacuation success.

4. *Consider evacuation drills*—Conducting regular mock evacuations better prepared agencies to manage evacuation difficulties when they arose.

SUMMARY AND CONCLUSIONS

Over 55 million Americans are persons with one or more disabilities, representing nearly 20% of the population. In any given disaster, odds are that one in five people will have a disability that requires both specialized planning for preparedness and specialized interventions for responders to meet the needs of these individuals. A review of the evidence base for these interventions reveals a number of important issues.

Perhaps most importantly, the data suggests that individuals with disabilities are among the most vulnerable during a disaster. However, persons with disabilities are typically less likely to have developed a personal evacuation plan, prepared an emergency kit, or established an effective social support network to assist in disaster. This points to a great need to find effective ways to improve preparedness among persons with disabilities.

Multiple local, state, and national organizations have developed guidelines for personal preparedness and responder interventions for persons with disabilities. Although these guidelines have been developed with careful attention to the reported problems and needs of the disabled, there remains a need for further empirical studies to evaluate the efficacy of these recommendations to validate them as best practices.

It is critical that individuals with disabilities are prepared as well as possible in advance of a disaster and that responders have been trained to assist and evacuate this population in a disaster. For a significant component of the population, such measures will improve the ability to save lives and ensure optimal health and well-being for persons with disabilities. In addition, during a disaster, efficient use of time, resources, and personnel is at a premium. Failure to effectively intervene with members of this vulnerable population has the potential to threaten the overall ability to respond adequately to all members of a community affected by disaster.

REFERENCES

Ablah, E., Konda, K., & Kelley, C. L. (2009). Factors predicting individual emergency preparedness: A multi-state analysis of 2006 BRFSS data. *Biosecurity and Bioterrorism: Biodefense Strategy, Practice and Science, 7*(3), 317–330. doi:10.1089/bsp.2009.0022

American Academy of Ophthalmology (AAO). (2011). *Eye statistics at a glance.* Retrieved March 24, 2014 from http://www.aao.org/newsroom/upload/Eye-Health-Statistics-April-2011.pdf

American Red Cross (ARC). (2004). *Preparing for disaster for people with disabilities and other special needs.* Retrieved September 19, 2013, from http://www.redcross.org/images/MEDIA_CustomProductCatalog/m4240199_A4497.pdf

American Red Cross (ARC). (2014). *Anatomy of a first aid kit.* Retrieved March 8, 2014, from http://www.redcross.org/prepare/location/home-family/get-kit/anatomy

Bethel, J. W., Foreman, A. N., & Burke, S. C. (2011). Disaster preparedness among medically vulnerable populations. *American Journal of Preventative Medicine, 40*(2), 139–143. doi:10.1016/j.amepre.2010.10.020

Bloodworth, D. M., Kevorkian, C. G., Rumbaut, E., & Chiou-Tan, F. Y. (2007). Impairment and disability in the Astrodome after Hurricane Katrina: Lessons learned about the needs of the disabled after large population movements. *American Journal of Physical and Rehabilitative Medicine, 86,* 770–775.

Bruck, D., & Thomas, I. (2009). Smoke alarms for sleeping adults who are hard-of-hearing: Comparison of auditory, visual, and tactile signals. *Ear and Hearing, 30*(1), 73-80. doi:10.1097/AUD.0b013e3181906f89

Calgaro, E., Allen, J., Craig, N., Craig, L., & Dominey-Howes, D. (2013). Increasing the resilience of the deaf community in NSW to natural hazards. Report to the New South Wales State Government. Retrieved March 24, 2014, from http://deafsocietynsw.org.au/documents/milestone_2__3_assessment_report.pdf

California Department of Rehabilitation (CDR). (1997). Disaster preparedness for persons with disabilities improving California's response. Retrieved September 12, 2013, from http://www.preventionweb.net/files/7966_disasterpreparednessforpeoplewithdisabilties1202797803789963.pdf

Campbell, V. A., Gilyard, J. A., Sinclair, L., Sternberg, T., & Kailes, J. I. (2009). Preparing for and responding to pandemic influenza: Implications for people with disabilities. *American Journal of Public Health, 99*(S2), S294–S300. doi:10.2105/AJPH.2009.162677

Center for Independence of the Disabled in New York (CIDNY). (2004). Lessons learned from the World Trade Center disaster: emergency preparedness for people with disabilities in New York. Retrieved September 13, 2013, from http://www.nobodyleftbehind2.org/resources/pdf/lessons_learned_from_the_world_trade_center_disaster.pdf

Centers for Disease Control and Prevention (CDC). (2011). Blindness and vision impairment. Retrieved March 25, 2014, from http://www.cdc.gov/healthcommunication/ToolsTemplates/EntertainmentEd/Tips/Blindness.html

Centers for Disease Control and Prevention (CDC). (2012). Disabilities: Emergency preparedness training. Retrieved September 11, 2013, from http://www.cdc.gov/Features/EmergencyPreparedness/

Centers for Disease Control and Prevention (CDC). (2014). Emergency preparedness and you. Retrieved March 8, 2014, from http://emergency.cdc.gov/preparedness/

Chaffee, M. (2009). Willingness of health care personnel to work in a disaster: An integrative review of the literature. *Disaster Medicine and Public Health Preparedness, 3*(1), 42–56.

Chou, Y.-J, Huang, N., Lee, C.-H., Tsai, S.-L., Chen, L.-S., & Chang, H.-J. (2004). Who is at risk of death in an earthquake? *American Journal of Epidemiology, 160*(7), 688–695. doi:10.1093/aje/kwh270

Dyer, C. B., Regev, B. A., Burnett, J., Festa, N., & Cloyd, B. (2008). SWiFT: A rapid triage tool for vulnerable older adults in disaster situations. *Disaster Medicine and Public Health Preparedness, 2*(Suppl. 1), S45–S50. doi:10.1097/DMP.0b013e3181647b81

Eisenman, D. P., Zhou, Q., Ong, M., Asch, S., Glik, D., & Long, A. (2009). Variations in disaster preparedness by mental health, perceived general health, and disability status. *Disaster Medicine and Public Health Preparedness, 3*(1), 33–41. doi:10.1097/DMP.0b013e31819be89

Engelman, A., Ivey, S. L., Tseng, W., Dahrouge, D., Brune, J., & Neuhauser, L. (2013). Responding to the deaf in disasters: Establishing the need for systematic training for state-level emergency management agencies and community organizations. *BMC Health Services Research, 13,* 84. http://www.biomedcentral.com/1472-6963/13/84

Erikson, W., Lee, C., & von Schrader, S. (2012). *2011 Disability Status Report.* United States. Ithaca, NY, Cornell University Employment and Disability Institute (EDI). Retrieved March 25, 2014, from http://www.disabilitystatistics.org/StatusReports/2011-PDF/2011-StatusReport_US.pdf?CFID=8942968&CFTOKEN=63f1b8c3de4fa1c8-F3007066-5056-B400-0D4125680F52DDDE&jsessionid=8430e4afad45194cd1a03451d7c5c2951475

Federal Emergency Management Agency (FEMA). (2010). *Guidance on planning for integration of functional needs support services in general population.* Retrieved September 9, 2013, from http://www.fema.gov/pdf/about/odic/fnss_guidance.pdf

Federal Emergency Management Agency (FEMA). (2011). *Planning for the whole community: Integrating and coordinating the functional needs of children and adults with disabilities in preparation, response, recovery and mitigation.* Retrieved January 2, 2014, from http://www.fema.gov/pdf/about/odic/all_hands_0411.pdf

Federal Emergency Management Agency (FEMA). (2012). *Prepare for emergencies now: Information for people with disabilities.* Retrieved September 11, 2013, from http://www.ready.gov/sites/default/files/FEMA_Disabilities_R-6_web_june2012.pdf

Federal Emergency Management Agency (FEMA). (2014). *Ready. Prepare. Plan. Stay informed.* Retrieved March 5, 2014, from http://www.ready.gov

Fox, M. H., White, G. W., Rooney, C., & Cahill, A. (2010). The psychological impact of Hurricane Katrina on persons with disabilities and independent living center staff living on the American Gulf Coast. *Rehabilitation Psychology, 55*(3), 231–240.

Fox, M. H., White, G. W., Rooney, C., & Rowland, J. L. (2007). Disaster preparedness and response for persons with mobility impairments. *Journal of Disability Policy Studies, 17*(4):196–205.

Gerber, B. J., Norwood, F., & Zakour, M. (2010). Disasters, evacuations and persons with disabilities: An assessment of key issues facing individuals and households. A cooperative project funded by the National Institute on Disability and Rehabilitation Research, Disability Rehabilitation Research Projects. United States Department of Education. Retrieved January 4, 2014, from http://www.ohsu.edu/xd/research/centers-institutes/institute-on-development-and-disability/public-health-programs/upload/NIDRR_Indiv_Finding_Report_Disaster_Evacuations_FINAL_6-10.pdf

Gershon, R. R. M., Qureshi, K. A., Stone, P. W., Pogorzelska, M., Silver, A., Damsky, M. R., Burdette, C., . . . Raveis, V. H. (2007). Home health care challenges and avian influenza. *Home Health Care Management and Practice, 20*(1), 58–69.

Greenough, P. G., Lappi, M. D., Hsu, E. B., Fink, S., Hsieh, Y., Vu, A., . . . Kirsch, T. D. (2008). Burden of disease and health status among Hurricane Katrina-displaced persons in shelters: A population-based cluster sample. *Annals of Emergency Medicine, 51*(4), 426–432.

Hall, J. R., Jr., (2013). *U.S. National Fire Prevention Association Report: U.S. experience with sprinklers.* Retrieved September 24, 2013, from http://www.nfpa.org/research/statistical-reports/fire-protection-systems/us-experience-with-sprinklers

Hammitt, J. (1994). EARTHQUAKE! Coping with the aftermath can be a disaster too, for people with disabilities. Originally published in the May 1994 issue of *Mainstream Magazine*. Retrieved September 16, 2013, from http://www.accessiblesociety.org/topics/independentliving/quake.htm

Hogaboom, N. S., Oyster, M. L., Riggins, M. S., & Boninger, M. L. (2013). Evacuation preparedness in full-time wheelchair users with spinal cord injury. *The Journal of Spinal Cord Medicine, 36*(4), 290–295.

Hogan, T. P., Holmes, S. A., Rapacki, L. M., Evans, C. T., Lindblom, L., Hoenig, H., Goldstein, B., . . . Weaver, F. M. (2011). Disaster preparedness and response practices among providers from the Veterans Health Administration and Veterans with spinal cord injuries and/or disorders. *The Journal of Spinal Cord Medicine, 34*(4), 353–361.

Hurricane Katrina Community Advisory Group (HKCAG), Kessler, R. C. (2007). Hurricane Katrina's impact on the care of survivors with chronic medical conditions. *Journal of General Internal Medicine, 22*(9), 1225–1230.

Illinois Terrorism Task Force (ITTF). (2004). *Emergency preparedness for those with functional needs*. Retrieved January 18, 2014, from http://www.illinois.gov/ready/Site CollectionDocuments/PreparednessTips_FunctionalNeeds.pdf

Kailes, J. I. (2002). *Evacuation Preparedness: Taking responsibility for your safety: A guide for people with disabilities and other activity limitations*. Center for Disability Issues and the Health Professions, Western University of Health Sciences, California (CDIHP). Retrieved March 25, 2014, from http://webhost.westernu.edu/hfcdhp/wp-content/uploads/Emergency_Evacuation.pdf

Kef, S., Hox, J. J., & Habekothé, H. T. (2000). Social networks of visually impaired and blind adolescents. Structure and effect on well being. *Social Networks, 22*, 73–91.

Kett, M., Stubbs, S., & Yeo, R. (2005). *Disability in conflict and emergency situations: Focus on Tsunami-affected areas*. International Disability and Development Consortium (IDDC) Report. Retrieved March 25, 2014, from http://www.iddc.org.uk

Kirkpatrick, D. V., & Bryan, M. (2007). Hurricane emergency planning by home health providers serving the poor. *Journal of Health Care for the Poor and Underserved, 18*(2), 299–314.

Knebel, A., & Phillips, S. J. (Eds.). (2008). *Home health care during an influenza pandemic. Issues and resources*. Agency for Healthcare Research and Quality. AHRQ Publication No. 08-0018. U.S. Department of health and Human Services, Rockville, MD. Retrieved February 17, 2014, from http://healthvermont.gov/emerg/documents/homehealthcare.pdf

Lemyre, L., Gibson, S., Zlepnig, J., Meyer-Macleod, R., & Boutette, P. (2009). Emergency preparedness for higher risk populations: Psychosocial considerations. *Radiation Protection Dosimetry, 134*(3/4), 207–214.

Markenson, D., Fuller, E. J., & Redlener, I. E. (2007). *Emergency preparedness: Addressing the needs of persons with disabilities*. National Center for Disaster Preparedness. Retrieved January 4, 2014, from http://academiccommons.columbia.edu/item/ac:155353

McCormick, L. C. (2013). Measuring levels of citizen public health emergency preparedness, Jefferson County, Alabama. *Journal of Public Health Management and Practice, 19*(3),266–273. doi:10.1097/PHH.0b013e318264ed8c

McClure, L. A., Boninger, M. L., Oyster, M. L. Roach, M. J., & Nagy, J. (2011). Emergency evacuation readiness of full-time wheelchair uses with spinal cord injury. *Archives of Physical Medicine and Rehabilitation, 92*(3), 491–498.

McGuire, L. C., Ford, E. S., & Okoro, C. A. (2007). Natural disasters and older U.S. adults with disabilities: Implications for evacuation. *Disasters, 31*(1), 49–56.

Melledy, A. M. (2001, October). The day the world changed. *Able News.*

Mokdad, A. H., Mensah, G. A., Posner, S. F., Reed, E., Simoes, E. J., & Engelgau, M. M. Chronic diseases and vulnerable populations in natural disasters working group. (2005). When chronic conditions become acute: prevention and control of chronic diseases and adverse health outcomes during natural disasters. *Preventing chronic disease.* Retrieved September 24, 2013, form http://www.cdc.gov/pcd/issues/2005/nov/05_0201.htm

National Council on Disability (NCD). (2005). *Saving lives: Including people with disabilities in emergency planning.* Retrieved July 12, 2014, from http://www.ncd.gov/publications/2005/04152005

National Council on Disability (NCD). (2009). *Effective emergency management: Making improvements for communities and people with disabilities.* Retrieved March 25, 2014, from http://files.eric.ed.gov/fulltext/ED507740.pdf

National Fire Prevention Association (NFPA). (2013). *Home safety for people with disabilities.* Retrieved September 24, 2013, from http://www.nfpa.org/safety-information/for-consumers/populations/people-with-disabilities/home-safety-for-people-with-disabilities

National Institute on Deafness and Other Communication Disorders (NIDCD). (2010). Quick statistics. Retrieved March 25, 2014, from https://www.nidcd.nih.gov/health/statistics/Pages/quick.aspx

National Institute of Standards and Technology (NIST). (2005). *Final report on the collapse of the World Trade Center Towers.* Retrieved March 25, 2014, from http://www.nist.gov/customcf/get_pdf.cfm?pub_id=909017

National Organization on Disability (NOD). (2004). 2004 NOD/Harris Survey document-strends impacting 54 million Americans. Retrieved March 24, 2014, from http://www.nod.org/research_publications/surveys_research/harris/

National Organization on Disability (NOD). (2005). Report on special needs assessment for Katrina evacuees (SNAKE) project. Retrieved September 16, 2013, from https://nod.org/assets/downloads/Special-Needs-For-Katrina-Evacuees.pdf

National Organization on Disability (NOD). (2009a). Disaster mobilization initiative: response to September 11th. Retrieved September 16, 2013, from http://www.nod.org/index.cfm?fuseaction=page.viewPage&pageID=1430&nodeID=1&FeatureID=457&redirected=1&CFID=11169012&CFTOKEN=5090464

National Organization on Disability (NOD). (2009b). Functional needs of people with disabilities: A guide for emergency managers, planners, and responders. Retrieved September 16, 2014, from http://nod.org/assets/downloads/Guide-Emergency-Planners.pdf

Oregon Office on Disability and Health (OODH). (2009). Emergency preparedness tool kit for people with disabilities. Retrieved March 28, 2014, from http://www.ohsu.edu/xd/outreach/occyshn/upload/ReadyNowToolkit.pdf

Peek, L., & Stough, L. M. (2010). Children with disabilities in the context of a disaster: A social vulnerability perspective. *Child Development, 81*(4), 1260–1270.

Rahimi, M. (1994). Behavior of mobility-disabled people in earthquakes: A simulationexperiment. *Earthquake Spectra, 10*(2), 381–401.

Renne, J. L., Sanchez, T. W., & Litman, T. (2011). Carless and special needs evacuation planning: A literature review. *Journal of Planning Literature, 26*(4), 420–431. doi:10.1177/0885412211412315

Riddex, L., & Dellgar, U. (2001). The ice storm in eastern Canada 1998 KAMEDO-Report No. 74. *Prehospital and Disaster Medicine, 16*(1), 50–52.

Rowland, J. L., White, G. W. Fox, M. J., & Rooney, C. (2007). Emergency response training practices for people with disabilities: Analysis of some current practices and recommendations for future training programs. *Journal of Disability Policy Studies, 17*(4), 216–222.

Spence, P. R., Lachlan, K., Burke, J. M., & Seeger, M. W. (2007). Media use and information needs of the disabled during a natural disaster. *Journal of Health Care for the Poor and Underserved, 18*(2), 394–404.

Smith, D. L., & Notaro, S. J. (2009). Personal emergency preparedness for people with disabilities from the 2006–2007 Behavioral Risk Factor Surveillance System. *Disability and Health Journal, 2*(2), 86–94.

Sullivan, H. T., & Häkkinen, M. T. (2006). Disaster preparedness for vulnerable populations: Determining effective strategies for communicating risk, warnings, and response. *Third Annual Magrann Research Conference at Rutgers University, 4*, 21–24.

State Independent Living Council (SILC). (2013). The impact of the 2003 wildfires on people with disabilities. Retrieved September 13, 2013, from http://www.nobody leftbehind2.org/resources/pdf/impact_of_2003_ca_wildfires_4-30-04.pdf

Tomio, J., Sato, H., & Mizumura, H. (2012). Disparity in disaster preparedness among rheumatoid arthritis patients with various general health, functional, and disability conditions. *Environmental Health & Preventive Medicine, 17*(4):322–331. doi:10.1007 /s12199-011-0257-3

United States Department of Homeland Security (DOH). (2005). Individuals with disabilities in emergency preparedness, Executive Order 13347. Annual Report. Retrieved January 5, 2014, from http://www.dhs.gov/xlibrary/assets/CRCL_IWDEP_Ann ualReport_2005.pdf

United States Department of Labor (DOL), Office of Disability Employment Policy (ODEP), Job Accommodation Network (JAN). (2013). Employer's guide to including employees with disabilities in emergency evacuation plans. Retrieved September 9, 2013, from http://askjan.org/media/EmployersGuideEmergencyEvacuation.pdf

White, G. W., Fox, M. H., & Rooney, C. (2007). Nobody left behind: report on exemplary and best practices in disaster preparedness and emergency response for people with disabilities. Research and Training Center on Independent Living, University of Kansas. Retrieved September 11, 2013, from http://www.nobodyleftbehind2.org /findings/pdfs/bestpractices_3-21-072.pdf

Older Adults and Disasters

CASE STUDY: Hurricane Katrina

When Hurricane Katrina hit, Cheryl Pettypool was living in a nursing home in Kenner, Louisiana. "They didn't evacuate us until 4 days after the hurricane," said Pettypool. "The staff left. We had nobody to watch us except the [nursing home's] four maintenance men."

Pettypool, who relies on a wheelchair to get around, said she was one of 60 residents left behind. For 3 days, the residents remained in the hallway, Pettypool noted. No one received showers and, after a couple of days, their only source of nourishment came from bottled water. "There was no electricity and no water. Wednesday, we ran out of food," she said.

The residents were finally rescued on Friday and sent by ambulance to the airport. They were then taken by Army helicopter to a makeshift trauma center located on the basketball court at Louisiana State University. Pettypool was ultimately transferred to another nursing home about 3 hours away. "My family and my friends couldn't find me," Pettypool recalls. To make matters worse, the nursing home was subsequently hit by Hurricane Rita, and residents had to evacuate for 3 weeks before they could return (National Organization on Disability, 2009).

Older adults represent a significant and growing percentage of the American population. In both the scholarly literature and in the popular vernacular, those who are 65 or older are generally classified as elderly. For any given individual, reaching age 65 does not necessarily mean that he or she is facing issues that create greater risks during a disaster. However, statistically, as adults age, they do begin to experience difficulties with health, mobility, cognition, hearing, and vision at greater rates than their younger counterparts. The term "frail elderly" is often used in the literature to differentiate between healthy older adults and those with significant health difficulties. As such, the frail elderly share much in common with persons with disabilities, as discussed in Chapter 5.

Globally, almost 500 million people are aged 65 or older, and that number is projected to reach 1 billion by 2030 (NIA, 2007a). In the United States, 41.4 million adults are aged 65 or older, representing 13.3% of the population, or approximately one in eight individuals (AOA, 2012). By 2030, it is estimated that one in five adults in the United States will be aged 65 or older (Aldrich & Benson, 2008). Worldwide, those over 65 years of age outnumber those under 5 years of age for the first time in history (NIA, 2007a). The percentage of adults aged 65 or older has increased 18% in the United States just since 2000 (AOA, 2012). People over 85 are now the fastest-growing segment of many national populations (NIA, 2007a). The growth of the population of older adults is due both to increased life expectancy and the births of fewer children in households. As such, family structures are changing that may leave older people with fewer options for care.

Older adults are not a uniform group and differ by education level, socioeconomic status, race/ethnicity, and sex. The National Institute on Aging's Health and Retirement Study (2007b) found that the pattern of disease at age 50 for people with less than a high school education is similar to that at age 60 for people with a college degree. To some extent, education and income are linked, but older adults as a whole tend to rank at lower levels of socioeconomic status. The median income for the U.S. elderly population in 2011 was $27,707 for males and $15,362 for females, with 8.7% of older adults living below the poverty level (AOA, 2012). Health status also differs by race/ethnicity. Among noninstitutionalized older adults over the age of 65 who ranked their health as excellent or good, 44.7% were identified as White, 33% were identified as Asian, 29.7% were identified as Hispanic, and 25% were identified as African American (AOA, 2012). Sex is also a variable, with a greater percentage of older women than older men. Older women outnumber older men by 23.4 million to 17.9 million, and are less likely to be married (45% vs. 72%), with 37% widowed and 46% over age 75 living alone (AOA, 2012).

Overall, older adults are more likely to experience some type of health difficulty than their younger counterparts. One study estimated that 80% of older adults suffer from at least one chronic health condition (Aldrich & Benson, 2008). From 2009 to 2011, the most frequently occurring diagnosed conditions were hypertension (72%), arthritis (51%), heart disease (31%), cancer (24%), and diabetes (20%; AOA, 2012). Some type of hearing, vision, cognition, ambulation, or self-care issue was reported by 35% of men and 38% of elderly women (AOA, 2012). The rate of severe depression in those aged 85 or older is 20% (NIA, 2007b). Approximately 10% of those aged 70 or older suffer from moderate to severe cognitive impairment (NIA, 2007b). Approximately 14 million noninstitutionalized adults aged 65 or older have some level of disability, and 13 million adults aged 50 and older report that they would need help to evacuate; half of the latter need help outside their immediate household (Aldrich & Benson, 2008). Although many senior adults are active and healthy, as a whole, the aging population is vulnerable during disasters.

THE VULNERABILITY OF OLDER ADULTS IN DISASTERS

CASE STUDY: Hurricanes Charley and Francis, Director of Nursing Accounts of Evacuation of Nursing Home Residents to a Gymnasium

We couldn't get anybody up and sitting like in the dining room. The residents with dysphasia or swallowing problems, we would have to hold them up in the bed. Somebody would sit at one side and hold up the mattress and somebody else could feed.

Usually we use a lift [at our facility] if you cannot stand and pivot-transfer with only stand-by assist from a staff member . . . so what you are looking at is an employee injury, which is going to be, not only that they are tired and worn out and they have to work through a hurricane, but now they are lifting, repositioning people at a level that is not safe. So, technically, in order to do any kind of care safely, you have to get on your hands and knees to take care of that customer (Christensen, Brown, & Hyer, 2012).

Ample evidence exists that demonstrates the increased vulnerability of older adults in disasters compared to the general population. In one meta-analysis reviewing the literature from journal articles, government training materials, news reports, and materials from senior organizations, a number of factors were identified that contribute to the increased vulnerability of older adults (Fernandez, Byard, Lin, Benson, & Barbera, 2002). These issues include impaired mobility, diminished sensory awareness, chronic health conditions, and social and economic limitations, which make older adults both less likely to prepare for disasters and less likely to adapt during disasters. The study also found that the frail elderly with serious physical, cognitive, economic, and psychosocial problems were at especially high risk.

Accidents of geography also play a role in the extent to which older adults may be vulnerable in a disaster. Florida has the greatest percentage of elderly persons and has had the highest number of hurricanes (NOAA, 2011; U.S. Census Bureau, 2011a). California has the highest number of older adults and ranks second in the nation (behind Alaska) for frequency of earthquakes (U.S. Census Bureau, 2011a; USGS, 2012). The great Midwest floods of 1993 affected 6 of the 10 states with the highest percentage of persons aged 85 and older (Oriol, 1999). In the United States, almost one-half of the adults residing in nursing homes live in one of the 18 hurricane-prone Gulf and Atlantic Coast states (Dosa et al., 2008). Although older adults as a whole share similar characteristics that increase their vulnerability in a disaster, differences exist in the needs of the noninstitutionalized and institutionalized populations.

The Vulnerability of Noninstitutionalized Older Adults in Disaster

A number of studies have demonstrated that older adults are disproportionately affected when disaster strikes. During Hurricane Katrina, one study found that 49% of the deaths were among individuals over the age of 75 (Brunkard, Namulanda, & Ratard, 2008). Another study involving Hurricane Katrina reported that 74% of the deaths were among individuals older than 60 and half were over 75, although only 15% of the population was older than 65 (Sakauye et al., 2009). During a 1995 heat wave in the Midwest, the median age of the 465 heat-related deaths in Chicago was 75 (Aldrich & Benson, 2008). The increased vulnerability of older adults has also been demonstrated cross-culturally. In the 1995 Hanshin-Awaji earthquake in Japan that claimed over 6000 lives, 40% of the people who died were over 65 (Kailes, 2000). During the European heat wave of 2003, more than 13,000 French elderly died (Sakauye et al., 2009). Generally, age-related alterations in the thermoregulatory system put older adults at increased risk for developing both hyperthermia and hypothermia (e.g., Åström, Bertil, & Joacim, 2011; Chester & Rudolph, 2011; Hajat, O'Conner, & Kosatsky, 2010; Keim, Guisto, & Sullivan, 2002).

As discussed in Chapter 5 on disasters and persons with disabilities, health problems that are normally managed may exacerbate under the physical and psychological stresses of a disaster situation. In some cases, the negative health effects may not be immediately apparent. For example, following the 1995 Hanshin-Awaji earthquake in Japan, one study found increased hypertension among older adults living near the epicenter (Kario, Matsuo, Kobayashi, Yamamoto, & Shimada, 1997). The blood pressure of 42 elderly persons with controlled hypertension found elevations that did not return to pre-quake parameters until 4 to 6 months after the incident. In addition, the study suggested that such elevations likely contribute to cardiovascular incidents. In one district, 10 cardiovascular incidents or sudden deaths were recorded in the 6 weeks following the earthquake (population 11,500) compared with only 3 in the year before, suggesting a more than three-fold increase.

Several studies have demonstrated increased risk for mental health issues in the wake of a disaster. Older adults may experience a multiple loss effect (Oriol, 1999). Before the disaster, older adults have often already experienced the loss of a spouse, reduced income, and a decline in health or physical abilities. A disaster can compound these losses if property or personal items are lost or damaged that have nostalgic or economic value. An observational study in India compared psychiatric symptoms between older adults aged 60 and older (n = 75) and those aged 19 to 59 (n = 363) who had experienced a 2004 tsunami involving the Andaman and Nicobar Islands (Viswanath et al., 2012). At 3 months following the tsunami, the older adults experienced greater levels of adjustment disorder than their younger counterparts.

Older adults may be particularly vulnerable for experiencing posttraumatic stress disorder (PTSD) after a disaster. One longitudinal prospective study examined the effect of floods among adults aged 60 or older (n = 274) in Australia (Bei et al., 2013). The researchers employed several instruments to examine mental and physical health of older adults both pre- and post-event: Impact of Event Scale, Revised (IES-R), Geriatric Anxiety Inventory (GAI), Center for Epidemiological Studies Depression Scale, SF-12 Health Survey, Satisfaction with Life Scale (SWLS), Liverpool Stoicism Scale (LLS), and Brief Cope Questionnaire. They found significantly higher PTSD scores among those personally affected by flooding compared to those not personally affected. Another study investigated the mental health effects of adults aged 60 or older (n = 193) in the Galveston Bay area 2 to 5 months following Hurricane Ike (Pietrzak, Southwick, Tracy, Galea, & Norris, 2011). The researchers found that the weighted prevalence of PTSD was 7.6% and 8.6% for depression. Even higher rates of PTSD were found in a study of older adults after the 2008 Sichuan earthquake in China (Jia et al., 2010). Here, a population-based study was conducted 15 months after the earthquake using a multistage system-atic sampling design (n = 152 elders, n = 175 older adults). The rate of PTSD was 22.5% for older adults compared to 8.0% for their younger counterparts.

The poor elderly may be at even greater risk during a disaster. An exploratory-descriptive study of older public housing evacuees from Hurricane Andrew in Florida in 1992 found a number of negative consequences (Sanders, Bowie, & Bowie, 2004). The study participants were 58 low-income African Americans with a mean age of 67 years who lived in public housing in the Miami-Dade County area, 70% of whom were female. The residents had a wide range of physical and mental health issues that were greatly exacerbated when they had to evacuate for the storm. Relocation resulted in separation from key support ser-vices including family, friends, social services, and health care facilities that they depended upon. The authors of the study recommend that more attention be given to training public housing property managers and the recognition of the increased need for social workers to assist this population in the post-disaster period.

The Vulnerability of Institutionalized Older Adults in Disasters

Older adults in institutional environments, such as nursing homes, face unique challenges in a disaster situation. The United States has approximately 2 million people housed in 17,000 nursing homes who may have multiple health care needs, including frailty, lack of mobility, dementia, vision/hearing difficulties, activities of daily living (ADL) limitations, increased susceptibility to infectious disease, mental health issues, and a wide variety of potential other medical conditions (Dosa et al., 2008).

The stress of a disaster and the disruption of care have been demonstrated to adversely affect older adults in institutions. One study of the cognitively impaired in nursing homes who were evacuated from the Gulf Coast during the 2008 Hurricane Gustav demonstrated an increase in mortality rate (Brown et al., 2012). In this study, 21,555 elderly adults with severe dementia who were liv-ing in 119 nursing homes were observed over 3 years. In comparing the 2 years before the storm to after Gustav, there was a 2.8% increase in deaths after 30 days and a 3.9% increase in deaths after 90 days. Mental health issues are also common among nursing home residents. One study found that the prevalence of clinical depression was 12% to 16% in nursing home patients, with 50% experiencing some depressive symptoms (Dosa et al., 2008).

Another issue for the institutionalized elderly who must be evacuated is that the evacuation site may not have the resources to adequately care for this population, adversely affecting health. A qualitative study involving focus groups with nursing home administrators (n = 15) and directors of nursing (n = 15) during the 2004 to 2005 hurricane season in Florida revealed a number of difficulties with evacuees (Christensen, Brown, & Hyer, 2012). The primary problem they reported was that the type of buildings designated for evacuation such as churches and school gymnasiums were not designed to support the types of nursing services that the patients required. The evacuation situation adversely affected resident feeding, sleeping, movement, and security. In addition, the focus group participants indicated that serious occupational health concerns existed for nursing staff members, who were at increased risk of injury due to the lack of appropriate equipment for lifting, moving, and transporting patients. Similar findings were reported in a study using qualitative and quantitative methods to evaluate the experiences of 291 Florida nursing homes during the 2004 hurricane season (Hyer, Brown, Christensen, & Thomas, 2009). One of the primary concerns reported was finding facilities to evacuate that were appropriate for nursing home residents. Difficulties were also reported in having ambulance transportation contracts honored. For those who sheltered in place, one of the main concerns was the length of time it took for power to be restored.

Even when the facility sheltering evacuees is a nursing home, housing and caring for new patients can overwhelm the resources of a facility. A qualitative study of administrators (n = 4) and employees (n = 38) from 14 nursing homes that sheltered evacuees from Hurricane Katrina revealed a number of significant problems (Laditka et al., 2008a). One of the major issues reported was that nursing homes had not been included in community planning or recognized as a community health care resource. They also reported that there was insufficient communication about the patients who were evacuated to provide appropriate care. Further, the sheltering nursing homes had inadequate supplies and medications to care for the evacuees. Both the nursing home evacuees and the staff that cared for them had increased mental health needs after the storm. Further, a long-term consequence was difficulty maintaining adequate staffing after the crisis was over due to loss of personnel from nursing homes.

THE DISASTER FRAMEWORK AND OLDER ADULTS

CASE STUDY: Northridge Earthquake

After the Northridge earthquake in California, older residents in many of the 1,500 mobile homes in the area were having symptoms of panic, disorientation, fear, sleeplessness, and anger. Thirteen senior centers became central points for phone calls, walk-ins, referrals, and triage. Outreach teams that sought out the elders who might otherwise have not received assistance made the centers their base for visits to mobile home parks and for stress management activities (Oriol, 1999, citing Fain 1998 and Project Cope, 1992a).

A recent review of older adults and disasters outlined a number of issues that they face that may present obstacles to effective planning, response, and recovery in the wake of a disaster, including mobility, sensory, economic, and psychosocial issues (Banks, 2013). For individuals experiencing mobility issues, disasters can compound these problems. Disasters often create damage to living structures and the surrounding community infrastructures. Older adults who are frail or disabled may have difficulty in engaging in protective or avoidance maneuvers, putting them at greater risk for illness, injury, or death. Cognitive and sensory deficits may also create difficulties in the ability of some elders to appropriately respond to instructions that are given for evacuating or sheltering in place during a disaster. Hearing loss, visual impairments, or various forms of dementia may make it difficult to understand important communication during disasters including weather warnings, disaster orders, and the instructions of responders who may be providing assistance. Older adults may depend on medication, special nutrition, and medical supplies to manage health conditions. Physical and cognitive impairments may make it difficult for some older adults to organize and prepare essential health care materials that are needed for sheltering in place or evacuating. Moreover, limited financial reserves may make it difficult to meet daily needs, much less purchase extra reserve supplies to prepare for a potential disaster.

The loss of ability to drive or the lack of transportation can result in older adults being left behind if mandatory evacuation orders are given. Further, psychosocial issues may come into play. Social isolation may make it difficult for older adults to seek out help during an evacuation and older adults may also be reluctant or unwilling to evacuate the perceived safety of their home environments when instructed to evacuate.

Planning, Preparedness, and Mitigation for Older Adults

Broadly, the key variables that may make it difficult for older adults to adequately prepare for a disaster include physical impairments, sensory deficits, cognitive disorders, and social and economic limitations (Aldrich & Benson, 2008). Given these challenges, a logical inference would be that older adults are less prepared for a disaster than the general population. Research studies have actually provided rather mixed results, with some revealing that older adults are less likely to prepare and others revealing that they are more likely to prepare. Unfortunately, we do not yet have a broad base of empirical studies on this topic to draw clear conclusions. Further study is needed to elucidate the key variables that are either inducing or impeding preparedness in this population.

Two studies suggest that older adults are less likely to adequately prepare for disasters. One study involving a survey of Hurricane Katrina evacuees found that older adults were less likely to have either an evacuation plan or an emergency kit than their younger counterparts (Spence, Lachlan, Burke, & Seeger, 2007). A random-digit-dial survey in Jefferson County, Alabama, after recently experiencing tornados found that those over 65 were no more likely to have an emergency kit than younger adults (McCormick, 2013). However, a Behavioral Risk Factor Surveillance System (BRFSS) found that older adults were more likely to be prepared (Ablah, Konda, & Kelley, 2009). The study involved five states that used the preparedness modules developed by the Centers for Disease Control (CDC; Arizona, Connecticut, Montana, Nevada, and Tennessee). Respondents were defined as prepared if they were deficient in no more than six preparedness measures: evacuation planning, water supply, food supply, medication supply, radio, and flashlight. Relative to the overall preparedness rate of 45.1%, those between 55 and 64 years of age (55.2%) and those 65 or older (56.2%) were significantly more likely to be prepared.

Social isolation of older adults has been identified as a potential obstacle to effective preparation for and recovery from disaster (Banks, 2013). Some support does exist verifying the general benefits of a strong social support network in older adults. For example, a longitudinal study derived from data from the National Social Life, Health, and Aging Project (NSHAP) demonstrated that addition of members to one's social network was associated with improvements in ratings of functional and psychological health (Cornwell & Laumann, 2013). Research specifically investigating the relationship of disaster outcomes and strength of social networks would be instructive in revealing the extent to which social isolation may differentially affect older adults in disasters.

An additional issue relevant to older adults involves reliance on home health care. A number of other populations may rely on home health care including persons with disabilities, the chronically ill, and those recovering from surgery or acute illness. However, older adults are the major recipients of home health care services. Approximately 69% of recipients were over the age of 65 (NAHC, 2010). Disasters have the potential to significantly disrupt these essential services to older adults.

One early study of 30 home health care agencies in San Diego found a number of problems in disaster preparedness (Phreaner, Jacoby, Dreier, & McCoy, 1994). Although 53 agencies were sent questionnaires, only 30 responded. Of those, 90% had written disaster plans, but only 33% conducted regular drills to practice their plans. Among hospital-sponsored agencies, only 18% had backup agreements with other agencies to provide care in the event of a disaster. Among public and nonprofit agencies, only 38% had backup care plans. Private agencies were the best prepared in this regard, with 92% having backup plans for care. In addition, 31% of home health care agencies indicated that they would not be able to meet the needs of their patients in the event of a disaster.

A more recent study involving home health and personal care providers in South Carolina demonstrated similar results (Laditka, Laditka, Cornman, Davis, & Chandlee, 2008b). Nine public officials responsible for preparedness for home care patients and administrators from 16 agencies were interviewed in a telephone survey. Although the degree of preparedness varied, most were categorized as "less" prepared or "moderately" prepared. The study found that there was a general lack of preparedness in several areas: identifying clients at high risk and assisting them with planning, providing written materials and/or recommendations, protecting records, educating staff and patients, and coordinating disaster planning and response across agencies. Overall, home health care agencies were better prepared than personal care agencies.

The three essentials of disaster preparedness for older adults are the same as for the general population: be informed, make a plan, and build a kit. However, older adults may have a number of additional needs that are important for basic disaster planning and preparedness. Table 6.1 provides guidelines for older adults

TABLE 6.1 Personal Preparedness for Older Adults

BE INFORMED

- Be aware of the types of disasters that occur in your area and county warning procedures, evacuation plans, and shelters before disaster strikes
- Be aware of evacuation procedures in your workplace; know the location of fire extinguishers and emergency alarms
- Monitor television, radio, Internet, and social media news reports as able for information from authorities on local conditions and official instructions
- Know your community's response and evacuation plans

MAKE A PLAN

General
- Keep by your bedside a charged phone, a flashlight, and prescription glasses
- Make an assessment of any limitations you may have that will require assistance in an emergency evacuation, including: mobility issues; fatigue or reduced stamina; respiratory conditions; emotional, cognitive, thinking, or learning difficulties; vision loss; hearing loss; temporary limitations such as recent surgery or accident; reliance on technology or medication that may not work in an emergency, such as hearing aids, wheelchair, gas mask, elevator, lighting, sounds
- Register with the local emergency services organization if special warning procedures, evacuation assistance, and/or special shelter facilities are needed; some fire departments also have registries for people who may need extra assistance
- Check the accessibility of local shelters and hotels and the availability of support services in those areas
- Contact your local Area Agency on Aging to see if they have a special needs registry
- If you undergo routine treatments administered by a clinic or hospital or if you receive regular services such as home health care, treatment, or transportation, talk to your service provider about their emergency plans
- People living in nursing homes, assisted living facilities, or similar supervised settings should be aware of the disaster plans in place and how relatives will be notified if evacuation is necessary
- Perform routine mock drills and update plan as necessary
- Complete an Emergency Health Information Card and keep it with you at all times
- Fire safety:
  - Keep batteries charged in smoke alarms
  - Know where fire extinguishers are and how to operate them
  - Test smoke alarms once a month
  - For added safety, interconnect all the smoke alarms so that when one sounds, they all sound
  - If possible, purchase alarms with nonreplaceable (life-long) batteries designed to be effective for up to 10 years; these can be helpful for people who have difficulty changing batteries
  - If you are deaf, use strobe light smoke alarm alert devices; pillow and bed shakers can also be used
  - If you are hard of hearing, but not deaf, a smoke alarm accessory that produces a loud, mixed low-pitch sound is most effective; pillow and bed shakers can also be used
  - If possible, choose an apartment with a sprinkler system or install the system in your home

SHELTERING IN PLACE AND EVACUATION

- Develop a plan to shelter in place
  - Be prepared to shelter in place in the event that you are unable to evacuate or are advised by local officials to stay where you are, including an emergency kit (see below)
  - If you use medical equipment at home that requires electricity, develop a backup plan for its use during a power outage
- Develop a plan to evacuate
  - Plan two ways out of every room
  - Know your community's response and evacuation plans and plan an evacuation route from your home
  - Plan for transportation if you need to evacuate to a shelter
  - Always evacuate if you are told by medical or other official personnel to evacuate or seek treatment

(continued)

TABLE 6.1 Personal Preparedness for Older Adults (*continued*)

- ○ Keep equipment with you in an evacuation; if you use a wheelchair and cannot take it, bring the cushion
- ○ If there is sufficient time, shut off valves for household utilities (gas, electricity, water)
- ○ Recommendations for mitigating potential impairments for evacuating: bolt bookshelves to walls; anchor outdoor items that can be projectiles in high winds and hurricanes; install hurricane shutters (if appropriate to area); trim trees that overhang roofs; repair cracks in ceilings and foundations; store flammable materials away from heat sources

COMMUNICATION—FAMILY, FRIEND, AND NEIGHBOR COMMUNICATION PLAN

- Make a list of family, friends, and others who will be part of your personal support network and communication plan
- Include a friend or relative from another area who would not be affected by the same emergency and can help if needed
- Decide where to meet your household members if you should become separated
- Notify members of your personal support network if you plan to go out of town
- Inform your personal support network how you plan to evacuate your home, workplace, or other facility, and where you will go in the event of a disaster
- Make sure someone in your personal network has an extra key to your home and knows where you keep your emergency supplies
- If you use medical devices such as a wheelchair, oxygen, or other medical equipment, make sure several people in your personal support network know how to operate these devices
- If you receive support services such as meals, transportation, and home health care, talk with service providers about potential backup service providers in the area to which you will evacuate
- Make sure a trusted friend or relative has copies of important medical and any other important documents

BUILD A KIT

- Basic supplies:
  - ○ A 3-day supply of food and water
  - ○ Flashlight and batteries
  - ○ Hand-crank or battery-operated radio
  - ○ Cell phone with charger, inverter, or solar charger
- Basic first aid kit (American Red Cross for a family of four):
  - ○ Bandages and dressings: 2 absorbent compress dressings (5.9 inches); 25 adhesive bandages (assorted sizes); 1 adhesive cloth tape (10 yards × 1 inch); 1 roller bandage (3 inches wide); 1 roller bandage (4 inches wide); 5 sterile gauze pads (3 × 3 inches); 5 sterile gauze pads (4 × 4 inches); 2 triangular bandages
  - ○ Medications/wound care: 2 packets of aspirin (for adults only), 5 antibiotic ointment packets (approximately 1 gram); 5 antiseptic wipe packets; 2 hydrocortisone packets
  - ○ Other supplies and equipment: blanket; breathing barrier (with one-way valve); instant cold compress; 2 pairs of nonlatex gloves (large); scissors; oral thermometer; tweezers
  - ○ First aid instruction booklet
- Medical supplies:
  - ○ Medications: a 3- to 7-day supply of prescription medications if possible
  - ○ Equipment: as applicable, an extra pair of prescription glasses; hearing aid batteries and spare hearing aids (if available); incontinence supplies; battery charger for motorized wheelchairs or other battery-operated medical/assistive devices; list of style, serial number, and operating instructions for medical devices
  - ○ Documentation: copies of important documents in a waterproof container including a list of all medications, prescriptions, doctor's orders, medical records and history, insurance cards and/or Medicare/Medicaid cards, physician contact information, list of allergies, and list of nonprofit or community-based organizations that may be able to assist you with health needs

(*continued*)

TABLE 6.1 Personal Preparedness for Older Adults (*continued*)

- ○ Other medical information: medical alert tags or written descriptions of your health/disability needs; if you have a communication disability, include information for responders on the best way to communicate, pen and paper or a laminated communication board
- Other supplies for home emergency kit: whistle to signal for help; dust mask to help filter contaminated air and plastic sheeting and duct tape to shelter in place; sanitation items (moist towelettes, toilet paper, garbage bags); local maps; wrench or pliers to turn off utilities; manual can opener; extra cash or traveler's checks if possible; extra batteries; extra blankets
- Finances: Federal Emergency Management Association suggests making arrangements for direct deposit of paycheck and federal benefits and use of the Direct Express® prepaid credit card
- Other documents: consider including records such as social security number, charge and bank account information, tax records, will, etc. A portable thumb drive is an option for storing important information
- Pets and service animals: food, water, first aid, and other supplies if you have a pet or service animal (see Chapter 9)

Sources: ARC (2004, 2013, 2014); CDC (2014); CDR (1997); Kailes (2002); CIDNY (2004); DOEA (2011); FEMA (2012a, 2012b, 2013, 2014); HHS-AOA (2013); NIA (2012); ITTF (2004); Markenson, Fuller, and Redlener (2007); NCD (2005); NFPA (2013); NOD (2009); White, Fox, and Rooney (2007).

that include recommendations from a number of organizations that include a focus on elderly persons including the American Red Cross (ARC), the California Department of Rehabilitation (CDR), the CDC, the Federal Emergency Disaster Association (FEMA), and the Health and Human Services Administration on Aging (HHS-AOA).

One important recommendation for disaster planning for older adults is to make a personal assessment of one's specific limitations that would necessitate additional assistance during a disaster. This includes mobility issues, frailty or decreased stamina, sensory deficits, cognitive deficits, and reliance on any medication or equipment that would be needed in a disaster. Before disaster strikes, older adults should make sure that they have made plans so that their basic needs can be met. It is particularly important for older adults to plan for any medical needs. If financially possible, older adults should have at least 3 days and, optimally, a week of medications on hand. It is also important to have a list of prescription medications, physician contact information, and written information on health needs. Keeping an Emergency Health Information Card on one's person at all times is helpful to be able to relay critical information to responders or health care personnel in an evacuation shelter. If evacuating, information should be supplied on any medical equipment an older person may need. If sheltering in place, a backup power source is critical for any type of medical equipment that relies on electricity. Other essentials such as eyeglasses, hearing aids, and extra batteries should be kept at the bedside so that they can be quickly retrieved in a disaster.

The support network for older adults should include not only friends, family, and neighbors, but also providers of care. In some areas, older persons may be able to register with the local emergency services organization so that they are alerted to potential special needs during a disaster. Many communities also have a local branch of the Area Agency on Aging with a special needs registry. Before a disaster, older adults who receive services such as home health care should investigate support services at area evacuation shelters or in an area where they may eventually evacuate. Older adults should also discuss alternate plans for care in the event of a disaster with local health care or service providers.

An additional mitigation measure for older adults is to assess their living environments and to make them as safe as possible in the event of a disaster. Normal household items can create obstacles when attempting to evacuate or move to a safe area of the home. For example, bookshelves should be bolted to the walls, outdoor items that can become projectiles should be anchored, and flammable materials should be stored away from heat sources.

Response and Recovery for Older Adults

A number of moderating variables contribute to the post-disaster health and well-being of older adults, including the severity of the trauma; baseline health and functional status; varying social, economic, and cultural factors, including gender; and the availability of social support and psychosocial resources (Elmore & Brown, 2007/2008). A number of stressors can lead to the development of health issues or the exacerbation of health issues among older adults, including experiencing lack of food or water, exposure to extremes of heat or cold, exposure to infectious diseases, or interruption in medications or health care services (Aldrich & Benson, 2008). Disaster recovery for older adults may involve a number of people including health and mental health professionals, volunteer emergency workers, family members who may be caregivers, and professionals involved in aging (Oriol, 1999). The decision for whether to evacuate or shelter in place can be complicated for the institutionalized elderly. As previously described, studies have demonstrated that transferring elderly patients to sheltering facilities poses a number of potential health risks, beyond what would be found in the general population. The level of acuity of patients in nursing homes has increased as the length of stay in hospitals has decreased (Dosa et al., 2008), making this population more medically fragile than they have been in the past.

One general concern with older adults is their willingness to evacuate during a disaster. As previously described, a number of studies have indicated that older adults have increased mortality rates in a disaster. Given that failure to evacuate when ordered also places individuals at risk, it might be assumed that older adults are less willing to evacuate. Little research is available on this topic, but the key issue may not so much be unwillingness, but inability. Such inability may relate to impairments in mobility that make it difficult to evacuate or impairments in communication that make it difficult to receive the message to evacuate.

One study that was identified that dealt specifically with the willingness of older adults to evacuate involved 765 voluntary participants in the Midwest (Gray-Graves, Turner, & Swan, 2011). Participants were administered the Disaster Evacuation Survey, and survey results indicated that older adults reported that they would be more likely to comply with a mandatory evacuation order than their younger counterparts. Here again, willingness and ability are two different issues. Another study investigated dyads of caregivers and patients with Alzheimer's disease or an Alzheimer's related disorder (ADRD) and hurricane evacuation in South Florida (Christensen, Richey, & Castañeda, 2013). The study involved 186 such dyads and found that a variety of variables differentially affected plans to evacuate. Predictors of dyad evacuation for a category 1 to 3 hurricane included (a) a younger age of the person with an ADRD diagnosis, (b) the caregiver living in a different residence from the person with ADRD, (c) lack of hurricane shutters, and (d) lower income. A dyad was found to be more likely to evacuate in a 4 to 5 hurricane if there was (a) a younger age person with an ADRD diagnosis, (b) a more recent ADRD diagnosis, (c) a residence in an evacuation zone, and (d) a report of needing a shelter.

When responders to a disaster assist older persons, one of the most important considerations is the awareness that health issues that may have been under control before a disaster may worsen under the stress of a disaster. Care should be taken to make sure that medical records are obtained when evacuating elderly adults. One problem that arose during Florida's Hurricane Andrew (1992) was that older adults who were evacuated to a nursing home facility arrived without any medical records or histories (Silverman, Weston, Llorente, Beber, & Tam, 1995). Responders should also be aware that older adults may require special assistance and equipment in order to evacuate. Data derived from the BRFSS from the New Orleans–Metairie–Kenner area in Louisiana was used to estimate the number of community-dwelling people aged 65 or older with a disability, who required special equipment (McGuire, Ford, & Okoro, 2007). The researchers found that approximately 16.6% of older adults who required special equipment were community dwelling and might require assistance to evacuate.

General guidelines for responders to older adults are provided in Table 6.2, derived from a number of organizations that have a focus on responding to older adults in a disaster. Effective communication is an important element due to potential hearing impairments, visual impairments, or cognitive impairments. Broadly, responders should speak slowly, calmly, and provide information as simply as possible. Disorientation is possible among older adults without a previously diagnosed cognitive impairment under the stress of the disaster. It is helpful to have pen and paper or a communication board available to write out information for the hearing impaired. If an individual wears eyeglasses, responders should make sure they are located for evacuation.

Responders should assess any medical needs an older adult may have. This includes asking them about any medical problems, medications they are taking, and medical devices they use. Responders should help older adults gather any medications, equipment, or documentation of health information to take with them to an evacuation site. It is also helpful to ask older adults if they need any assistance with ADL, such as walking, eating, bathing, dressing, toileting, or medication administration. Older adults with mobility issues should also be asked to explain the best way for transporting, transferring, and assisting them. In addition, responders should obtain contact information for individuals in an older adult's support system. It is important not only for social support, but for providing any health or other information that an older adult may not have

TABLE 6.2 Responder Guidelines for Older Adults in Disasters

COMMUNICATION STRATEGIES
• General 　○ Include on medical forms any information about special needs the person may have • Hearing impaired 　○ Have a communication board or notepads, pens, and pencils available 　○ Face the individual directly and speak slowly 　○ Make sure the individual evacuates with hearing aids, if applicable • Visually impaired 　○ Learn how to guide persons with visual impairments 　○ Make sure the individual evacuates with eyeglasses, if applicable • Cognitive impairment 　○ Assess cognitive status by asking to name and repeat three ordinary items, such as "apple, table, penny" and ask the senior what year it is 　○ Present information slowly, use simple language, speak in short sentences, and repeat if needed 　○ Be aware that older adults may have more difficulty in remembering or responding to disaster instructions 　○ Limit unnecessary conversation if the person becomes confused or disoriented; the primary focus should be on the action needed to evacuate

HEALTH ISSUES
• Ask seniors if they have any medical problems including diabetes, heart disease, high blood pressure, or memory difficulties • Ask seniors if they take medicine and if they have their medicine with them • Ask seniors if they require assistance with walking, eating, bathing, dressing, toileting, or medication administration • Assist evacuees in gathering necessary medicines, assistive equipment (glasses, walkers, hearing aids, etc.), and other medical supplies or equipment before evacuating • Obtain a list of medicines, names of doctor(s), family contact phone numbers, and important documents • Be aware that common health problems among older adults may become worse in a disaster situation, such as heart disease, arthritis, poor vision and hearing, depression and dementia, and acute illnesses

EVACUATION AND RESCUE
• Ask seniors if they use any assistive devices: cane, walker, wheelchair, bath bench • Ask persons with mobility issues to explain the best way for transporting, transferring, and assisting them • Ask seniors what their major need is right now • Ask seniors if they have a plan for where they will go and when they leave the residence • Ask seniors if they need assistance to find family and friends • Learn the use of wheelchairs and other specialized mobility equipment • Learn how to move and transfer the bedridden and frail elderly • Learn how to rescue persons from paratransit vans and buses • Track the transfer of residents from group homes to relocation sites

Sources: CDR (1997); CIDNY (2004); Dyer et al. (2008); FEMA (2010); Markenson et al. (2007); SILC (2013); White, Fox, and Rooney (2007).

available or be able to provide at the time of evacuation. Dyer, Regev, Burnett, Festa, and Cloyd (2008) have developed an extremely useful 13-item rapid triage tool for vulnerable older adults in disaster situations called the Seniors Without Families Team (SWiFT; see Figures 6.1 and 6.2).

CURRENT DATE:		WORKER'S NAME:	
NAME:		DOB:	
DO YOU HAVE FAMILY OR FRIENDS WITH YOU HERE? □ Y □ N			CONFIRMED? □ Y □ N

Level 1: Health/Mental Health Priority GOES TO SOCIAL WORK BOOTH IN MEDICAL CLINIC	**A.** Do you have any of the following medical problems? □ Y □ N Diabetes □ Y □ N Heart Disease □ Y □ N High Blood Pressure □ Y □ N Memory □ Other Note: **B.** Do you take medicine? □ Y □ N Do you have your medicine? □ Y □ N If no, treat as Level 1		**C.** Do you need someone to help you with: □ Y □ N Walking □ Y □ N Eating □ Y □ N Bathing □ Y □ N Dressing □ Y □ N Toileting □ Y □ N Medication administration Any checks, treat as Level 1 Do you use something to help you get around: □ Cane □ Walker □ Wheelchair □ Bath Bench
D. Where are you right now? If senior cannot or does not answer correctly treat as Level 1	**E.** Name three ordinary items and have them repeat them; for example, "apple, table, penny."	**F.** What year is it? If senior cannot/does not answer correctly, treat as Level 1	**G.** Ask them to repeat the three items you previously mentioned. If more than one item is missed, treat as Level 1
Level 2: Case Management Needs IS REFERRED TO A CASE MANAGER	**A.** Ask them what their major need is right now.	**B.** Do you have a plan for where you will go when you leave here? □ Y □ N	C. Income/Entitlements Are you on: □ Y □ N Medicare □ Y □ N Medicaid □ Y □ N SSI □ Y □ N Social Security □ Y □ N Food Stamps □ Y □ N VA Benefits □ Y □ N Section 8 Housing funds Do you have your documents? □ Y □ N
Level 3: Only needs to be linked to family or friends DIRECTED TO RED CROSS VOLUNTEER	**A.** Family Do you need help to find your family/ friends? □ Y □ N	**B.** Names: Relationship: Location:	*WHERE IS THE SENIOR LOCATED?*

FIGURE 6.1 SWiFT: A rapid triage tool for vulnerable older adults.

Source: Dyer, Regev, Burnett, Festa, and Cloyd (2008, p. S47).

SWIFT LEVEL	EXPLANATION	RECOMMENDED PRE-DISASTER ACTIONS
1 Health/mental health priority	Exhibits cognitive impairment, at least one activities of daily living (ADL: eating, bathing, dressing, toileting, walking, continence) impairment and/or has one or more serious untreated medical conditions	Evacuate early rather than late depending on the circumstance. If possible, stay with family member, companion, or caregiver Get assistance gathering all assistive devices including glasses, walkers, hearing aids, list of medicines, and names of doctor(s), family contact phone numbers, and important papers together so that they are accessible
2 Case management needs	Trouble with instrumental ADL (i.e., finances, benefits management, assessing resources)	Gather, with assistance if necessary, all assistive devices including glasses, walkers, hearing aids, list of medicines, and names of doctor(s), family contact phone numbers, and important papers together so that all are accessible
3 Only needs to be linked to family or friends	Needs to maintain contact with family or care providers	Ensure all assistive devices including walkers, glasses, hearing aids, list of medicines, and names of doctor(s), family contact phone numbers, and important papers are together and accessible

FIGURE 6.2 SWiFT tool use in disaster preparedness.

Source: Dyer, Regev, Burnett, Festa, and Cloyd (2008, p. S49).

A few additional issues are relevant for disaster response and recovery among older adults. Many people across populations may require counseling or psychological treatment after a disaster. Older adults may be hesitant to accept mental health services due to the stigma of mental illness and the fear that they will lose independence and be transferred to a nursing home if their problems become known to health professionals (Aldrich & Benson, 2008; Oriol, 1999).

Diet is also a concern for older adults. The Meal, Ready-to-Eat (MRE) packages that are offered to evacuees may be high in sodium, fat, and calories, which can compromise the nutrition of older adults with certain pre-existing health conditions such as hypertension or coronary artery disease (Aldrich & Benson, 2008; Banks, 2013). Although this chapter is primarily geared toward caring for older adults, many older adults have responsibilities for the care of others. Today, one in five relatives who provide care for preschoolers is a grandparent (U.S. Census Bureau, 2011b). Finally, one additional resource for friends and families of an older person is the Eldercare Locator (1-800-677-1116), provided by the AOA, which can be searched by location or topic (AOA, 2014).

SUMMARY AND CONCLUSIONS

Older adults represent a significant and growing segment of the American population. Today, one in eight persons are over the age of 65 and it is projected that the percentage will reach one in five by 2030. While many older adults are healthy and active, a variety of health issues affect adults as they age, making them vulnerable to disasters. The primary issues involve issues of mobility, diminished sensory awareness, cognitive impairments, social and economic limitations, and decline in overall health. The majority of the adult population over the age of 65 have at least one chronic health care issue.

Research studies have demonstrated that older adults are vulnerable in disasters, suffering differentially high rates of mortality in multiple types of disasters. The special needs and circumstances of older adults may make it difficult for them to adequately plan and prepare for a disaster. Older adults may also have more difficulty in evacuating during a disaster or safely sheltering in place. The physical and psychological stressors of a disaster may exacerbate existing health care issues in older adults or may contribute to the development of new health problems.

The best way for older adults to increase the probability of having positive outcomes in the event of a disaster is effective preparedness. A number of organizations have provided guidelines to assist older adults in disaster planning and preparation. The data to date is insufficient to draw any conclusions about whether or not older adults are better prepared than the general population, although it is known that they do not fare as well in disaster as their younger counterparts. It is also unclear whether older adults are less willing to evacuate or just less able to evacuate. Further evidence-based research is needed to understand obstacles to disaster preparedness and to establish best practices for older adults in disasters.

REFERENCES

Ablah, E., Konda, K., & Kelley, C. L. (2009). Factors predicting individual emergency preparedness: A multi-state analysis of 2006 BRFSS data. *Biosecurity and Bioterrorism: Biodefense Strategy, Practice and Science, 7*(3), 317–330. doi:10.1089/bsp.2009.0022

Administration on Aging (AOA). (2012). A profile of older Americans: 2012. Department of Health and Human Services. Retrieved February 15, 2014, from http://www.aoa .gov/AoARoot/Aging_Statistics/Profile/2012/docs/2012profile.pdf

Aldrich, N., & Benson, W. F. (2008). Disaster preparedness and the chronic disease needs of vulnerable older adults. *Preventing Chronic Disease, 5*(1), A:27. Retrieved February 14, 2014.

American Red Cross (ARC). (2004). Preparing for disaster for people with disabilities and other special needs. Retrieved September 19, 2013, from http://www.redcross.org /images/MEDIA_CustomProductCatalog/m4240199_A4497.pdf

American Red Cross (ARC). (2013). Seniors. Retrieved September 19, 2013, from http:// www.redcross.org/prepare/location/home-family/seniors

American Red Cross (ARC). (2014). Anatomy of a first aid kit. Retrieved March 8, 2014, from http://www.redcross.org/prepare/location/home-family/get-kit/anatomy.

Åström, O., Bertil, F., & Joacim, R. (2011). Heat wave impact on morbidity and mortality in the elderly population: A review of recent studies, *Maturitas, 69*(2), 99–105.

Banks, L. (2013). Caring for elderly adults during disasters: Improving health outcomes and recovery. *Southern Medical Journal, 106*(1), 94–98.

Bei, B., Bryant, C., Gilson, K., Koh, J., Gibson, P., Komiti, A., . . . Judd, F. (2013). A prospective study of the impact of floods on the mental and physical health of older adults. *Aging and Mental Health, 17*(8), 992–1002. doi:10.1080/13607863.2013.799199

Brown, L. M., Dosa, D. M., Thomas, K., Hyer, K., Feng, Z., & Mor, V. (2012). The effects of evacuation on nursing home residents with dementia. *American Journal of Alzheimer's and Other Dementias, 27*(6), 406–412. doi:10.1177/1533317512454709

Brunkard, J., Namulanda, G., & Ratard, R. (2008). Hurricane Katrina deaths, 2005. *Disaster Medicine and Public Health Preparedness, 2*(4), 215–223. doi:10.1097/DMP.0b013 e31818aaf55

California Department of Rehabilitation (CDR). (1997). Disaster preparedness for persons with disabilities improving California's response. Retrieved September 12, 2013, from http://www.preventionweb.net/files/7966_disasterpreparednessforpeople withdisabilities1202797803789963.pdf

Center for Independence of the Disabled in New York (CIDNY). (2004). Lessons learned from the World Trade Center disaster: Emergency preparedness for people with disabilities in New York. Retrieved September 13, 2013, from http://www.nobody leftbehind2.org/resources/pdf/lessons_learned_from_the_world_trade_center _disaster.pdf

Centers for Disease Control and Prevention (CDC). (2014). Emergency preparedness and you. Retrieved March 8, 2014, from http://emergency.cdc.gov/preparedness/

Chester, J. G., & Rudolph, J. L. (2011). Vital signs in older patients: Age-related changes. *Journal of the American Medical Directors Association, 12*(5), 337–343.

Christensen, J. J., Richey, E. D., & Castañeda, H. (2013). Seeking safety: Predictors of hurricane evacuation of community-dwelling families affected by Alzheimer's disease or a related disorder in South Florida. *Journal of Alzheimer's Disease and Other Dementias.* Retrieved February 17, 2014, from http://aja.sagepub.com/content/early/2013 /07/16/1533317513500837

Christensen, J. J., Brown, L. M., & Hyer, K. (2012). A haven of last resort: The consequences of evacuating Florida nursing home residents to nonclinical buildings. *Geriatric Nursing, 33*(5), 375–383.

Cornwell, B., & Laumann, E. O. (2013). The health benefits of network growth: New evidence from a national survey of older adults. *Social Science and Medicine.* Retrieved October 21, 2013, from http://www.sciencedirect.com.ezproxy3.lhl.uab.edu /science/article/pii/S0277953613005170.

Dosa, D. M., Hyer, K., Brown, L. M., Artenstein, A. W., Polivka-West, L., & Mor, V. (2008). The controversy inherent in managing frail nursing home residents during complex hurricane emergencies. *Journal of the American Medical Directors Association, 9*(8), 599–604.

Dyer, C. B., Regev, B. A., Burnett, J., Festa, N., & Cloyd, B. (2008). SWiFT: A rapid triage tool for vulnerable older adults in disaster situations. *Disaster Medicine and Public Health Preparedness, 2*(Suppl. 1), S45–S50. doi:10.1097/DMP.0b013e3181647b81.

Elmore, D. L., & Brown, L. M. (2007–2008). Emergency preparedness and response: Health and social policy implications for older adults. *Generations,* 66–74.

Federal Emergency Management Agency (FEMA). (2010). Guidance on planning for integration of functional needs support services in general population. Retrieved September 9, 2013, from http://www.fema.gov/pdf/about/odic/fnss_guidance.pdf

Federal Emergency Management Agency (FEMA). (2012a). Prepare for emergencies now: Information for people with disabilities. Retrieved September 11, 2013, from http://www.ready.gov/sites/default/files/FEMA_Disabilities_R-6_web _june2012.pdf

Federal Emergency Management Agency (FEMA). (2012b). Prepare for emergencies now: Information for older Americans. Retrieved September 19, 2013, from http://www .ready.gov/sites/default/files/documents/files/olderamericans_quadfold.pdf

Federal Emergency Management Agency (FEMA). (2013). Seniors. Retrieved September 19, 2013, from http://www.ready.gov/seniors

Federal Emergency Management Agency (FEMA). (2014). Ready. Prepare. Plan. Stay informed. Retrieved March 5, 2014, from http://www.ready.gov/

Fernandez, L. S., Byard, D., Lin, C. C., Benson, S., & Barbera, J. A. (2002). Frail elderly as disaster victims: Emergency management strategies. *Prehospital and Disaster Medicine, 17*(2), 67–74.

Gray-Graves, A., Turner, K. W., & Swan, J. H. (2011). The level of willingness to evacuate among older adults. *Gerontology and Geriatrics Education, 32*(2), 107–121.

Hajat, S., O'Conner, M., & Kosatsky, T. (2010). Health effects of hot weather: From awareness of risk factors to effective health protection. *The Lancet, 375*(9717), 856–863.

Hyer, K., Brown, L. M., Christensen, J. J., & Thomas, K. S. (2009). Weathering the storm: Challenges to nurses providing care to nursing home residents during hurricanes. *Applied Nursing Research, 22,* e9–e14.

Illinois Terrorism Task Force (ITTF). (2004). Emergency preparedness for those with functional needs. Retrieved January 18, 2014, from http://www.illinois.gov/ready /SiteCollectionDocuments/PreparednessTips_FunctionalNeeds.pdf

Jia, Z., Tian, W., Liu, W., Cao, Y., Yan, C., Yan, J., & Shun, Z. (2010). Are the elderly more vulnerable to the psychological impact of natural disaster? A population-based survey of adult survivors of the 2008 Sichuan earthquake. *BMC Public Health, 10,* 172–183.

Kailes, J. I. (2000). Creating a disaster-resistant infrastructure for people at risk including people with disabilities. Committee for the Global Assessment of Earthquake Countermeasures. http://www.jik.com/Kobe-word%20version.doc

Kailes, J. I. (2002). *Evacuation preparedness: Taking responsibility for your safety: A guide for people with disabilities and other activity limitations.* Center for Disability Issues and the Health Professions, Western University of Health Sciences, California (CDIHP). Retrieved March 25, 2014, from http://webhost.westernu.edu/hfcdhp /wp-content/uploads/Emergency_Evacuation.pdf

Kario, K., Matsuo, T., Kobayashi, H., Yamamoto, K., & Shimada, K. (1997). Earthquake-induced potentiation of acute risk factors in hypertensive elderly patients: Possible triggering of cardiovascular events after a major earthquake. *Journal of the American College of Cardiology, 29*(5), 926–933.

Keim, S. M., Guisto, J. A., & Sullivan, J. B., Jr. (2002). Environmental thermal stress. *Annals of Agricultural and Environmental Medicine, 9*(2), 1–15.

Laditka, S. B., Laditka, J. N., Xirasagar, S., Cornman, C. B., Davis, C. B., & Richter, J. V. E. (2008a). Providing shelter to nursing home evacuees in disasters: Lessons from Hurricane Katrina. *American Journal of Public Health, 98*(7), 1288–1293.

Laditka, S. B., Laditka, J. N., Cornman, C. B., Davis, C. B., & Chandlee, M. J. (2008b). Disaster preparedness for vulnerable persons receiving in-home, long-term care in South Carolina. *Prehospital and Disaster Medicine, 23*(2), 134–142.

Markenson, D., Fuller, E. J., & Redlener, I. E. (2007). Emergency preparedness: Addressing the needs of persons with disabilities. National Center for Disaster Preparedness. Retrieved January 4, 2014, from http://academiccommons.columbia.edu/item /ac:155353

McCormick, L. C. (2013). Measuring levels of citizen public health emergency preparedness, Jefferson County, Alabama. *Journal of Public Health Management and Practice, 19*(3), 266–273. doi:10.1097/PHH.0b013e318264ed8c

McGuire, L. C., Ford, E. S., & Okoro, C. A. (2007). Natural disasters and older U.S. adults with disabilities: Implications for evacuation. *Disasters, 31*(1), 49–56.

Morrow, B. H. (1999). Identifying and mapping community vulnerability. *Disasters, 23*(1), 1–18.

National Institute on Aging (NIA). (2012). Alzheimer's disease and disaster preparedness. Retrieved March 28, 2012, from http://www.nia.nih.gov/alzheimers/publication/alzheimers-disease-and-disaster-preparedness

National Association of Home Care & Hospice (NAHC). (2010). Basic statistics about home care. Retrieved March 1, 2014, from http://nahc.org/assets/1/7/10HC_Stats.pdf

National Council on Disability (NCD). (2005). *Saving lives: Including people with disabilities in emergency planning.* Retrieved March 25, 2014, from http://www.ncd.gov/publications/2005/04152005

National Fire Prevention Association (NFPA). (2013). Home safety for people with disabilities. Retrieved September 24, 2013, from http://www.nfpa.org/~/media/Files/Safety%20information/Safety%20tip%20sheets/disabilitysafetytips.pdf

National Institute on Aging (NIA). (2007a). *Why population aging matters. A global perspective.* U.S. Department of Health and Human Services. Bethesda, MD. Retrieved February 15, 2014, from http://www.nia.nih.gov/sites/default/files/WPAM.pdf

National Institute on Aging (NIA). (2007b). *Growing older in America: The health and retirement study.* U.S. Department of Health and Human Services. Bethesda, MD. Retrieved February 15, 2014, from http://www.nia.nih.gov/sites/default/files/health_and_retirement_study.pdf

National Oceanic and Atmospheric Administration (NOAA). (2011). U.S. mainland hurricane strikes by state, 1851–2004. Retrieved March 1, 2014, from http://www.nhc.noaa.gov/paststate.shtml

National Organization on Disability (NOD). (2009). Functional needs of people with disabilities: A guide for emergency managers, planners, and responders. Retrieved July 12, 2014, from http://nod.org/assets/downloads/Guide-Emergency-Planners.pdf

Oriol, W. (1999). *Psychosocial issues for older adults in disasters.* U.S. Department of Health and Human Services, Substance Abuse and Mental Health Services Administration, Center for Mental Health Services. Retrieved July 12, 2014, from http://store.samhsa.gov/shin/content//SMA99-3323/SMA99-3323.pdf

Phreaner, C., Jacoby, I., Dreier, S., & McCoy, N. (1994). Disaster preparedness of home health care agencies in San Diego County. *Journal of Emergency Medicine, 12*(6), 811–818.

Pietrzak, R. H., Southwick, S. M., Tracy, M., Galea, S., & Norris, F. H. (2011). Posttraumatic stress disorder, depression, and perceived needs for psychological care in older persons affected by Hurricane Ike. *Journal of Affective Disorders, 138*(1/2), 96–103.

Sakauye, K. M., Streim, J. E., Kennedy, G. J., Kirwin, P., Llorente, M. D., Schultiz, S. K., & Srinivasan, S. (2009). American Academy of Geriatric Psychiatry (AAGP) position statement: Disaster preparedness for older Americans: Critical issues for the preservation of mental health. *American Journal of Geriatric Psychiatry, 17*(11), 916–924.

Sanders, S., Bowie, S. L., & Bowie, Y. D. (2004). Chapter 2 lessons learned on forced relocation of older adults. The impact of Hurricane Andrew on health, mental health, and social support of public housing residents. *Journal of Gerontological Social Work, 40*(4), 23–35.

Silverman, M. A., Weston, M., Llorente, M., Beber, C., & Tam, R. (1995). Lessons learned from Hurricane Andrew: Recommendations for care of the elderly in long-term care facilities. *Southern Medical Journal, 88*(6), 603–608.

Spence, P. R., Lachlan, K., Burke, J. M., & Seeger, M. W. (2007). Media use and information needs of the disabled during a natural disaster. *Journal of Health Care for the Poor and Underserved 18*(2), 394–404.

State Independent Living Council (SILC). (2013). The impact of the 2003 wildfires on people with disabilities. Retrieved September 13, 2013, from http://www.nobodyleft behind2.org/resources/pdf/impact_of_2003_ca_wildfires_4-30-04.pdf

State of Florida Department of Elder Affairs (DOEA). (2011). Disaster preparedness. Retrieved March 28, 2014, from http://elderaffairs.state.fl.us/doea/disaster.php

United States Administration on Aging (AOA). (2014). Eldercare locator. Retrieved March 1, 2014, from http://www.eldercare.gov/Eldercare.NET/Public/Index.aspx

United States Census Bureau. (2011a). Sixty-five plus in the United States. Retrieved March 1, 2014, from http://www.census.gov/population/socdemo/statbriefs /agebrief.html

United States Census Bureau. (2011b). Child care, an important part of American life. Retrieved March 1, 2014, from http://www.census.gov/how/pdf/child_care.pdf

United States Department of Health and Human Services Administration on Aging (HHS-AOA). (2013). National family caregiver support program, emergency readiness for older adults and caregivers. Retrieved July 12, 2014, from http://www.agin ginstride.org/emergencyprep/docs/Just_in_Case.pdf

United States Geological Survey. (2012). Top earthquake states. Retrieved July 12, 2014, from http://earthquake.usgs.gov/earthquakes/states/top_states.php

Viswanath, B., Maroky, A. S., Math, S. B., John, J. P., Benegal, V., Hamza, A., & Chaturvedi, S. K. (2012). Psychological impact of the tsunami on elderly survivors. *American Journal of Geriatric Psychiatry, 20*(5), 402–407.

White, G. W., Fox, M. H., & Rooney, C. (2007). Nobody left behind: Report on exemplary and best practices in disaster preparedness and emergency response for people with disabilities. Research and Training Center on Independent Living, University of Kansas. Retrieved September 11, 2013, from http://www.nobodyleftbehind2.org /findings/pdfs/bestpractices_3-21-072.pdf

Persons With Chronic Mental Health Issues and Disasters

CASE STUDY

"Clinical field experience has shown that disaster survivors with mental illness function fairly well following a disaster, if essential services have not been interrupted. Many demonstrate an increased ability to handle this stress without an exacerbation of their mental illness, especially when they are able to maintain their medication regimens. However, some survivors with mental illness have achieved only a tenuous balance before the disaster. The added stress of the disaster disrupts this balance; for some additional mental health support services, medications or hospitalization may be necessary to regain stability" (CIDNY, 2004, citing Training Manual for Mental Health and Human Service Workers in Major Disasters. Deborah J. DeWolfe for FEMA and the Center for Mental Health Services at the Substance Abuse and Mental Health Services Administration [SAMHSA], 2000).

A considerable body of literature has been produced involving the relationship between mental illness and disaster. However, the bulk of this research is devoted to the psychological consequences of experiencing a disaster in the general population and among first responders, particularly the development of posttraumatic stress disorder (PTSD). Comparatively little empirical research has been conducted on disaster preparedness and responder interventions in addressing the specific needs of those with pre-existing mental illness. Although addressing PTSD and other long-term mental health consequences among those who have experienced disaster is a vital component in disaster recovery, it is also important to address the specific needs of persons with mental illness in order to help them prepare and to address how professionals respond to this population during the critical hours of the onset of a disaster.

Mental illness is quite common in the United States. The chances are approximately one in four that a person facing a disaster will also be facing some form of mental illness. According to the National Institute of Mental Health, 26.2% of the U.S. population is diagnosable with one or more mental disorders in a given year (NIMH, 2014). Persons with severe mental illness (SMI) suffer the most serious adverse effects. According to the National Survey on Drug Use and Health, 96 million adults (4.1% of the population) suffer from SMI (NSDUH, 2012). The survey defines an SMI as a mental, behavioral, or emotional disorder, diagnosable currently or within the last year, of sufficient duration to meet the diagnostic criteria of the *Diagnostic and Statistical Manual of Mental Disorders (DSM-IV)*, and resulting in serious functional impairment, which substantially interferes with or limits one or more major routines in life. Similarly, the severe functional impairment criterion of SMI is consistent with the Americans with Disabilities Act (ADA), which describes psychiatric disability as a mental impairment that substantially limits one or more of major life activities (EEOC, 1990).

Person and Fuller (2007) have aptly noted that disaster care for persons with mental illness is complex for a variety of reasons. The term "mental illness" covers a wide range of disorders that vary by their nature in both onset and long-term outcomes. In addition, a wide variation also exists in an individual's response to any given mental illness in terms of the context of illness exacerbation and the degree of psychiatric disability experienced. Depending on both the type of mental illness and an individual's unique response, some may function well with community support, medications, and the aid of mental health professionals. Others may always experience significant disability, even when they have access to high-quality care. This presents a challenge to developing appropriate guidelines for preparedness and response, for considerable variability exists from person to person with mental illness. Nonetheless, with over one-quarter of the population facing a diagnosable mental illness, it is crucial to develop evidence-based guidelines to address their needs.

THE VULNERABILITY OF PERSONS WITH CHRONIC MENTAL HEALTH ISSUES IN DISASTERS

CASE STUDY

Agron suffered from a long-term paranoid psychosis and was cared for by his family in a rural village in Kosovo. He received antipsychotic medicine, although he remained delusional, and lived quite comfortably in a small hut in the garden of the villa belonging to his extended family. . . . When Serb forces arrived at the village in the spring of 1999, the family fled but could not persuade Agron to go with them. He was shot in his bed and was discovered when his family returned to the village 2 months later (Jones et al., 2009, citing Kosovo, 1999).

One important question that has received attention in the literature is the extent to which persons with mental illness may be more vulnerable than the general population in a disaster. Although it may seem counterintuitive, persons with mental illness do not necessarily fare worse than the general population. The studies that have been conducted have mixed results, with some indicating that persons with mental illness are more vulnerable, some indicating that there are no differences, and, surprisingly, some studies indicating that those with mental illness (even SMI) may even fare better than the general population. Two potential factors accounting for these mixed results have been suggested.

One is that outcomes may vary according to the type of pre-existing mental illness. As will be discussed further, some evidence supports that persons with a pre-existing psychotic illness, such as schizophrenia, cope better than those with pre-existing PTSD. Again, surprisingly, individuals with anxiety disorders, such as panic disorder (PD), do not necessarily have an exacerbation of symptoms with a disaster. One explanation is that the fears of those with PD are internally generated rather than due to an actual external source of danger.

A second potential explanation that has been given is that an individual with a pre-existing mental illness may already have a support system in place to help manage his or her condition. Although that support system is not specifically geared to disaster situations, due to the nature of some mental illnesses, individuals may have developed plans for dealing with personal crises during times of exacerbation of mental illness. One potential limitation of that explanation is that those individuals who are already in treatment and being monitored by health care professionals are more likely to be the subjects of studies due to their involvement in the health care system and available records to assess pre- and post-disaster response. It is much more difficult to obtain analyzable data for individuals who may not be in treatment, such as the homeless or those who choose not to be involved in treatment.

Evidence for Worsening of Mental Health Symptoms in Disasters

Conventional wisdom has held that those with pre-existing mental illness are more vulnerable than the general population when experiencing disaster. Several studies have supported this premise. When evaluating these studies, and those that appear to contradict this assumption, it is important to keep in mind that the body of literature exploring pre-existing mental illness and disaster is limited. In one 2007 literature review of studies involving pre-existing mental illness and disaster, the authors found only 12 relevant articles (Person & Fuller, 2007).

One early, but wide scale, study that looked at the relationship between mental illness and response to disaster investigated the reactions to toxic oil syndrome (TOS) in Spain (Lopez-Ibor, Carras, & Rodriguez-Gamazo, 1985). TOS involved a food poisoning epidemic, probably from contaminated rapeseed oil, that affected more than 20,000 people and caused 350 deaths. The clinical symptoms of TOS included pulmonary, neuromuscular, and systemic symptoms that could lead to severe physical disabilities. Approximately 6,000 people were identified as experiencing negative psychological consequences and the authors found that a personal history of psychological disturbance was a risk factor. One complicating factor in this study is determining the extent that victims experienced difficulties to the disaster itself versus difficulty coping with the rather extreme medical problems that were experienced by many. Another study that broadly describes mental health sequelae was a population-based cohort study identifying risk factors for mortality among those who had experienced a 1999 earthquake in Taiwan (Chou, Huang, Lee, Tsai, Chen, & Chang, 2004). The authors of the study found that those with pre-existing mental health disorders were the most vulnerable. Another study examined the differences in response to the September 11 World Trade Center (WTC) attacks between medical patients and psychiatric patients (Franklin, Young, & Zimmerman, 2002). Psychiatric and medical patients (n = 308) living approximately 150 to 200 miles from the attack sites were administered questionnaires to assess background information, health care utilization, and PTSD symptoms. The researchers found that psychiatric patients were significantly more likely (33%) than medical patients (13%) to report PTSD symptoms.

Two studies reported negative psychological effects in response to disaster according to several different types of mental illness. One study investigated the role of pre-existing mental illness in the response to a jet crash accident (Smith, North, Carol, McCool, & Shea, 1990). In 1987, an Air Force jet fighter crashed into the lobby of a Ramada Inn in Indianapolis. Within 4 to 6 weeks of the accident, 46 victims of the accident were interviewed with the Diagnostic Interview Schedule/ Disaster Supplement. More than half met the criteria for one of four mental illness disorders after the accident: PTSD, major depression, generalized anxiety disorder, and alcohol abuse/dependence. Of those who met the criteria for mental illness, two-thirds had a pre-existing mental health disorder. Another study compared outcomes of veterans who had experienced Hurricane Katrina both with (n = 249) and without (n = 250) a pre-existing mental illness (Sullivan et al., 2013). The veterans were screened for PTSD, depression, generalized anxiety disorder, and PD. Overall, they found the odds of developing a new mental disorder were 6.8 times greater for those with a pre-existing mental illness. These results varied to some extent with the type of pre-existing illness. The odds of developing a new mental illness were 11.9 times greater in those with pre-existing PTSD, 9.1 times greater in those with schizophrenia, and 4.4 times greater in those with affect disorder.

Evidence for No Significant Change in Mental Health Symptoms in Disasters

Despite the data indicating that persons with chronic mental illness are at risk for exacerbation of symptoms or development of new symptoms, some studies seem to contradict these findings. One early study examined the responses to patients in the community mental health system to the 1979 Three Mile Island nuclear accident in Middletown, Pennsylvania (Bromet, Schulbert, & Dunn, 1982). A sample of 151 patients from the Three Mile Island area was compared with a sample of 61 patients from another area where a nuclear power plant is located. The authors found no significant differences in changes in mental health symptoms between these two groups. Another investigated mental health changes among 63 individuals with chronic schizophrenia who had experienced the 2009 earthquake in L'Aquila Italy (Pollice et al., 2012). Pre-earthquake and post-earthquake scores were compared for positive symptoms of schizophrenia and changes in cognitive function using the Wisconsin Card Sorting Test (WCST). No differences were found in either schizophrenia symptoms or memory function as measured by the WCST.

Several studies investigated changes in mental health functioning in disaster among individuals with anxiety disorders. One study investigated the response of individuals with PD to the NATO air strikes in Belgrade (Starcevic, Kolar, Latas, Bogojevic, & Kelin, 2002). Scores on the Panic and Agoraphobia Scale (PAS) were compared before and after the air strikes for those in complete or partial remission (n = 84). Symptoms of PD *decreased* after the air strikes in terms of overall severity of symptoms, health concerns, level of disability, and level and frequency of anticipatory anxiety. No significant differences were found in PAS scores. These results suggest that experiencing the air strikes did not disrupt the recovery of these individuals or cause deterioration in functioning. Another study compared individuals with obsessive–compulsive disorder (OCD; n = 25) to normal controls (n = 27) in their response to the September 11 WTC attacks (Riemann, Braun, Greer, & Ullman, 2004). All were administered a 15-item questionnaire (Consequences of Terrorist Activity) after the attacks. Patients with OCD reported only minor changes in mood, behavior, and somatic complaints. Interestingly, the controls actually reported a slight increase in cognitive symptoms in comparison to the individuals with OCD in terms of uncertainty about the future, intrusive recollections, and greater desire to be with loved ones. Another study compared symptoms among patients with OCD and PD both before and after the 1994 Northridge Earthquake in California (Bystritsky, Vapnik, Maidment, Pynoos, & Steinberg, 2000). Participants in the study were individuals with OCD involved in a partial hospitalization program (n = 19) and patients involved with ongoing PD studies (n = 22). Patients were assessed according to the Hamilton Anxiety (HAMA) and Hamilton Depression (HAMD) rating scales before and after the earthquake. OCD patients were also rated on the Yale-Brown Obsessive Compulsive Scale (YBOC) and PD patients were rated with the Cornell-Yale Panic Attack Scale (CY-PAS). Neither group experienced an exacerbation of their primary symptoms after the earthquake. The YBOC score did not change significantly for individuals with OCD and the CY-PAS score did not change significantly for those with PD. However, the HAMA and HAMD scores did change significantly for PD patients, but not in OCD patients. The authors suggest that a potential reason why there was no change in primary symptomology for either group is because the real disaster of the earthquake did not trigger the core fears that were part of the patients' anxiety disorders.

One interesting study involved the response to a disaster in Enschede, the Netherlands, involving the explosion of a fireworks depot in 2000 (Soeteman et al., 2006). The disaster resulted in the deaths of 18 residents, injury to approximately 1,000 people, and loss of homes for 1,200. This controlled-cohort study involved two time frames: pre-disaster (1 year) and post-disaster (2.5 years); victims of the explosion at the fireworks depot (n = 2,518) were matched with controls (n = 2,512) who were not victims. Outcome measures were evaluated using medical records of general practitioners (GP) in terms of attendance and physical and psychological symptoms registered. Individuals with pre-existing psychological problems had no increase in visits to their GP, but those without such pre-existing conditions did. In comparing controls, the study found that being a victim of disaster had a greater effect than the existence of pre-disaster psychological problems in post-disaster presentation of *psychological* problems. The existence of pre-disaster psychological problems had more of an effect than being a victim in post-disaster presentation of *physical* problems.

Another intriguing study demonstrates some degree of improvement of symptoms in individuals with pre-existing mental health disorders in the wake of a disaster. In this study, the effects of Hurricane Iniki on psychiatric inpatients at Hawaii State Hospital found that most patients showed no decompensation during the crisis, and some even improved in some respects (Godleski, Luke, DiPreta, Kline, & Carlton 1994). The study employed a sample of 22 patients, most of whom (73%) had a diagnosis of schizophrenia. Data recorded in the medical charts of patients indicated that none of the patients experienced decompensation during the crisis of the storm in terms of the need for additional medication; aggressive/self-destructive behavior; or increases in hallucinations, delusions, or bizarre behaviors. Improvement in the amount of participation in ward activities was documented for 55% of the patients; 45% stayed the same, and none decreased in participation levels. The authors attribute the positive outcome to the staff's guidance in directly involving the patients in preparing for the disaster and keeping them informed by having radios in patient areas, so they were able to listen to broadcasts.

The experiences of the psychiatric inpatients during Hurricane Iniki are thought provoking, for they may suggest that the presence of social support is what makes the difference in coping with a disaster for persons with mental illness. Assertive Community Treatment (ACT) involves a multidisciplinary team of professionals who serve patients who do not regularly use clinic-based services, but are at high risk for psychiatric hospitalization; its effectiveness has been demonstrated in 25 randomized controlled trials (Bond, Drake, Mueser, & Latimer, 2001). One study investigated the response of SMI patients involved in ACT from Southeastern Canada during a 1998 ice storm (McMurray & Steiner, 2000). The ice storm lasted 12 days, shutting down schools and businesses and leaving many without heat or electricity. The researchers found that SMI patients (n = 33) were no more likely to be seen at an emergency room during the disaster than they were at any other time. The authors suggest that SMI patients are able to respond well in disasters if they have sufficient support and if their support is not disrupted.

Evidence for Differences in Response by Type of Mental Illness in Disaster

A few studies are available that suggest differences may exist in disaster response depending on the type of mental illness a person is experiencing. In one early review article of the relationship between pre-existing mental illness and disaster response, it was found that pre-existing mood and anxiety disorders appeared to be a risk factor for pathology after a disaster (Katz, Pellegrino, Pandya, Ng, & DeLisi, 2002). However, individuals with psychotic illnesses did not appear to be at any greater risk for increase in psychopathology after a disaster. It should be noted that the authors of the review make it clear that the data to date on this topic was very limited.

Two other studies identified were also suggestive that those with pre-existing mental disorders may fare better than those with other types of mental illness. One involved the assessment of 20 survivors of a major bus crash who were patients at a day treatment center (Chubb & Bisson, 1996). Although a bus crash is not the typical situation that would be identified as representing a disaster, the level of trauma experienced is similar enough to be at least instructive. Of the 43 patients, staff, and relatives on the day trip, 10 people were killed in the accident. Several instruments were administered to the patients who were survivors, including the Clinician Administered PTSD Scale, the Hospital Anxiety and Depression Scale, and the Impact of Event Scale (IES) between 4 to 8 weeks of the accident. Half of the patients (n = 10) met the criteria for PTSD. The sample was also divided into categories of those with chronic schizophrenia (a psychotic disorder) versus those with anxiety or depressive disorders; those with schizophrenia displayed less marked psychological sequelae than the anxiety/depressive group.

A second study that is suggestive that those with psychotic disorders may fare better than those diagnosed with other types of mental illness involved the 2009 earthquake that struck L'Aquila, Italy (Strata & Rossi, 2010). This study demonstrated only slight differences between those with a psychotic disorder and those with an affective disorder. The Clinical Global Impression (CGI) instrument was administered to 65 patients who were previously engaged in a mental health program. The CGI involved a subjective self-evaluation that asked the question: "How do you mentally feel after the earthquake?" (better, equal, worse). For the sample, among those who rated their symptoms as worse, 25% had schizophrenia and 26% had affective disorders. Among those who rated their symptoms as equal, 57.1% had been diagnosed with schizophrenia and 57.9% had been diagnosed with affective disorders. Among those who described their symptoms as better, 17.9% had been diagnosed with schizophrenia and 15.8% had been previously diagnosed with affective disorders.

Although these studies suggest that individuals with a pre-existing psychotic disorder may fare better than those with other pre-existing mental health conditions, several other studies present data contradictory to that assumption. For example, a study of New York City psychiatric inpatients examined the differences between those who had the opportunity to view the disaster directly through a hospital window and those who did not (n = 156; DeLisi, Cohen, & Maurizio, 2004). The researchers found no differences in post-disaster symptomology between viewers and nonviewers. However, for both groups, those with a schizophrenia spectrum diagnosis (broadly, a psychotic disorder) showed more evidence of their symptoms worsening than those with an affective (mood) disorder. Affective or mood disorders include conditions such as bipolar disorder and major depression (NIMH, 2014).

Another study examined the difference in response to the California Northridge Earthquake survivors among those with a diagnosis with schizophrenia (n = 96), those with a diagnosis with bipolar disorder (n = 18), and healthy controls (n = 18; Horan et al., 2007). All participants completed the IES instrument to measure subjective stress at weeks one and five post-event. Individuals diagnosed with schizophrenia and bipolar disorder reported higher IES avoidance symptoms than healthy controls after the earthquake. Individuals with schizophrenia reported lower scores in coping, self-esteem, and social support than individuals diagnosed with bipolar disorder.

An additional study that examined the differences between psychotic and affective disorders involved the sequelae to the fall of the Berlin Wall in 1989 (Bohlken & Priebe, 1991). Although this was more a major political event than a disaster per se, the results here are instructive because they are analogous in documenting a major external disruption in normal life activities. In this study, the psychological aftermath was assessed among 67 patients in long-term treatment with schizoaffective disorders and affective disorders. The affective disorder group was subdivided into those diagnosed with unipolar (major) depression and those diagnosed with bipolar disorder. Comparing symptoms of the three groups, those with bipolar disorder did not demonstrate any significant differences in pre- versus post-event symptoms. Those with unipolar depression had improvement in symptomology between pre- and post-event. Those with schizoaffective disorder showed a significantly worse course of illness when comparing pre-event and post-event symptoms.

Two additional studies merit attention in examining pre-event and post-event symptoms of those with pre-existing psychological conditions. One involved the psychological consequences of individuals with pre-existing psychological symptoms following the 2011 Fukushima disaster (Matsumoto et al., 2013). The Fukushima disaster was a complex event. It first involved an earthquake, the earthquake spawned a tsunami, and the tsunami was responsible for a meltdown at the Fukushima nuclear power plant. Psychiatric outpatients at the Fukushima Medical University Hospital were surveyed 1 month after the disaster and the medical records of 1,286 outpatients were examined. Among those with bipolar disorder, exacerbations were more likely to switch to depressive than manic symptoms.

CASE STUDY: Hurricane Katrina

A 33-year-old man with a history of schizoaffective disorder presented to DePaul via the New Orleans Police Department Crisis Unit following an episode in which he approached police requesting assistance for finding his home, a home in which he has not resided since the time of Hurricane Katrina. Instead, the patient currently resides with his mother in another home. The patient also believed himself to be Jesus and requested to be addressed as such . . . On exam, he displayed thought blocking, grandiose delusions, and an expansive affect. At the time of Katrina, the patient was trapped in his home due to the floodwaters and had to wade through the water to higher ground at the interstate (Pletch, Rodgman, Leímbach, Erwin, & Johnson, 2013).

Another study involved the psychological sequelae of a 2009 swine influenza epidemic (Page, Seetharaman, Suhail, Wessely, Pereira, & Rubin, 2011). This study is significant because there is extremely scant evidence that evaluates the disaster response to epidemic disease, particularly for vulnerable populations. The study involved a narrative, thematic analysis of patient records from the South London & Maudsley Foundation/NHS Foundation Trust (SLAM) using the Case Register Interactive Search (CRIS) program. The results from the study indicated that both children and adults with neurotic and somatoform disorders were over-represented among those expressing moderate/severe swine flu concerns.

THE DISASTER FRAMEWORK AND PERSONS WITH CHRONIC MENTAL HEALTH ISSUES

As just described, the data is mixed regarding the way that individuals with chronic mental illness respond to a disaster, with varied studies indicating worsening of symptoms, no change in symptoms, and in some cases, improvement in symptoms. Differences in outcomes may depend to some degree on the type of mental illness an individual experiences. The studies that document individuals who fare well are suggestive that being involved in a supportive treatment environment may help in coping with a disaster. Thus, planning ahead to minimize potential disruptions in medication, counseling, and other support services is important for the chronically mentally ill to maintain pre-disaster levels of functioning post-disaster.

Planning, Preparedness, and Mitigation for Persons With Chronic Mental Health Issues

Rabins, Kass, Rutkow, Vernick, and Hodge, Jr. (2011) have described it as a "moral mandate" to develop preparedness strategies for individuals with pre-existing mental illness and others who are at greater risk in disasters. Without planning, these individuals may not receive necessary mental health services and have the potential to decompensate in a crisis. The authors of the study also stress the importance of having professionals with mental health training available in a disaster, not only to assist the chronically mentally ill, but also to recognize individuals who may experience a new onset of mental illness under the stress of disaster conditions.

Very little research exists to document disaster planning and preparation among individuals with SMIs. One study suggests that this population is less likely to have prepared than the general population (Eisenman et al., 2009). The researchers conducted a random-digit-dial telephone survey of the noninstitutionalized population in Los Angeles County. Significant differences were found between people who have a serious mental illness having an emergency kit (29.5%) and those who do not have a serious mental illness (49.2%). A study of Hurricane Katrina survivors also suggests that individuals with mental illness may not be preparing adequately for disasters (Greenough et al., 2008). A two-state, 18-cluster sample survey was conducted with 499 evacuees residing in American Red Cross shelters in Louisiana 2 weeks after Hurricane Katrina.

The study results indicated that 13.5% of the evacuees suffered from some form of psychiatric illness. Of those, 42.4% arrived without any of their prescribed medications.

For personal disaster preparedness among those with chronic mental illness, the basic triad of being informed, making a plan, and building a kit applies. However, there are also special considerations for those with pre-existing mental illness. Some individuals may need assistance from mental health professionals in making disaster plans, depending on the type of mental illness and the severity of the symptoms. Since symptoms may exacerbate during a crisis, it is wise as standard practice for mental health professionals to incorporate disaster preparedness as a core component of any individual's treatment plan. One information source for both individuals with mental illness and professionals who work with them is the Disaster Technical Assistance Center (DTAC; SAMHSA, 2013).

Table 7.1 provides recommendations for personal disaster preparedness from a number of organizations that include a focus on individuals with mental illness. One of the most important steps to take is for an individual to conduct a personal assessment of his or her needs and the types of assistance that are anticipated during a disaster, ideally in collaboration with a mental health professional. The emergency disaster kit should include the name and phone number of one's mental health professional(s) and other members of one's support system. To plan ahead, one should discuss with family, friends, or health professionals the common reactions that individuals have to a disaster, such as increased anxiety and sadness, and discuss ways to cope with these types of feelings ahead of time.

Individuals with chronic mental illness should also prepare for continuity in care during a disaster. The emergency kit should include at least a 3-day supply of medication and other important medical information including names and phone numbers of mental health professionals; important medical documents including a list of medications, prescriptions, physician's orders, medical and records; and any other relevant information. An Emergency Health Information Card should be completed and kept on one's person at all times. It is also important to work with mental health providers to identify backup support services in the event of a disaster.

Response and Recovery for Persons With Chronic Mental Health Issues

Three of the most important elements for helping professionals in assisting individuals with mental illness in disaster are recognizing mental illness, managing symptoms through a crisis, and ensuring continuity of care. Disaster responders should be trained to identify individuals with pre-existing mental health conditions because such individuals may not be capable of communicating information about their condition during a crisis (Nauert, 2011). Some individuals with chronic mental illness are dependent on caretakers and may not be able to relate this type of information even under normal circumstances. For others, a crisis may exacerbate symptoms or create new symptoms, making it difficult to communicate effectively with responders.

TABLE 7.1 Personal Preparedness for Persons With Chronic Mental Illness

BE INFORMED
• Be aware of the types of disasters that occur in your area and county warning procedures, evacuation plans, and shelters before disaster strikes • Be aware of evacuation procedures in your workplace; know the location of fire extinguishers and emergency alarms • Monitor television, radio, Internet, and social media news reports as able for information from authorities on local conditions and official instructions • Know your community's response and evacuation plans

MAKE A PLAN

General
- Keep by your bedside a charged phone, a flashlight, and prescription glasses
- Check the accessibility of local shelters and hotels and the availability of support services in those areas
- Perform routine mock drills and revise plan as necessary
- Create a personal assessment of what you will be able to do for yourself and what assistance you may need during or after a disaster
- Include in your emergency disaster kit the name and phone number of your local mental health professional(s) and/or other persons you can rely on for support
- Meet with your family members, friends, and residence manager to review community hazards and emergency plans and emergency supplies
- Know the signs and symptoms of common reactions to a disaster and develop and discuss coping skills with your family and friends
- Check the accessibility of local shelters and hotels and the availability of support services in those areas
- Notify first responders of any mental health issues you may have
- Complete an Emergency Health Information Card and keep it with you at all times
- Fire safety:
  - Keep batteries charged in smoke alarms
  - Know where fire extinguishers are and how to operate them
  - Test smoke alarms once a month
  - For added safety, interconnect all the smoke alarms so that when one sounds, they all sound
  - If possible, purchase alarms with nonreplaceable (life-long) batteries designed to be effective for up to 10 years; these can be helpful for people who have difficulty changing batteries
- If possible, choose an apartment with a sprinkler system or install the system in your home

Mental Health Needs
Sheltering in Place and Evacuation
- Develop a plan to shelter in place
  - Be prepared to shelter in place in the event that you are unable to evacuate or are advised by local officials to stay where you are, including an emergency kit (see below)
  - If you use medical equipment at home that requires electricity, develop a backup plan for its use during a power outage
- Develop a plan to evacuate
  - Plan two ways out of every room
  - Know your community's response and evacuation plans and plan an evacuation route from your home
  - Plan for transportation if you need to evacuate to a shelter
  - Always evacuate if you are told by medical or other official personnel to evacuate or seek treatment
  - If there is sufficient time, shut off valves for household utilities (gas, electricity, water)
  - Recommendations for mitigating potential impairments for evacuating: bolt bookshelves to walls; anchor outdoor items that can be projectiles in high winds and hurricanes; install hurricane shutters (if appropriate to area); trim trees that overhang roofs; repair cracks in ceilings and foundations; store flammable materials away from heat sources

(continued)

TABLE 7.1 Personal Preparedness for Persons With Chronic Mental Illness (*continued*)

Communication—Family, Friend, and Neighbor Communication Plan • Make a list of family, friends, and others who will be part of your personal support network and communication plan • Include a friend or relative from another area who would not be affected by the same emergency and can help if needed • Decide where to meet your household members if you should become separated • Notify members of your personal support network if you plan to go out of town • Inform your personal support network of how you plan to evacuate your home, school, or workplace and where you will go in the event of a disaster • Make sure someone in your personal network has an extra key to your home and knows where you keep your emergency supplies • Make sure a trusted friend or relative has copies of important medical and any other important documents
BUILD A KIT

• Basic supplies:
  o A 3-day supply of food and water
  o Flashlight and batteries
  o Hand-crank or battery-operated radio
• Cell phone with charger, inverter, or solar charger
• Basic first aid kit (American Red Cross for a family of four):
  o Bandages and dressings: 2 absorbent compress dressings (5.9 inches); 25 adhesive bandages (assorted sizes); 1 adhesive cloth tape (10 yards × 1 inch); 1 roller bandage (3 inches wide); 1 roller bandage (4 inches wide); 5 sterile gauze pads (3 × 3 inches); 5 sterile gauze pads (4 × 4 inches); 2 triangular bandages
  o Medications/wound care: 2 packets of aspirin (for adults only); 5 antibiotic ointment packets (approximately 1 gram); 5 antiseptic wipe packets; 2 hydrocortisone packets
  o Other supplies and equipment: blanket; breathing barrier (with one-way valve); instant cold compress; 2 pairs of nonlatex gloves (large); scissors; oral thermometer; tweezers
  o First aid instruction booklet
• Medical supplies: keep a 3- to 7-day supply of prescription medication and documentation of any medical records, prescriptions, insurance information, etc.
• If you have been prescribed medication for mental health, keep a copy of information about where you received the medication, the name of the medication, and the dosage
• Other supplies for home emergency kit: whistle to signal for help; dust mask to help filter contaminated air and plastic sheeting and duct tape to shelter in place; sanitation items (moist towelettes, toilet paper, garbage bags); local maps; wrench or pliers to turn off utilities; manual can opener; extra cash or traveler's checks if possible, extra batteries; extra blankets
• Other documents: consider including records such as social security number, charge and bank account information, tax records, will, etc. A portable thumb drive is an option for storing important information
• Create an emergency Health Information Card, update it regularly, and keep it with you at all times
• Pets and service animals: food, water, first aid, and other supplies if you have a pet or service animal (see Chapter 9)
• Prepare a kit for sheltering in place and a smaller, lightweight kit if you need to evacuate

Sources: ARC (2014); CDC (2012, 2014); CDR (1997); FEMA (2014); ITTF (2004); Markenson, Fuller, and Redlener (2007); Reyers/NAMI (2012); SAMHSA (2013).

As a general rule, responders should utilize the principles of psychological first aid when assisting individuals in a disaster situation (CDC, 2012; WHO, 2011). It is useful as a global response, for even those who do not have a pre-existing mental illness may experience significant stress in a crisis. The ABCs of psychological first aid are:

- **A**rousal: Decrease excitement (provide safety, comfort, consolation)
- **B**ehavior: Assist survivors to function effectively in disaster
- **C**ognition: Provide reality testing and clear information

The aims of psychological first aid are to provide practical care and support, to address basic needs, to help people connect to information services and social supports, and to protect people from further harm.

Table 7.2 provides responder guidelines for persons with chronic mental illness in disasters derived from a variety of organizations with a focus on mental illness. Assessment should include monitoring an individual for extreme distress reaction, poor reality testing, or signs of an individual being a danger to himself or herself or others. Signs and symptoms of extreme stress reaction may include anxiety, crying, agitation, fear, anger, and not responding to questions. Signs and symptoms of poor reality testing may include confusion, disorientation, delusions, or hallucinations. Indications that a person may be a danger to himself or herself or others include suicidal ideation, homicidal ideation, or observation of a person engaging in dangerous behavior. This is a particular concern for those who are responsible for caring for children.

Effective communication is also key for those who may be experiencing symptoms of mental illness in a crisis. An offer of practical assistance, such as food, water, or blankets, may help ease stress. Responders should assist with reality orientation if an individual appears to be disoriented or confused. This includes identifying oneself as being there to help, speaking slowly and calmly, providing factual information in simple terms, and explaining what is happening and the plan for evacuation. If an individual appears to be in distress, responders should help the person to remain calm. Strategies include keeping the tone of one's voice soft and calm, acknowledging feelings and indicating understanding, and encouraging the person to focus on breathing slowly. As the person is able, responders should ask the person about any mental or physical health conditions, gather information about medication and current treatments, and assist the person in getting access to mental health services if needed.

Provision of continuity of care is fundamental for maintaining pre-disaster levels of functioning for those with chronic mental illness. Maintaining a daily routine with scheduled medications, access to a health provider, and a stable environment may all be disrupted during a disaster and in its aftermath (Milligan & McGuinness, 2009). A report from the Center for Independence of the Disabled in New York reported a number of problems with the response to individuals with serious mental illness including professionals insufficiently trained in mental health and lack of strategies for outreach to and evacuation of individuals with psychiatric conditions (CIDNY, 2004). Hurricane Katrina severely disrupted mental health services, including Charity Hospital, which had been a major provider of psychiatric services in New Orleans (Milligan & McGuinness, 2009). A telephone survey of Katrina survivors (n = 1043) found that among those with pre-existing mental disorders, 22.9% experienced either a reduction or termination of services (Wang et al., 2008). In a cross-sectional survey involving a convenience sample (n = 222) in New Orleans, 52% of respondents reported poor

TABLE 7.2 Responder Guidelines for Persons With Chronic Mental Illness in Disasters

GENERAL
• As a general rule, utilize the ABCs of psychological first aid when assisting individuals in a disaster situation, who may or may not have chronic mental illness o **A**rousal: decrease excitement (provide safety, comfort, consolation) o **B**ehavior: assist survivors to function effectively in disaster o **C**ognition: provide reality testing and clear information • Be aware that persons with mental illness may need additional reassurance and support during an emergency situation • Be aware that persons with severe mental illness (SMI) do not necessarily have an adverse reaction to disaster if continuity of care is provided • Be aware that those without prior SMI may have an extreme distress response in times of disaster

ASSESSMENT
• Assess for extreme distress reaction o Symptoms may include shaking, crying, not responding to questions, anxiety, fear, irritability, anger, and agitation • Assess for signs of poor reality testing o Symptoms may include, confusion, disorientation, delusions, and/or hallucinations • Assess for signs of the individual being a potential danger to himself or herself, or others o Symptoms may include verbalizations of suicidal or homicidal ideation, behaviors that put the individual or those around him or her at risk, or overt attempts to harm self or others

COMMUNICATION STRATEGIES
• Provide practical assistance to make contact (offer food, water, blankets) • Assist with reality orientation if the individual appears confused or disoriented o Explain that you are there to help o Provide accurate, factual information o Speak slowly, in simple, concrete terms o Explain what is happening and the plan for evacuation o Offer to write down information if needed • Assist individuals in remaining calm if in distress o Be patient, calm, and demonstrate understanding o Keep tone of voice soft and calm o Acknowledge feelings o Encourage to focus on breathing, breathing slowly

HEALTH ISSUES
• Ask about any mental or physical health issues an individual may have • Inquire whether or not the individual is currently taking any medications and assist in gathering medications for evacuation • Mental health providers should make additional support and services available if it appears that a person with SMI is experiencing increased distress

EVACUATION AND RESCUE
• Ensure immediate physical safety • Assist the individual in evacuating to a safe place • Assist in accessing available mental health providers and support services if it appears that a person with SMI is experiencing increased distress • Assist the individual in contacting friends, family, or other supports • For the persons with mental illness who are institutionalized, track the transfer of patients from psychiatric facilities to relocation sites

Sources: CDC (2012); Janowski and Hamblen (2014); Minnesota Department of Health (2013); NCTSN (2006); SAMHSA (2013); WHO (2011); YCPHP (2008).

mental health 15 months after the event. Although continuity of care is critical for individuals with chronic mental illness, it is often difficult to achieve in the midst of a crisis. Planning ahead is central to mitigating negative outcomes for persons with mental illness during a disaster.

SUMMARY AND CONCLUSIONS

Unfortunately, the research to date on disaster response among persons with pre-existing mental health conditions is scant, contradictory, and understudied. There is a clear need for empirical research that is specifically geared toward assessing how persons with pre-existing mental illness respond to disaster, how to best establish guidelines to help them prepare, and to establish evidence-based guidelines for professionals responding to those with pre-existing mental health conditions.

At this point, a few general assessments can be posited. First, given the statistics that nearly one person in four of the general American population suffers from some form of diagnosable mental illness, it is critical that generalized mental health screening be incorporated into first responder interventions during the time of crisis. This is relevant both for those with pre-existing mental health conditions and for those who may develop serious psychological sequelae after experiencing a disaster. Second, the assumption that those with pre-existing mental health conditions are more vulnerable in disaster needs further critical evaluation and empirical research to be justified. There is sufficient evidence to suggest at least a re-evaluation of the premise that individuals with mental illness are always more vulnerable. Although the empirical evidence to date is meager, what is available does suggest that persons with pre-existing mental illness who are tapped into a strong support system fare no worse than the general population. Moreover, the pre-disaster development of a strong support system may even make those with pre-existing support systems more resilient than the general population. Finally, there is the question of whether the category of "mental illness" is too broad to differentiate between the differing mental health outcomes of those with specific mental illnesses. Although to date there are only a handful of studies that address this issue, there is intriguing evidence to suggest that those with SMI who are psychotic, perhaps the most severe form of SMI, are not necessarily more vulnerable than other persons with SMI or the general population. Rather, a potential critical factor is the development and availability of a solid and sound support system, which is integral to the effective disaster response of any population, whether or not diagnosed with a pre-existing mental health condition.

REFERENCES

American Red Cross (ARC). (2014). Anatomy of a first aid kit. Retrieved March 8, 2014, from http://www.redcross.org/prepare/location/home-family/get-kit/anatomy

Bohlken, J., & Priebe, S. (1991). Political change and course of affective psychoses: Berlin 1989–90. *Psychiatry Research, 37*(1), 1–4.

Bond, G. R., Drake, R. E., Mueser, K. T., & Latimer, E. (2001). Assertive community treatment for people with severe mental illness. *Disease Management and Health Outcomes, 9*(3), 141–159.

Bromet, E., Schulbert, H. D., & Dunn, L. (1982). Reactions of psychiatric patients to the Three Mile Island nuclear accident. *Archives of General Psychiatry, 39*(6), 669–673.

Bystritsky, A., Vapnik, T., Maidment, K., Pynoos, R. S., & Steinberg, A. M. (2000). Acute responses of anxiety disorder patients after a natural disaster. *Depression and Anxiety, 11*, 43–44.

California Department of Rehabilitation (CDR). (1997). Disaster preparedness for persons with disabilities improving California's response. Retrieved September 12, 2013, from http://www.preventionweb.net/files/7966_disasterpreparednessforpeople withdisabilties1202797803789963.pdf

Center for Independence of the Disabled in New York (CIDNY). (2004). Lessons learned from the World Trade Center disaster: Emergency preparedness for people with disabilities in New York. Retrieved on September 13, 2013, from http://www.nobodyleftbehind2 .org/resources/pdf/lessons_learned_from_the_world_trade_center_disaster.pdf

Centers for Disease Control and Prevention (CDC). (2014). Emergency preparedness and you. Retrieved March 8, 2014, from http://emergency.cdc.gov/preparedness/

Chou, Y. J., Huang, N., Lee, C. H., Tsai, S. L., Chen, L. S., & Chang, H. J. (2004). Who is at risk of death in an earthquake? *American Journal of Epidemiology, 160*(7), 688–695. doi:10.1093/aje/kwh270

Chubb, H. L., & Bisson, J. I. (1996). Early psychological reactions in a group of individuals with pre-existing and enduring mental health difficulties following a major coach accident. *British Journal of Psychiatry, 169*, 430–433.

DeLisi, L. E., Cohen, T. H., & Maurizio, A. M. (2004). Hospitalized psychiatric patients view the World Trade Center disaster. *Psychiatric Research, 129*(2), 201–207.

Eisenman, D. P., Zhou, Q., Ong, M., Asch, S., Glik, D., & Long, A. (2009). Variations in disaster preparedness by mental health, perceived general health, and disability status. *Disaster Medicine and Public Health Preparedness, 3*(1), 33–41. doi:10.1097 /DMP.0b013e31819be89

Federal Emergency Management Agency (FEMA). (2014). Ready. Prepare. Plan. Stay informed. Retrieved March 5, 2014, from http://www.ready.gov/

Franklin, C. L., Young, D., & Zimmerman, M. (2002). Psychiatric patients' vulnerability in the wake of the September 11th terrorist attacks. *The Journal of Nervous and Mental Disease, 190*(12), 833–838.

Godleski, L. S., Luke, K. N., DiPreta, J. E., Kline, A. E., & Carlton, B.S. (1994). Responses of state hospital patients to Hurricane Iniki. *Hospital and Community Psychiatry, 45*(9), 931–933.

Greenough, P. G., Lappi, M. D., Hsu, E. B., Fink, S., Hsieh, Y., Vu, A., . . . Kirsch, T. D. (2008). Burden of disease and health status among Hurricane Katrina-displaced persons in shelters: A population-based cluster sample. *Annals of Emergency Medicine, 51*(4), 426–432.

Horan, W. P., Ventura, J., Mintz, J., Kopelowicz, A., Wirshing, D., Christian-Herman, J., . . . Liberman, R. P. (2007). Stress and coping responses to a natural disaster in people with schizophrenia. *Psychiatry Research, 151*(1–2), 77–86.

Illinois Terrorism Task Force (ITTF). (2004). *Emergency preparedness for those with functional needs.* Retrieved January 18, 2014, from http://www.illinois.gov/ready /SiteCollectionDocuments/PreparednessTips_FunctionalNeeds.pdf

Janowski, K., & Hamblen, J. (2014). The effects of disaster on people with severe mental illness. PTSD: National Center for PTSD. U.S. Department of Veterans Affairs. Retrieved March 8, 2014, from http://www.ptsd.va.gov/professional/trauma /disaster-terrorism/effects-disaster-mental-illness.asp

Jones, L., Asare, J. B., El Masri, M., Mohanraj, A., Sherief, H., & van Ommeren, M. (2009). Severe mental disorders in complex emergencies. *The Lancet, 374*(9690), 654–661.

Katz, C. L., Pellegrino, L., Pandya, A., Ng, A., & DeLisi, L. E.(2002). Research on psychiatric outcomes and interventions subsequent to disasters: A review of the literature. *Psychiatry Research, 110*(3), 201–217.

Kim, S. C., Plumb, R., Gredig, Q., Rankin, L., & Taylor, B. (2008). Medium-term post-Katrina health sequelae among New Orleans residents: Predictors of poor mental and physical health. *Journal of Clinical Nursing, 17*(17), 2335–2342.

Lopez-Ibor, J. J., Jr., Carras, S. F., & Rodriguez-Gamazo, M. (1985). Psychopathological aspects of the toxic oil syndrome catastrophe. *British Journal of Psychiatry, 147*, 352–365. doi:10.1192/bjp.147.4.352

Markenson, D., Fuller, E. J., & Redlener, I. E. (2007). Emergency preparedness: Addressing the needs of persons with disabilities. National Center for Disaster Preparedness. Retrieved January 4, 2014, from http://academiccommons.columbia.edu/item/ac:155353

Matsumoto, J., Kunii, Y., Wada, A., Mashiko, H., Yabe, H., & Niwa, S. (2013). Mental disorders that exacerbated due to the Fukushima disaster, a complex radioactive contamination disaster. *Psychiatry and Clinical Neurosciences, 68*(3), 182–187. doi:10.1111/pcn.12112

McMurray, L., & Steiner, W. (2000). Natural disasters and service delivery to individuals with severe mental illness—ice storm, 1998. *Canadian Journal of Psychiatry, 45*(4), 383–385.

Milligan, G., & McGuinness, T. M. (2009). Mental health needs in a post-disaster environment. *Journal of Psychosocial Nursing and Mental Health, 47*(9), 23–30.

National Institute of Mental Health (NIMH). (2014). Statistics. Retrieved January 18, 2014, from http://www.nimh.nih.gov/statistics/index.shtml?utm_source=winter-inside-nimh&utm_medium=email&utm_campaign=staff

Minnesota Department of Health. (2013). Psychological first aid (PFA). Retrieved March 8, 2014, from http://www.health.state.mn.us/oep/responsesystems/pfa.html

National Child Traumatic Stress Network (NCTSN). (2006). *Psychological first aid: Field operations guide* (2nd edition). Retrieved March 8, 2014, from http://www.ptsd.va.gov/professional/manuals/manual-pdf/pfa/PFA_V2.pdf

National Survey on Drug Use and Health (NSDUH). (2012). Results from the 2012 national survey on drug use and health: Mental health findings. Retrieved January 20, 2014, from http://www.samhsa.gov/data/NSDUH/2k12MH_FindingsandDetTables/2K12MHF/NSDUHmhfr2012.htm

Nauert, R. (2011). Disaster plans should include those with mental illness. Retrieved March 8, 2014, from http://psychcentral.com/news/2011/05/24/disaster-plans-should-include-those-with-mental-illness/26432.html

Page, L. A., Seetharaman, S., Suhail, I., Wessely, S., Pereira, J., & Rubin, G. J. (2011). Using electronic patient records to assess the impact of swine flu (influenza H1N1) on mental health patients. *Journal of Mental Health, 20*(1), 60–69.

Person, C., & Fuller. (2007). Disaster care for persons with psychiatric disabilities. *Journal of Disability Policy Studies, 17*(4), 238–248.

Pletsch, G., Rodgman, C. Leímbach, E., Erwin, K., & Johnson, J. (2013). The road home: Returning to pre-Katrina homes during episodes of psychosis. *Open Journal of Psychiatry, 3*, 1–4. Retrieved March 25, 2014, from http://dx.doi.org/10.4236/ojpsych.2013.31001

Pollice, R., Bianchini, V., di Mauro, S., Mazza, M., Verni, L., Roncone, R., & Casacchia, M. (2012). Cognitive function and clinical symptoms in first-episode psychosis and chronic schizophrenia before and after the 2009 L'Aquila earthquake. *Early Intervention in Psychiatry, 6*, 153–158. doi:10.1111/j.1751-7893.2011.00319x

Rabins, P. V., Kass, N. E., Rutkow, L., Vernick, J. S., & Hodge J. G., Jr. (2011). Challenges for mental health services raised by disaster preparedness: Mapping the ethical and therapeutic terrain. *Biosecurity and Bioterrorism: Biodefense Strategy, Practice, and Science, 9*(2), 175–179. doi:10.1089/bsp.2010.0068

Riemann, B. C., Braun, M. M., Greer, A., & Ullman, J. M. (2004). Effects of September 11 on patients with obsessive compulsive disorder. *Cognitive Behaviour Therapy, 33*(2), 60–67.

Reyers, C. (2012). In Sandy's wake: Managing mental illness after a disaster and finding support. National Alliance on Mental Illness (NAMI). Retrieved March 8, 2014, from http://www.nami.org/Content/NavigationMenu/Top_Story/In_Sandy's_Wake _Managing_Mental_Illness_after_a_Disaster_and_Finding_Support.htm

Smith, E. M., North, C. S., McCool, R. E., & Shea, J. M. (1990). Acute postdisaster psychiatric disorders: Identification of persons at risk. *American Journal of Psychiatry, 147*(2), 202–206.

Soeteman, R. J. H., Yzermans, C. J., Kerssens, J. J. Dirkzwager, A. J. E., Donker, G. A., van den Bosch, W. J. H. M., & van der Zee, J. (2006). The course of post-disaster health problems of victims with pre-disaster psychological problems as presented in general practice. *Family Practice, 23*(3), 378–384.

Starcevic, V., Kolar, D., Latas, M., Bogojevic, G., & Kelin, K. (2002). Panic disorder patients at the time of air strikes. *Depression and Anxiety, 16*, 152–156.

Substance Abuse and Mental Health Services Administration (SAMHSA).(2013). Disaster Technical Assistance Center (DTAC). Retrieved February 15, 2014, from http://www.samhsa.gov/dtac/

Strata, P., & Rossi, A. (2010). Subjective adjustment of individuals with psychiatric disorders in the aftermath of the L'Aquila Earthquake. *American Journal of Psychiatry, 167*(3), 352–353.

Sullivan, G. Vasterling, J. J., Han, X., Tharp, A. T., Davis, T., Deitch, E. A., & Constans, J. I. (2013). Preexisting mental illness and risk for developing a new disorder after Hurricane Katrina. *The Journal of Nervous and Mental Disease, 201*(2), 161–166.

United States Equal Opportunity Commission (EEOC). (1990). *The Americans with Disabilities Act of 1990, As Amended.* Retrieved January 15, 2014, from http://www .ada.gov/pubs/ada.htm

Wang, P. S., Gruber, M. J., Powers, R. E., Schoenbaum, M., Speier, A. H., Wells, K. B., & Kessler, R. C. (2008). Disruption of existing mental health treatments and failure to initiate new treatment after Hurricane Katrina. *American Journal of Psychiatry, 165*(1), 34–41. doi:10.1176/appi.ajp.2007.07030502

World Health Organization (WHO). (2011). *Psychological first aid: Guide for field workers.* Retrieved March 8, 2014, from http://whqlibdoc.who.int/publications/2011 /9789241548205_eng.pdf

Yale Center for Public Health Preparedness (YCPHP). (2008). Disaster preparedness for people with serious mental illness. Retrieved March 8, 2014, from http://www .ctschoolhealth.org/images/Disasters_and_Mental_Illness.pdf

Persons With Alcohol and Substance Use/Abuse and Disasters

CASE STUDY: Hurricane Katrina, Experiences of Evacuees

As a use, as a parent, as a father, as a street person I've seen people come to Houston and go to other habits. The younger generation didn't do what they call x-pills (ecstasy). They was not popular with the younger generation. Now you got these younger generations, got FEMA money and you see what I'm saying, even the youngsters—they got money, they making money. Now they selling and buying out there. (Cepeda, Valdez, Kaplan, & Hill, 2010, p. 434)

I got a little assistance from the Red Cross. They give me $360 on a debit card and that helped me a little bit. You know but I don't know nobody. I start getting high and then drinking. Seem like the drinking was all that everybody did. People that I ran across, I mean people that didn't drink in their life was now drinking. (Cepeda et al., 2010, p. 435)

Dealing with persons with substance abuse and dependency is one of the most neglected areas in the literature involving empirical evidence and guidelines for appropriate response in a disaster. Nonetheless, the problem is quite real. Approximately 22 million U.S. citizens (9%) meet the diagnostic criteria for substance dependence (Substance Abuse and Mental Health Services Administration [SAMHSA], 2010). That translates into nearly 1 in 10 individuals in any given relief effort suffering from addiction to one or more substances. Few studies have attempted to document the number of people with substance abuse who are part of evacuation efforts. One study found relatively low numbers in a two-stage cluster sample survey of 499 evacuees residing in American Red Cross shelters in Louisiana 2 weeks after Hurricane Katrina (Greenough et al., 2008). In this study, it was estimated that 4.3% of the evacuees were suffering from substance abuse.

Given that the SAMHSA national average is twice what this study found, it suggests that either people are reluctant to report substance abuse in such surveys, or perhaps, that individuals with substance abuse may be less willing to evacuate. One study (Dunlap & Golub, 2011) supports the latter in describing the reluctance of illegal drug users and dealers to evacuate during Hurricane Katrina.

Developing appropriate guidelines and interventions presents a thorny set of problems for both addicted individuals and emergency responders. Individuals with substance abuse problems may not give truthful responses to questions from responders, health care personnel, or researchers conducting surveys due to denial of addiction, the stigma attached to addiction, and the illegality of some of the substances that are abused. In addition, withdrawal symptoms may not manifest until well after the evacuation has taken place. Where evidence-based research exists on addictive disease, much of the focus has been on substance abuse that may begin or increase in the aftermath of a disaster. Relatively little information is available by comparison on appropriate steps for disaster preparedness and appropriate interventions for responders to members of the population who may be addicted to drugs or alcohol.

Contributing to the problem is the wide array of substances that can be abused with intoxication and withdrawal symptoms that may vary widely (SAMHSA, 2005). Commonly abused substances include alcohol, opioids, sedative-hypnotics (such as benzodiazepines), stimulants (including cocaine and methamphetamine), club drugs and hallucinogens (such as ecstasy, marijuana, ketamine, and phencyclidine [PCP]), and inhalants and solvents (such as airplane glue and gasoline). It should also be mentioned that some studies include the study of changes in nicotine use, particularly in the form of cigarettes, in disasters. Although nicotine is highly addictive, it does not produce the serious health threats of withdrawal that may occur with alcohol and benzodiazepine addiction.

THE VULNERABILITY OF PERSONS WITH SUBSTANCE ABUSE IN DISASTERS

CASE STUDY: Post-Katrina Drug Boom

Opioid user:
Uh, my drug was opiates before Katrina . . . Methadone wafers, $20 apiece, um, Lortab, $6 apiece. But right after Katrina, there was just a whole bunch. It just came out of everywhere. The prices dropped. You get a bargain for $5. Um, the wagers dropped to like $10 and that went on for like 3 months after Katrina. But we just, pills everywhere. (Bennett, Golub, & Dunlap, 2011)

Heroin user:
Man, coz we had so much drugs in our [neighborhood] . . . the dealers were just passin' it out. [They] wasn't selling it. But they was coming back with so much drugs from Texas, Atlanta. Wherever they went, they came back with quantity. And they was like, "Aw man, we got this, ya'll try it and tell me how it is." "Man, you gotta look at [what I] come back with . . . here, try this." (Bennett et al., 2011)

The social stress model of substance abuse suggests that the likelihood of an individual engaging in drug abuse is influenced by the level of stress and offset by stress modifiers such as social networks, social resources, and social competence (e.g., Boardman, Finch, Ellison, Williams, & Jackson, 2001; Lindenberg, Reiskin, & Gendrop, 1994; Miczek, Yap, & Covington III, 2008; Rhodes & Jason, 1990; Seth, Murray, Braxton, & DiClemente, 2013). The evidence is mixed as to the extent to which the stress of a disaster situation may contribute to substance abuse. Some studies demonstrate at least a temporary increase in substance use/abuse following disasters. Others have indicated no significant changes following a disaster. A third consideration is that because some addictions involve illegal substances, criminal behavior can be associated with maintenance of an addiction during a disaster.

Evidence for Increase in Substance Abuse Following Disasters

Increases in alcohol abuse following a disaster have been reported in several studies. A study of the World Trade Center (WTC) disaster found increased alcohol use and abuse among residents of New York City after the attack (Boscarino, Adams, & Galea, 2006). A random-digit-dial survey was conducted of 1,681 New York City adults at 1 year and 2 years after the 9/11 attacks. Of the respondents, 12% reported an increase of two or more drinks per day between year 1 and year 2. Binge drinking was reported at a rate of 14% 1 month before 9/11, 16% 1 year after, and 15% 2 years after. In addition, differences were found in degree of exposure; those with greater exposure to the WTC reported higher levels of alcohol consumption and dependence than those with less exposure. DiMaggio and colleagues (2009a, 2009b) found similar results in a study of 9/11. Data from 31 population-based studies and examination of 11,298,266 outpatient visits in the months following 9/11 found that alcohol and substance abuse was related to proximity of exposure. Each 2-mile increment in distance from the WTC was associated with 18% more substance use-related diagnoses.

Several studies have looked at cigarette smoking or cigarette and alcohol abuse after disasters. Increases in both were found after the bombing of the Murrah Federal Building in Oklahoma City in 1995 (Smith, Chritiansen, Vincent, & Hann, 1999). Here, surveys were conducted in the Oklahoma City metropolitan area and a control community. Those in the Oklahoma City group reported double the rate of alcohol use, smoked more, or started smoking. Similar results were found in another study of 209 Hurricane Katrina survivors in Columbia, South Carolina, and New Orleans, Louisiana (Flory, Hankin, Kloos, Cheely, & Turecki, 2009). Both alcohol consumption and cigarette smoking problems occurred at a much higher rate than would be expected based on pre-hurricane prevalence data. Among those surveyed, 53% reported smoking compared with the Centers for Disease Control (CDC) U.S. prevalence rate of 20.9%; 36% met the criteria for high level of nicotine dependence. In addition, 27% met the criteria for heavy drinking (two or more drinks per day) compared with the 4.6% CDC U.S. prevalence rate of 4.6%; 36% met the criteria for hazardous drinking. Although cigarette smoking may not be as serious an immediate threat as other forms of substance abuse, there are long-term consequences to health. In one review article of 62 studies related to trauma and cigarette smoking, it was found that approximately 45% of persons with posttraumatic stress disorder (PTSD; which can be a consequence of exposure to disaster) are current smokers (Feldner, Babson, & Zvolensky, 2007). Another study looked at cigarette smoking in the aftermath of a 2010 earthquake in Canterbury, New Zealand (Erskine, Daley, Stevenson, Rhodes, & Beckert, 2013). Semistructured interviews were conducted with 1,001 individuals 15 months after the earthquake. Prior to the earthquake, 41% never smoked, 27% were currently smoking, and 32% were ex-smokers. After the earthquake, 24% of ex-smokers had smoked at least one cigarette and 38.2% had smoked more than 100.

Several studies have investigated changes in substance abuse for a variety of substances, including cigarettes. Two studies investigated alcohol, cigarettes, and marijuana use following the 9/11 WTC attack. Vlahov and colleagues (2002) conducted a random-digit-dial telephone survey of 988 residents in Manhattan 5 to 8 weeks after the attack. Increases were found in the use of all substances: 28% increased in all three, 9.7% increased in smoking, 24.6% increased in alcohol consumption, and 3.2% increased in marijuana use. In addition, for those who did not use these substances in the week before 9/11, 3.3% used cigarettes the week after, 19.3% drank alcohol the week after, and 2.5% used marijuana the week after. Ahern et al. (2004) also conducted a random-digit-dial telephone survey of substance abuse among residents of New York City, 6 to 9 months after the attack (n = 1,570). Among those surveyed, 9.9% reported increased smoking, 17.5% reported increased alcohol consumption, and 2.7% reported an increase in marijuana use.

Two additional studies are examples of reports on increases in multiple substance use. One involved the Herald of Free Enterprise disaster off the coast of Belgium in 1987 that led to the deaths of almost 200 people (Joseph, Yule, Williams, & Hodgkinson, 1993). Cross-sectional data on 73 survivors using the General Health Questionnaire (GHO) and Impact of Event Scale (IES) found that many had an increase in their consumption of alcohol, cigarettes, sleeping tablets, antidepressants, and tranquilizers after the disaster. Levels of increase were higher at 6 months after the disaster than at 30 months after the disaster. Another study involving qualitative and quantitative data from semistructured interviews among Hurricane Katrina evacuees in Houston, Texas, also found increases in abuse of multiple substances (Cepeda, Valdez, Kaplan, & Hill, 2010). This study divided substance abuse into two main categories: alcohol and tobacco (AT) use and illicit drug (ID) use. The findings were that females and younger evacuees were the most likely to increase AT use, and that increase in ID use was associated with resource loss and leaving the city before the hurricane struck. In addition, for those using ID prior to the hurricane, 34% had increases in marijuana use, 29% increased AT use, 12% increased ecstasy use, 6% increased crack use, and 4% increased cocaine use.

Evidence for No Changes in Substance Abuse Following Disasters

A number of studies have demonstrated little to no change in substance abuse following disasters. Several studies have looked at changes in substance abuse following the 9/11 WTC attacks and found no significant changes. Weiss, Fabri,

McCoy, Coffin, Netherland, and Finkelstein (2002) conducted qualitative interviews of 57 current or former users of heroin, crack, and other forms of cocaine. They found that reductions in substance abuse were just as common as increases. Factor and colleagues (2002) surveyed street-recruited heroin and cocaine users in Harlem and the Bronx after 9/11 and found no increase in frequency of drug use. North et al. (2013) surveyed a volunteer sample of 379 individuals from New York City agencies affected by the 9/11 attacks 3 years afterwards. They found that increases in alcohol consumption were relatively small. Increases after the attacks tended to be temporary, and in the long term individuals returned to baseline levels of consumption. They authors argue that the effects of disaster on alcohol use are so negligible for the general population as to have little clinical relevance.

Several other studies of other disasters have found similar results. One study involved 162 survivors of the Great Midwestern Floods of 1993 in the St. Louisiana area (North et al., 2004). Structured diagnostic assessment was conducted at 4 and 16 months after the disaster. One-half of the sample had a pre-existing alcohol use disorder, but virtually no new substance abuse developed following the flood. Another study by North, Ringwalt, Downs, Derzon, and Galvin (2011) looked at substance abuse in 10 different disasters: mass murder episodes, floods, a tornado, an earthquake, a firestorm, a plane crash into a hotel, and the Oklahoma City terrorist bombing. The research found a prevalence rate of 19% post-disaster of alcohol use disorders, which is similar to the national average. Only 0.3% of the sample developed a new incident of alcohol use disorder in the first few months after the disaster. Another study looked at alcohol consumption among Norwegian adults (n = 899) who resided in areas affected by the 2004 Southeast Asia tsunami. They were administered the Impact of Event Scale-Revised (IES-R) 6 months after the event. This study produced unusual results. Individuals with greater exposure to the disaster were more likely to report changes in alcohol consumption than those less exposed. However, the reports were polarized with individuals reporting both increases and decreases. The authors suggest the findings may be due to attribution and recall bias.

Substance Abuse and Criminality Following Disasters

One further issue regarding vulnerable populations and substance abuse involves potential changes in drug marketing, distribution, and associated criminal activity following a disaster. Numerous studies of a wide variety of disasters and over time have demonstrated at least temporary increases in community prosocial behaviors, social cohesion, social solidarity, and various forms of altruism during a disaster (e.g., Harlow & Dundes, 2004; Hawdon & Ryan, 2011; Nurmi, Räsänen, & Oksanen, 2011; Siegel, Borque, & Shoaf, 1999; Sweet, 1998; Zahran, Shelley, Peek, & Brody, 2009). Although the evidence suggests that the normative behavior may be for community members to come together and help one another during a crisis, the few that engage in criminal or predatory behavior can create significant problems. Many studies have pointed to a problem of media exaggeration of looting and violent crime during a disaster (e.g., Barsky, Trainor, Torres, 2006; Sun, 2011; Tierney, Bevc, & Kiligowski, 2006). Arguably, media reports of chaos and criminal behavior may make more compelling headlines than reports of a large number of people behaving cooperatively. It has too often been the case that initial sensational reports have been either exaggerated or wrong. In addition, looting is not always criminal behavior. A difference exists between prosocial and antisocial looting (Sun, 2011; Tierney et al., 2006). In prosocial looting, disaster victims may be taking supplies that are necessary to sustain life and health. Antisocial looting involves taking unnecessary items such as electronics and luxury items in order to profit from a disaster.

Although looting and other criminal behavior may be exaggerated in many cases, it does occur. It has been documented in events from the 1977 New York City Blackouts (Genevie et al., 1987) to Hurricane Andrew (Lanza-Kaduce, Dunham, Akers, & Cromwell, 1998). According to one study, antisocial behaviors such as looting, price gouging, and violence have increased in more recent U.S. disasters, such as Hurricanes Hugo and Katrina (Brown, 2012). Another study found that sites of Hurricane Katrina evacuation in Houston, San Antonio, and Phoenix also experienced increases in crimes of murder, robbery, assault, rape, burglary, and auto theft (Varano, Schafer, Cancino, Decker, & Greene, 2010).

Various explanations have been given for these behaviors, including situations of temporary and localized redefinitions of property rights (Quarantelli & Dyers, 1968), breakdown in formal and informal mechanisms of social control (Varano et al., 2010), or preexisting social and economic problems in a community (Genevie et al., 1987). However, one study of Hurricane Katrina found that individuals addicted to illegal drugs engaged in the looting of stores and the breaking into homes of drug dealers primarily to find a way to maintain their drug habits when the normal drug market was disrupted (Dunlap & Golub, 2011). The study involved semistructured, open-ended interviews with 119 poor, predominantly African American drug users and sellers. They found that many drug users placed maintaining their drug habits and making money ahead of their personal safety. In order to continue drug use and sales, many did not evacuate before the storm, either avoided shelters or used drugs in shelters, to search out drug connections in the flooded, debris-strewn streets, to loot stores and drug dealer homes, and to use violence or threat of violence in order to continue their drug use.

Another interesting study involving focus groups looked at how the drug market changed in the wake of Katrina (Bennett, Golub, & Dunlap, 2011). The first initial change was that the drug trade was radically reduced immediately after the storm. However, it was quickly reconstituted in a different form. While it had previously been based on social connections in neighborhoods, with friends, and with families, it changed to a more freelance-style market. Some described an unintended consequence of distribution of Federal Emergency Management Association (FEMA) relief funds in being an influx of money to support the buying and selling of drugs. In addition, drug dealers made connections in the cities where they had evacuated, and when they returned to New Orleans, they brought back large quantities of high-quality drugs. More street drugs were available and that resulted in a price drop, fostering greater drug use.

THE DISASTER FRAMEWORK AND PERSONS
WITH SUBSTANCE ABUSE

CASE STUDIES: Hurricane Katrina

59-year-old female cocaine user:
See, they went in the stores. You know, I saw this firsthand. . . . They was in the Wal-Mart. They came down Jackson Avenue pushin' grocery carts with big-screen TVs. And we didn't have electricity. Now, I could understand they were getting clothes. . . . But we didn't have electricity so what would you need with TVs and, you know, stereos? . . . It was just like a open market for everybody for crime. (Dunlap & Golub, 2011)

35-year-old male crack user and dealer:
Yes, indeed. There was more lootin,' robbin,' and killin' and all kind of stuff was goin' on. It was just like the whole world was comin' to an end. (Dunlap & Golub, 2011)

40-year-old male crack and heroin user and dealer:
People was shooting. People was desperate. . . . People was going crazy. It was like the world was coming to a end. And-and-and-uh, you know, I'm on I-10 bridge, no water, no food. You know, if you had a gallon of water, a person would of give you $10 for a gallon of water. . . . I went to a Wagner to get some water. And, they had uh three guys, two of them with AK-47's and one with a sledge hammer and ax working on a ATM machine and told us, "Don't." I said, "Man, I'm just coming to get me some water. I ain't got nothing to do with what y'all doing." They told us like if I would've tried to get in they business or try to fool with ATM machine they was gone put some of them AK bullets in me. (Dunlap & Golub, 2011)

Scarce empirical evidence or other sources of information are available for helping individuals with substance abuse prepare for a disaster. It is perhaps the most neglected area in disaster research. As will be described for response and recovery, the two biggest concerns of the helping professionals who encounter those with substance abuse are acute intoxication and acute withdrawal. For those in recovery, helping professionals should assist in maintaining medical and support systems, which helps to keep them sober and drug free.

Planning, Preparedness, and Mitigation for Persons
With Substance Abuse

Unfortunately, no studies were located in the review of the literature that assessed levels of preparedness among individuals with substance abuse. Table 8.1 provides guidelines for personal preparedness for individuals with substance abuse during a disaster. Perhaps the most important step that an individual with

TABLE 8.1 Personal Preparedness for Persons With Substance Abuse

BE INFORMED
• Be aware of the types of disasters that occur in your area and county warning procedures, evacuation plans, and shelters before disaster strikes • Be aware of evacuation procedures in your workplace; know the location of fire extinguishers and emergency alarms • Monitor television, radio, Internet, and social media news reports as able for information from authorities on local conditions and official instructions • Know your community's response and evacuation plans
MAKE A PLAN

General
• Create a personal assessment of what you will be able to do for yourself and what assistance you may need
• Keep by your bedside a charged phone, a flashlight, and prescription glasses
• Check the accessibility of local shelters and hotels and the availability of support services in those areas
• Perform routine mock drills and revise plan as necessary
• Fire safety:
  ○ Keep batteries charged in smoke alarms
  ○ Know where fire extinguishers are and how to operate them
  ○ Test smoke alarms once a month
  ○ For added safety, interconnect all the smoke alarms so that when one sounds, they all sound
  ○ If possible, purchase alarms with nonreplaceable (life-long) batteries designed to be effective for up to 10 years; these can be helpful for people who have difficulty changing batteries
  ○ If possible, choose an apartment with a sprinkler system or install the system in your home

Sheltering in Place and Evacuation
• Develop a plan to shelter in place
  ○ Be prepared to shelter in place in the event that you are unable to evacuate or are advised by local officials to stay where you are, including an emergency kit (see below)
  ○ If you use medical equipment at home that requires electricity, develop a backup plan for its use during a power outage
• Develop a plan to evacuate
  ○ Plan two ways out of every room
  ○ Know your community's response and evacuation plans and plan an evacuation route from your home
  ○ Plan for transportation if you need to evacuate to a shelter
  ○ Always evacuate if you are told by medical or other official personnel to evacuate or seek treatment
  ○ If there is sufficient time, shut off valves for household utilities (gas, electricity, water)
  ○ Recommendations for mitigating potential impairments for evacuating: bolt bookshelves to walls; anchor outdoor items that can be projectiles in high winds and hurricanes; install hurricane shutters (if appropriate to area); trim trees that overhang roofs; repair cracks in ceilings and foundations; store flammable materials away from heat sources
  ○ Notify first responders that you have experienced substance abuse problems

Communication—Family, Friend, and Neighbor Communication Plan • Make a list of family, friends, and others who will be part of your personal support network and communication plan • Include a friend or relative from another area who would not be affected by the same emergency and can help if needed

(continued)

TABLE 8.1 Personal Preparedness for Persons With Substance Abuse (*continued*)

- Decide where to meet your household members if you should become separated
- Notify members of your personal support network if you plan to go out of town
- Inform your personal support network how you plan to evacuate your home, school, or workplace and where you will go in the event of a disaster
- Make sure someone in your personal network has an extra key to your home and knows where you keep your emergency supplies
- Make sure a trusted friend or relative has copies of important medical and any other important documents
- Know the signs and symptoms of common reactions to a disaster and develop and discuss coping skills with your family and friends
- If you have experienced a history of substance abuse: practice how to communicate your needs to avoid resuming substance abuse with your sponsor or other persons you rely on for support
- Avoid contact with persons or places that may trigger relapse

BUILD A KIT

- Basic supplies:
  - A 3-day supply of food and water
  - Flashlight and batteries
  - Hand-crank or battery-operated radio
  - Cell phone with charger, inverter, or solar charger
- Basic first aid kit (American Red Cross for a family of four):
  - Bandages and dressings: 2 absorbent compress dressings (5.9 inches); 25 adhesive bandages (assorted sizes); 1 adhesive cloth tape (10 yards × 1 inch); 1 roller bandage (3 inches wide); 1 roller bandage (4 inches wide); 5 sterile gauze pads (3 × 3 inches); 5 sterile gauze pads (4 × 4 inches); 2 triangular bandages
  - Medications/wound care: 2 packets of aspirin (for adults only), 5 antibiotic ointment packets (approximately 1 gram); 5 antiseptic wipe packets; 2 hydrocortisone packets
  - Other supplies and equipment: blanket; breathing barrier (with one-way valve); instant cold compress; 2 pairs of nonlatex gloves (large); scissors; oral thermometer; tweezers
  - First aid instruction booklet
- Medical supplies: keep a 3- to 7-day supply of prescription medication and documentation of any medical records, prescriptions, insurance information, etc.
- If you have been prescribed a medication for substance abuse, keep a copy of the information about where you received the medication, the name of the medication, and the dosage
- Include in your emergency disaster kit the name and phone number of your local mental health professional(s), your recovery sponsor, and/or other persons you can rely on for support
- Other supplies for a home emergency kit: whistle to signal for help; dust mask to help filter contaminated air and plastic sheeting and duct tape to shelter in place; sanitation items (moist towelettes, toilet paper, garbage bags); local maps; wrench or pliers to turn off utilities; manual can opener; extra cash or traveler's checks if possible; extra batteries; extra blankets
- Other documents: consider including records such as social security number, charge and bank account information, tax records, will, etc. A portable thumb drive is an option for storing important information
- Create an emergency Health Information Card, update it regularly, and keep it with you at all times
- Pets and service animals: food, water, first aid, and other supplies if you have a pet or service animal (see Chapter 9)
- Prepare a kit for sheltering in place and a smaller, lightweight kit if you need to evacuate
- Include in your emergency disaster kit the name and phone number of your local mental health professional(s), your recovery sponsor, and/or other persons you can rely on for support

Sources: ARC (2014); CDC (2014); FEMA (2014); ITTF (2004); SAMHSA (2006, 2013).

a substance abuse history can take is to create a personal assessment of the types of needs that one will experience during a disaster. If in recovery, it will be important to have at least a 3-day supply of any prescription medications one is taking and documentation of the need for the medication due to addiction. If one regularly receives counseling or support services, backup sources of treatment and support should be identified as part of disaster planning.

What remains to be a particularly difficult problem is how to effectively implement preparedness strategies for individuals who are actively abusing substances, particularly addictive substances. For most substances that are abused, a common symptom of intoxication is impairment in thinking and judgment. This makes motivating individuals with addictions to make disaster plans quite difficult, for many have difficulty giving sufficient attention to basic self-care needs and health needs due to the intrusion of the addiction in their daily lives.

Response and Recovery for Persons With Substance Abuse

According to the Substance Abuse and Mental Health Services Administration (SAMHSA, 2006), three basic steps should be taken in dealing with persons with substance abuse.

- Evaluation: testing for the presence of substances in the bloodstream, measuring their concentration, and screening for co-occurring mental and physical conditions. Evaluation also includes a comprehensive assessment of the patient's medical, psychological, and social situation.
- Stabilization: includes the medical and psychosocial process of assisting the patient through acute intoxication and withdrawal to the attainment of a medically stable, fully supported, substance-free state.
- Fostering the patient's entry into treatment: involves preparing a patient for entry into treatment by stressing the importance of following through with a complete continuum of care.

Although responders may not have the opportunity to thoroughly address aspects of these steps, the two most critical in a disaster are recognizing the symptoms of intoxication and providing medical attention in acute withdrawal. Table 8.2 provides guidelines for responding to individuals with substance abuse.

At times, responders to disaster who encounter a person intoxicated with drugs or alcohol may be dealing with a medical emergency in the event of an overdose. It is far more likely what the problem responders will face is assisting someone who is cognitively and physically impaired. Intoxication can result in physical/emotional changes, personal attitude/behavioral changes, and cognitive/mental changes as outlined in Table 8.2. The goal of the responder is to assist the person in remaining safe or evacuating to a shelter. Due to potential confusion, disorientation, and difficulty processing information, responders should speak slowly, give simple instructions, and repeat if necessary. Communications should be nonjudgmental, treating the person with respect and dignity. In this

TABLE 8.2 Responder Guidelines for Persons With Substance Abuse Disasters

GENERAL
<ul><li>Be aware that alcohol and benzodiazepine withdrawal can be life-threatening</li><li>Individuals who abuse alcohol, prescription drugs, or illicit drugs may be reluctant to admit addictions due to social stigma or illegality</li><li>Individuals who are legally prescribed medications for chronic pain may also experience withdrawal symptoms</li></ul>
ASSESSMENT
Be aware of possible indicators or warning signs associated with alcohol and drug intoxication <ul><li>Physical/emotional indicators</li><ul><li>Smell of alcohol on breath or marijuana on clothing</li><li>Presence of burned fingers, burns on lips, or needle track marks on arms</li><li>Slurs speech or stutters, is incoherent</li><li>Difficulty maintaining eye contact</li><li>Dilated (enlarged) or constricted (pinpoint) pupils</li><li>Tremors (shaking or twitching of hands and eyelids)</li><li>Hyperactive or overly energetic</li><li>Impaired coordination or unsteady gait (staggering, off balance)</li><li>Appears lethargic or falls asleep easily</li><li>Speaks very rapidly or very slowly</li><li>Experiences mood swings (highs and lows)</li><li>Appears fearful or anxious</li><li>Appears impatient, agitated, or irritable</li><li>Increasingly angry or defiant</li></ul><li>Personal attitude/behavioral indicators</li><ul><li>Talks about getting high, uses vocabulary among drug users</li><li>Behaves in an impulsive or inappropriate manner</li><li>Denies, lies, covers up</li><li>Takes unnecessary risks or acts in a reckless manner</li><li>Fails to comply with directions without easily verifiable reasons</li></ul><li>Cognitive/mental indicators</li><ul><li>Has difficulty concentrating, focusing, or attending to a task</li><li>Appears distracted or disoriented</li><li>Makes inappropriate or unreasonable choices</li><li>Has difficulty making decisions</li><li>Experiences short-term memory loss</li><li>Needs directions repeated frequently</li><li>Has difficulty recalling known details</li><li>Needs repeated assistance completing ordinary paperwork</li></ul></ul>
COMMUNICATION STRATEGIES
<ul><li>Treat persons with substance abuse with respect and dignity</li><li>Treat persons with substance abuse in a supportive and nonjudgmental manner</li><li>Services planning should be completed in partnership with the patient and his or her support network</li><li>Patients should be treated with due consideration for individual background, culture, preferences, sexual orientation, disability, vulnerabilities, and strengths</li><li>Educate individual about withdrawal symptoms</li></ul>
HEALTH ISSUES
<ul><li>**Alcohol**</li><ul><li>Intoxication signs and symptoms include: mood and behavioral changes; reduced coordination; speech impairment; difficulty walking; impairment of thinking and judgment; somnolence or combative behavior; nausea and/or vomiting</li></ul></ul>

(continued)

TABLE 8.2 Responder Guidelines for Persons With Substance Abuse Disasters (*continued*)

○ Withdrawal signs and symptoms include: restlessness, irritability, anxiety, agitation; anorexia, nausea, vomiting; tremor, elevated heart rate, increased blood pressure; insomnia, intense dreaming, nightmares; poor concentration, impaired memory and judgment; increased sensitivity to sound, light, and touch; hallucinations (auditory, visual, or tactile); delusions, usually of paranoid or persecutory varieties, hyperthermia; delirium/disorientation, fluctuation in level of consciousness, seizures • **Opioids** ○ Intoxication signs and symptoms include: slow pulse, low blood pressure, low body temperature, sedation, pinpoint pupils, slowed movement, slurred speech, head nodding, euphoria ○ Withdrawal signs and symptoms include: fast pulse, high blood pressure, elevated body temperature, insomnia, enlarged pupils, abnormally heightened reflexes, sweating, gooseflesh, increased respiratory rate, eye tearing, yawning, runny nose, muscle spasms, abdominal cramps, nausea/vomiting, diarrhea, bone/muscle pain, anxiety • **Benzodiazepines and other sedative-hypnotics** ○ Intoxication signs and symptoms (similar to alcohol): slurred speech, ataxia, poor physical coordination ○ Withdrawal signs and symptoms include: sleep disturbance, irritability, anxiety, hand tremor, sweating, nausea/vomiting, headache, palpitations, sweating, difficulty concentrating, muscle pain and stiffness • **Cocaine, methamphetamine, and other stimulants** ○ Intoxication signs and symptoms include: increased blood pressure, increased heart rate, paranoia, decreased appetite, increased activity ○ Withdrawal signs and symptoms include: depression, hypersomnia, or insomnia, fatigue, anxiety, irritability, poor concentration, psychomotor retardation, paranoia, drug craving
EVACUATION AND RESCUE
• Ensure immediate physical safety • Assist the individual in evacuating to a safe place • Assist in accessing available detoxification services, substance abuse counseling, and mental health services if needed • Assist the individual in contacting friends, family, or other supports

Sources: Dunlap and Golub (2011); Milligan and McGuinness (2009); NPF (2012); Pétursson (1994); SAMHSA (2006, 2013).

way, the individual will be more likely to share information about what he or she has used or consumed. Withdrawal from opiates can be most uncomfortable, but withdrawal from heavy addiction to alcohol or benzodiazepines can present a life-threatening condition (Milligan & McGuinness, 2009). Acute alcohol withdrawal symptoms can begin in as little as 6 hours after a person takes his or her last drink (SAMHSA, 2006).

Despite the potential life-threatening consequences of withdrawal from some substances, little research exists on withdrawal during disasters. After the WTC attacks, focus groups with methadone patients indicated that a major fear was experiencing withdrawal because they were unable to get to their clinics (CSAT, 2002). Another study involved opium addiction during the 2003 earthquake in Bam, Iran (Movaghar et al., 2005). Interviews with 163 individuals during the first two weeks of the earthquake reviewed that about half of opium users were suffering withdrawal symptoms. It is particularly difficult to obtain accurate information about substance abuse not only due to the stigma, but because many substances that are abused are illegal. Dunlap and Golub (2011) have gone so far as to recommend suspending the "war on drugs" during a disaster and to establish guidelines for helping individuals maintain their habit during a disaster to prevent a potential medical crisis of acute withdrawal.

As previously described, the evidence is mixed as to whether or not a disaster increases the risk of new substance abuse or relapse among those who are sober or drug free. Nonetheless, an important role of the helping professionals among those with substance abuse is to help them maintain their current treatments for recovery, including prescribed medications, counselors, and support groups such as Alcoholics Anonymous. SAMHSA (2013) has a Disaster Technical Assistance Center (DTAC), which is a clearing house of information that is useful to both individuals with substance abuse and helping professionals who may be involved in response and recovery.

SUMMARY AND CONCLUSIONS

Nearly 1 in 10 individuals in the United States meets the criteria for a diagnosis of substance abuse. Nonetheless, substance abuse is one of the most neglected areas of disaster research. Most of the information available involves the extent to which a disaster contributes to substance abuse in its aftermath. Here, the results are mixed with some studies indicating that substance abuse increases during a disaster and others suggesting no change. Potential explanations for variance in the literature are differences in substance abuse related to the level of exposure to the disaster and bias in reporting one's substance abuse habits accurately. Such bias may occur because individuals are in denial about substance abuse, are embarrassed about their substance abuse, or are fearful of admitting abuse of an illegal substance. Another finding from some studies that could help explain the discrepancies is that increases in substance abuse were found to be temporary in some populations, with individuals returning to baseline levels after some time had passed since the event. Regardless, there is a clear need for further study to clarify these issues.

A more critical need is the lack of evidence-based information on how to best help individuals with substance abuse problems prepare for disasters. For those in recovery, recommendations are similar for those with any other health care issue, with efforts needed to ensure continuity of treatment, whether it be medication regimen, counseling, or support services. The more intractable population are those with active alcohol or drug addictions. Some studies have shown this population to present an obstacle to disaster relief efforts due to the unwillingness of many to evacuate because it will mean separation from the substances they use and abuse. Disaster planning presents an equal challenge, for many individuals with chronic addictions may have difficulty attending to basic self-care needs, much less be motivated to be informed, make a plan, and build a kit.

REFERENCES

Ahern, J., Boscarino, J. A., Bucuvalas, M., Galea, S., Gold, J., & Kilpatrick, D. (2004). Consumption of cigarettes, alcohol, and marijuana among New York City residents six months after the September 11 terrorist attacks. *American Journal of Drug and Alcohol Abuse, 30*(2), 385–407.

American Red Cross (ARC). (2014). Anatomy of a first aid kit. Retrieved March 8, 2014, from http://www.redcross.org/prepare/location/home-family/get-kit/anatomy

Barsky, L., Trainor, J., & Torres, M. (2006). Disaster realities in the aftermath of Hurricane Katrina: Revisiting the looting myth. University of Delaware Disaster Research Center, Miscellaneous Report #53. Retrieved March 15, 2014, from http://udspace.udel.edu/bitstream/handle/19716/2367/Misc%20Report%2053.pdf?sequence=1

Bennett, A. S., Golub, A., & Dunlap, E. (2011). Drug market reconstitution after Hurricane Katrina: Lessons for drug abuse control initiatives. *Justice Research and Policy, 13*(1), 23–44.

Boardman, J. D., Finch, B. K., Ellison, C. G., Williams, D. R., & Jackson, J. S. (2001). Neighborhood disadvantage, stress, and drug use among adults. *Journal of Health and Social Behavior, 42*(2), 151–165.

Boscarino, J. A., Adams, R. E., & Galea, S. (2006). Alcohol use in New York after the terrorist attacks: A study of the effects of psychological trauma drinking behavior. *Addictive Behaviors, 31*(4), 606–621.

Brown, B. L. (2012). Disaster myth or reality: Developing a criminology of disaster. *Sociology of Crime Law and Deviance, 17*, 3–17.

Centers for Disease Control and Prevention (CDC). (2014). Emergency preparedness and you. Retrieved March 8, 2014, from http://emergency.cdc.gov/preparedness/

Center for Substance Abuse Treatment (CSAT). (2002). *Impact of the World Trade Center disaster on treatment and prevention services for alcohol and other drug abuse in New York: Immediate effects, lingering problems, and lessons learned.* U.S. Department of Health and Human Services. Retrieved February 15, 2014, from http://www.samhsa.gov/csatdisasterrecovery/lessons/impactWTCtreatment.pdf

Cepeda, A., Valdez, A., Kaplan, C., & Hill, L. E. (2010). Patterns of substance abuse among Hurricane Katrina evacuees in Houston, Texas. *Disasters, 34*(2), 426–446. doi:10.1111/j.0361-3666.2009.01136.x

DiMaggio, C., Galea, S., & Li, G. (2009a). Substance use and misuse in the aftermath of terrorism. A Bayesian meta-analysis. *Addiction, 104*(6), 894–904.

DiMaggio, C., Galea, S., & Vlahov, D. (2009b). Bayesian hierarchical spatial modeling of substance abuse patterns following a mass trauma: The role of time and space. *Substance Use & Misuse, 44*(12), 1725–1743.

Dunlap, E., & Golub, A. (2011). Drug markets during the Katrina disaster. *Disaster Prevention Management, 20*(3), 251–265. doi:10.1108/09653561111141709

Erskine, N., Daley, V., Stevenson, S., Rhodes, B., & Beckert, L. (2013). Smoking prevalence increases following Canterbury earthquakes. *The Scientific World Journal.* Retrieved February 15, 2014, from http://downloads.hindawi.com/journals/tswj/2013/596957.pdf

Factor, S. H., Wu, Y., Monserrate, J., Edwards, V., Cuevas, Y., Del Vecchio, S., & Vlahov, D. (2002). Drug use frequency among street-recruited heroin and cocaine users in Harlem and the Bronx before and after September 11, 2001. *Journal of Urban Health, 79*(3), 404–408.

Feldner, M. T., Babson, K. A., & Zvolensky, M. J. (2007). Smoking, traumatic event exposure, and posttraumatic stress: A critical review of the empirical literature. *Clinical Psychology Review, 27*(1), 14–45.

Federal Emergency Management Agency (FEMA) (2014). Ready. Prepare. Plan. Stay informed. Retrieved March 5, 2014, from http://www.ready.gov/

Flory, K., Hankin, B. L., Kloos, B., Cheely, C., & Turecki, G. (2009). Alcohol and cigarette use and misuse among Hurricane Katrina survivors: psychosocial risk and protective factors. *Substance Use &Misuse, 44*, 1711–1724.

Genevie, L., Kaplan, S. R., Peck, H., Struening, E. L., Kallos, J. E., Muhlin, G. L., & Richardson, A. (1987). Predictors of looting in selected neighborhoods of New York City during the blackout of 1977. *Sociology and Social Research, 71*(3), 228–231.

Greenough, P. G., Lappi, M. D., Hsu, E. B., Fink, S., Hsieh, Y., Vu, A., . . . Kirsch, T. D. (2008). Burden of disease and health status among Hurricane Katrina-displaced persons in shelters: a population-based cluster sample. *Annals of Emergency Medicine, 51*(4), 426–432.

Harlow, R., & Dundes, L. (2004). "United" we stand: Responses to the September 11 attacks in black and white. *Sociological Perspectives, 47*(4), 439–464.

Hawdon, J., & Ryan, J. (2011). Social relations that generate and sustain solidarity after a mass tragedy. *Social Forces, 89*(4), 1363–1384.

Illinois Terrorism Task Force (ITTF). (2004). Emergency preparedness for those with functional needs. Retrieved January 18, 2014, from http://www.illinois.gov/ready/SiteCollectionDocuments/PreparednessTips_FunctionalNeeds.pdf

Joseph, S., Yule, W., Williams, R., & Hodgkinson, P. (1993). Increased substance use in survivors of the Herald of Free Enterprise disaster. *British Journal of Medical Psychology, 66*(2), 185–191.

Lanza-Kaduce, L., Dunham, R., Akers, R. L., & Cromwell, P. (1998). Policing in the wake of Hurricane Andrew comparing citizens and police priorities. *Criminology and Law Enforcement, 21*(2), 330–338.

Lindenberg, C. S., Reiskin, H. K., & Gendrop, S. C. (1994). The social stress model of substance abuse among child-bearing age women: A review of the literature. *Journal of Drug Education, 24*(3), 253–268.

Miczek, K. A., Yap, J. J., & Covington, H. E., III. (2008). Social stress, therapeutics and drug abuse: Preclinical models of escalated and depressed intake. *Pharmacology and Therapeutics, 120*(2), 102–128.

Milligan, G., & McGuinness, T. M. (2009). Mental health needs in a post-disaster environment. *Journal of Psychosocial Nursing and Mental Health, 47*(9), 23–30.

Movaghar, A. R., Goodarzi, R. R., Izadian, E., Mohammadi, M. R., Hosseini, M., & Vazirian, M. (2005). The impact of Bam Earthquake on substance users in the first two weeks: A rapid assessment. *Journal of Urban Health, 82*(3), 370–377.

National Pain Foundation (NPF). (2012). Abrupt withdrawal from pain medications— Information and caution. Retrieved February 15, 2014, from http://www.samhsa.gov/csatdisasterrecovery/featuredReports/Abrupt%20Withdrawal.pdf

North, C. S., Adinoff, B., Pollio, C. E., Kinge, S., Downs, D. L., & Pfefferbaum, B. (2013). Alcohol use, disorders and drinking among survivors of the 9/11 attacks on the World Trade Center in New York City. *Comprehensive Psychiatry, 54*(7), 962–969.

North, C. S., Kawaski, A., Spitzhagel, E. L., & Hong, B. A. (2004). The course of PTSD, major depression, substance abuse, and somatization after a natural disaster. *The Journal of Nervous and Mental Disease, 192*(12), 823–829.

North, C. S., Ringwalt, C. L., Downs, D., Derzon, J., & Galvin, D. (2011). Postdisaster course of alcohol use disorders in systematically studied survivors of 19 disasters. *Archives of General Psychiatry, 68*(2), 173–180.

Nurmi, J., Räsänen, P., Oksanen, A. (2011). The norm of solidarity: Experiencing negative aspects of community life after a school shooting tragedy. *Journal of Social Work, 12*(3), 300–319. doi:10.1177/1468017310386426

Pétursson, H. (1994). The benzodiazepine withdrawal syndrome. *Addiction, 89*(11), 1455–1459.

Quarantelli, E. L., & Dynes, R.R. (1968). Looting in civil disorders: An index of social change. *American Behavioral Scientist, 5*, 7–10.

Rhodes, J. E., & Jason, L. A. (1990). A social stress model of substance abuse. *Journal of Consulting and Clinical Psychology, 58*(4), 395–401.

Seth, P., Murray, C. C., Braxton, N. D., & DiClemente, R. J. (2013). The concrete jungle: City stress and substance abuse among young adults African American men. *Journal of Urban Health, 90*(2), 307–313.

Siegel, J. M., Borque, L. B., & Shoaf, K. I. (1999). Victimization after a natural disaster: Socialization or community cohesion. *International Journal of Mass Emergencies and Disasters, 17*(3), 265–294.

Smith, D. W., Chritiansen, E. H., Vincent, R., & Hann, N. E. (1999). Population effects of the bombing of Oklahoma City. *The Journal of the Oklahoma State Medical Association, 92*(4), 193–198.

Substance Abuse and Mental Health Services Administration (SAMHSA). (2013). Disaster Technical Assistance Center (DTAC). Retrieved February 15, 2014, from http://www.samhsa.gov/dtac/

Substance Abuse and Mental Health Services Administration (SAMHSA). (2010). *Results from the 2009 National Survey on Drug Use and Health: Volume 1.* Rockville, MD, SAMHSA. Retrieved March 26, 2014, from http://www.samhsa.gov/data/NSDUH/2k9NSDUH/2k9Results.htm

Substance Abuse and Mental Health Services Administration (SAMHSA). (2006). Quick guide for clinicians based TIP 45 detoxification and substance abuse treatment. Retrieved February 15, 2014, from http://www.samhsa.gov/csatdisasterrecovery/featuredReports/03-QG%20Clinicians_Tip%2045.pdf

Substance Abuse and Mental Health Services Administration (SAMHSA). (2005). Tips for first responders. Possible alcohol and substance abuse indicators. Retrieved February 15, 2014, from http://store.samhsa.gov/shin/content/NMH05-0212/NMH05-0212.pdf

Sun, L. G. (2011). Disaster mythology and the law. *Cornell Law Review, 96*(5), 1131–1208.

Sweet, S. (1998). The effect of a natural disaster on social cohesion: A longitudinal study. *International Journal of Mass Emergencies and Disasters, 16*(3), 321–331.

Tierney, K., Bevc, C., & Kiligowski, E. (2006). Metaphors matter: Disaster myths, media frames, and their consequences in Hurricane Katrina. *The Annals of the American Academy of Political and Social Science, 604*(1), 57–81.

Varano, S. P., Schafer, J. A., Cancino, J. M., Decker, S. H., & Greene, J. R. (2010). A tale of three cities: Crime and displacement after Hurricane Katrina. *Journal of Criminal Justice 38*(1):42–50.

Vlahov, D., Galea, S., Resnick, H., Ahern, J., Boscarino, J. A., Bucuvalas, M., . . . Kilpatrick, D. (2002). Increased use of cigarettes, alcohol, and marijuana among Manhattan, New York, residents after the September 11th terrorist attacks. *American Journal of Epidemiology, 155*(11), 988–996.

Weiss, L., Fabri, A., McCoy, K., Coffin, P., Netherland, J., & Finkelstein, R. (2002). A vulnerable population in a time of crisis: Drug users and the attacks on the World Trade Center. *Journal of Urban Health, 79*(3), 392–403.

Zahran, S., Shelley, T. O., Peek, L., & Brody, S. D. (2009). Natural disasters and social order: Modeling crime outcomes in Florida. *International Journal of Mass Emergencies and Disasters, 27*(1), 26–52.

Persons With Animals and Pets in Disasters

CASE STUDY: Hurricane Katrina, 2005

At the front of the line, the weary refugees waded through ankle-deep water, grabbed a bottle of water from state troopers and happily hopped on buses that would deliver them from the horrendous conditions of the Superdome. At the end of the line, people jammed against police barricades in the rain. Refugees passed out and had to be lifted hand-over-hand to medics. Pets were not allowed on the bus, and when a police officer confiscated a little boy's dog, the child cried until he vomited. "Snowball, Snowball," he cried. (Irvine, 2007, citing Mary Foster of the Associated Press)

The majority of households in the United States include pets. According to the Humane Society, 62% have pets (HSUS, 2014), with a trend toward increasing pet ownership over the past 40 years. Since the 1970s, the number of households with pets has tripled from 67 million to 164 million today. Most of these pets are dogs (83.3 million) and cats (95.6 million). Similar numbers were found in a recent Gallup poll that found that 6 in 10 Americans own a pet, typically a dog or cat (Gallup, 2006). To a lesser extent, animals such as fish, birds, reptiles, snakes, lizards, hamsters, guinea pigs, horses, and rabbits are kept as pets. The percentage of households with pets in the United States actually exceeds the percentage of households with children (Austin, 2013).

Although arguably human lives should be prioritized over the lives of companion animals, past disasters have demonstrated that it is imperative to include animals in disaster planning for a number of reasons to be discussed in this chapter. One is that studies have demonstrated that many people are unwilling to evacuate without their pets and that some return to unsafe conditions in an attempt to save a pet that has been left behind. Another is that failure to plan for evacuation of pets can create a number of public health concerns, including the spread of disease and the potentially dangerous behavior of frightened lost or abandoned animals. Pets that are not properly cared for during a disaster are at risk for injury, which is not only a threat to the animal, but can make an animal dangerous to evacuees or responders who may encounter them. In addition, some companion animals serve as service animals that have been trained to aid individuals with visual, hearing, or other disabilities.

Depending on the severity of the disaster, the potential for loss of pets can be quite significant. After Hurricane Katrina, the online source, petfinder.com, listed more than 17,000 pets found that had been separated from their owners and 22,000 requests for help in locating a lost pet (Hunt, Bogue, & Rohrbaugh, 2012). The Humane Society estimated that during Hurricane Katrina as many as 50,000 pets were left behind when owners moved to higher ground (Nolen, 2005).

Farm animals are also vulnerable during disasters. Some, such as horses, may be considered as much a pet or companion animal as a cat or dog. However, most farm animals are used as agricultural livestock. While owners of livestock may not experience the same emotional attachment to these animals, livestock can present challenges during an evacuation. Logistically, farm animals are harder to protect and evacuate than small pets due to the difficulty in relocating large numbers of large-sized animals. It is often difficult to arrange transportation to evacuate them to a place of shelter away from the disaster. Loose and frightened farm animals can be dangerous, presenting a hazard to both the general public and to responders.

A final consideration is the role of pets in disaster recovery. As will be described below, the loss of a pet for many is just as traumatic as the loss of home and possessions during a disaster. Uncertainty about the fate of a pet may cause evacuees to return to a disaster site before conditions are safe. Pets may also play an important psychological role in coping with the aftermath of a disaster. Although human lives should be put above the lives of animals, one of the important lessons learned from disaster research is that failure to make accommodations for animals during a disaster puts both humans and animals at greater risk.

THE VULNERABILITY OF PERSONS WITH ANIMALS AND PETS IN DISASTERS

> **CASE STUDY: "Black Friday" Bushfires of 2009 in Victoria and Queensland Floods of 2010 (Australia)**
>
> Juliet Moore leapt from the safety of a police rescue helicopter to return to her dog Poncho, Dr. Chris Towie died saving his pet dogs, and sisters Melanie and Penny Chambers died trying to save their horses. In the Queensland floods of December 2010 and January 2011, farmer David Kelly was last seen alive heading off with his dog to save his cattle. (Thompson, 2013)

The most significant issue that qualifies individuals with animals as a vulnerable population is the unwillingness to evacuate without animals. It is well documented that people form strong emotional attachments to pets, often considering them to be members of the family. Similar emotional attachments are found among people with service animals, but these individuals may depend on animals for their physical well-being. Farm animals also present challenges for disaster planning and response. Here, some may be unwilling to evacuate in order to protect their economic well-being when they depend on livestock to make a living. Although the evidence is limited, preparing ahead of time increases the likelihood for a successful evacuation of pets and their owners.

Companion and Service Animals

Humans and companion animals often share a close bond. Many consider pets to be members of the family (Cohen, 2002). A 2005 Pew Research Center Poll found that 85% of dog owners and 78% of cat owners considered their pets to be family (Pew, 2006). According to a recent Gallup poll, 68% of American pet owners had given presents to their pets at Christmas (Gallup, 2006). In addition, the poll found that among pet owners and non-pet-owners alike, 60% felt that pet owners had more satisfying lives than those who did not. An American Kennel Club (AKC) survey found that 21% of dog owners report that their dogs sleep with them and 18% indicated that they either have or would have included their dog in their wedding ceremony (AKC, 2006).

Most strikingly, the survey found that 62% of respondents indicated that they would disobey mandatory evacuation orders in order to remain with their pets. Concern for pets may also affect health care personnel. A literature review of 25 quantitative and 2 qualitative studies investigated the willingness of health care personnel to work during a disaster (Chaffee, 2009). The study found that pet care needs was one of the main barriers to willingness to report for work.

The unwillingness to evacuate without pets has presented a major obstacle to disaster relief and recovery and has made it clear that effective disaster planning must include companion animals. Several studies have demonstrated differences in willingness to evacuate between pet owners and nonpet-owners. One study investigated the issue among residents in Yuba County, California, who had been ordered to evacuate due to flooding in 1997 (Heath, Kass, Beck, & Glickman, 2001a).

The study involved a random-digit-dial telephone survey of 397 households 6 months after the flooding event. A greater percentage of households with pets (20.9%) failed to evacuate than households without pets (16.3%). The study also found that the greater the number of pets, the less likely the household was to evacuate. It should be noted that contrary to these two studies, a study of 2011 Hurricane Irene evacuees did not show a difference in failure to evacuate by pet owners (Hunt et al., 2012). A survey of 90 pet owners and 27 nonpet-owners found no statistical difference related to pet ownership and failure to evacuate. However, many pet owners in the study stated that the reason they did not evacuate was because of difficulties in evacuating their pets.

Despite the problems presented by disobeying evacuation orders to stay with pets, some households do leave pets behind. One study of Louisiana evacuees displaced from Hurricane Gustav in 2008 attempted to determine the percentages of people who evacuated with pets compared to those who evacuated without pets

(Thompson, Brommer, & Sherman-Morris, 2012). A convenience sample of 183 evacuees was conducted at rest stops along two major evacuation routes. Among those interviewed, 65% had at least one pet in the household. Of those, 71% evacuated with pets and 29% left at least one pet behind. Another study attempted to determine differences among individuals who evacuated with pets and those who leave them behind. Here, a mandatory evacuation was ordered in the vicinity of Weyauwega, Wisconsin, after several cars carrying propane gas caught fire (Heath, Voeks, & Glickman, 2001b). This cross-sectional study compared pet-owning households that evacuated with their pets (n = 19) versus those who evacuated without their pets (n = 122). A mail survey administered the Lexington Attachment to Pets Scale (LAPS). Overall, the researchers found that 49.4% evacuated with pets and 60.3% evacuated without them; 40.7% evacuated without them, but later attempted to rescue them, and 10% neither evacuated with pets nor attempted to rescue them. Failure to evacuate pets was associated with having many animals, low levels of pet attachment on the LAPS instrument, and having low levels of preparedness.

Making preparations for pets ahead of time is important due to federal guidelines for responders. Federal disaster relief organizations prohibit animals, except service animals, from rescue vehicles and the American Red Cross (ARC) will only allow service animals in shelters (ARC, 2013; FEMA, 2008; Nolen, 2005). Frightened pets that are left behind during a disaster may also pose health risks. One survey found that animal bites were one of the top three trauma complaints among Disaster Medical Assistance Team (DMAT) workers during Hurricane Ike in Texas (Warner, 2010). Of the animal bites, 55% were dog bites, 40% were cat bites, and 5% were snake bites. Most of the bites were serious, requiring suturing. Similarly, following the Japanese earthquake/tsunami of 2011, the median monthly incidence of dog bites for patients in one city increased from a 0.21 per 100 visits pre-disaster to 6.5 per 100 visits post-disaster (Mori et al., 2013). If animals are not properly tagged, rabies treatment may be required for individuals who receive animal bites.

Disease may also be transferred among abandoned and free-roaming pets in the wake of a disaster. For example, an outbreak of canine distemper virus (CDV) occurred in the months after the 2010 earthquake and series of tsunamis in Dichato, Chile (Garde, Pérez, Acosta-Jamett, & Bronsvoort, 2013). Some diseases carried by pets are zoonotic, meaning that they are able to be transferred to humans. A cross-sectional study of dogs (n = 414) and cats (n = 56) in the Gulf Coast region following Hurricane Katrina found high prevalence for several zoonotic diseases (Levy et al., 2011). Among dogs, prevalence was highest for anti-West Nile virus (WNV) antibodies (55.9%), *Dirofilaria immitis* antigen (48.8%), anti-*Toxoplasma gondii* antibodies (25.1%), and hemotropic mycoplasma DNA (11.9%). Among cats, prevalence was highest for antibodies against *Bartonella* spp. and DNA of *Bartonella* spp. combined (89.1%) and anti-*T. gondii* antibodies (23.6%), hemotropic mycoplasma DNA (10.6%), and anti-FIV antibodies (7.1%). In addition, 74.4% of dogs and 92.9% of cats had evidence of previous or current vector-borne infections.

Broadly, the issues concerning evacuation of pets also apply to service animals. However, service dogs are given special consideration due to their importance in aiding individuals with disabilities. There are approximately 20,000 service dogs in the United States, which include 10,000 guide dogs (AHA, 2013).

Service dogs most commonly assist people with hearing or visual impairments, but have also been trained to work with individuals with autism, seizure disorders, diabetes, balance issues, mobility issues, and cognitive or psychiatric disabilities (ADA, 2012; Hill, King, & Mrachko, 2013; Malamud, 2013). The definition of a service animal is "any dog that is individually trained to do work or perform tasks for the benefit of an individual with a disability, including a physical, sensory, psychiatric, intellectual, or other mental disability" (ADA National Network, 2012). At this time, the Americans with Disabilities Act requires that service dogs be given public access, but does not consider other species of animals to legally be service animals, such as monkeys who assist those with quadriplegia; some accommodations have been made for miniature horses (Adair, 2010; ADA National Network, 2012; AHA, 2013). It should also be mentioned that service animals often play a role in disaster response. They can be working partners with law enforcement and can assist in search and rescue, as well as locating cadavers (Hall et al., 2004).

Farm Animals and Livestock

The United States is home to approximately 2.2 million farms (FEMA, 2012b). The evacuation of farm animals and livestock also presents significant challenges in disaster planning and intervention. Farm animals are particularly vulnerable to disasters due to the logistics of evacuating large numbers of animals, which may also include large animals such as cattle and horses. A number of disasters have caused large-scale deaths of livestock. Examples include 1,200 cattle killed in the 1998 ice storms in New York, 15,000 cattle killed in the 2006 Colorado blizzard, 90,000 cattle that froze to death or drowned in the 1997 north-central U.S. blizzards and floods, thousands of pigs and poultry in North Carolina that were killed during Hurricane Floyd in 1999, and several million poultry killed by heat waves in the mid-Atlantic states in 2001 (FEMA, 2012b; Hall et al., 2004; Paul, Che, & Tinnon, 2007; Schmidt, 2000). Following a 2010 earthquake in Canterbury, New Zealand, no human lives were lost, but 3,000 animals died, primarily in poultry farms (Glassey & Wilson, 2011).

Sequelae to disaster may involve harm to livestock when grazing areas are damaged. Volcanic ash fall after the 1991 Hudson eruption in Patagonia led to severe effects on livestock in the long term when the natural vegetation could not be restored (Wilson et al., 2012). The Federal Emergency Management Agency (FEMA, 2012b) estimates that in the United States, 7 million acres are destroyed by wildfires every year, which also affects pastureland.

The effects of a disaster on livestock may also present public health concerns due to contamination from animal waste or animal carcasses. During Hurricane Floyd in North Carolina, 50 animal waste lagoons, some of them acres in size, were breached after being inundated by floodwaters (Schmidt, 2000). Subsequent analysis of agricultural soils found an increased presence of *Escherichia coli* and *Clostridium perfringens* spores (Casteel, Sobsey, & Mueller, 2006). In addition, animal carcasses can transfer disease to humans and other animals and contaminate surface and ground water, including *Clostridia, Cryptosporidium* spp., *Escherichia coli, Giardia* spp., *Listeria* spp., and *Salmonella* spp. (Murphy & Knight, 2009).

THE DISASTER FRAMEWORK AND PERSONS WITH ANIMALS AND PETS

CASE STUDY: Hurricane Katrina

Louisiana State Treasurer John Kennedy was helping people board buses near Baton Rouge and found himself intervening when some evacuees resisted because they had been ordered to leave their pets behind. One woman pleaded, "I've lost my house, my job, my car, and I am not turning my dog loose to starve." . . .

Shortly after leaving the bus loading area, Kennedy found a mixed-breed dog tethered near the road with an unopened can of dog food next to him. With the dog was a plaintive note that read, "Please take care of my dog, his name is Chucky." Kennedy said, "What else could I do? I am taking care of Chucky." (Coren, 2012)

Very little empirical evidence is available to assess the extent to which disaster preparedness plans are made for pets or for the effectiveness of the recommended guidelines. As described in the previous chapters on vulnerable populations, the general preparations for animals are similar to those recommended for humans, including having an adequate supply of food and water for sheltering in place, having a first aid kit on hand, and making preparations for evacuation. Additional measures described below involve tagging animals for identification, keeping vaccinations up to date, and most importantly, making plans ahead of time for how to evacuate with pets. Further research is needed to document more clearly the extent to which families with animals comply with these recommendations and the obstacles that may prevent them from adequately preparing.

Planning, Preparedness, and Mitigation for Persons With Animals

As previously stated, there is a need for further empirical research on disaster planning for individuals and families with pets. One survey by the AKC (2006) on the surface might seem encouraging. Of those surveyed, 97% indicated pet vaccinations were up to date, 91% had a copy of pet medical records, 89% had extra dog food, 79% had microchipped or tattooed animals for identification, and 61% had a pet evacuation plan. However, owners whose pets are registered with the AKC may not represent the general population of dog owners. Only pure-bred dogs with documented pedigrees may be registered. Many AKC dogs are used for breeding and dog shows, so these owners may have higher levels of motivation to keep up with vaccinations, medical records, and identification. Despite those preparedness measures, 76% in the AKC survey did not have a pet disaster kit and 55% did not have a list of hotels that accept pets outside their evacuation zone. Very little information is available regarding preparedness for cats. However, in two previously described studies involving the failure to evacuate from a 1997 flood in California (Heath et al., 2001a) and a 1996 chemical spill in Wisconsin (Heath et al., 2001b), one reason given for staying was the lack of a cat carrier. Little research has been conducted about levels of disaster preparedness among farmers, but one early survey of horse farm ranchers in Madison County, Kentucky, found that only 11.5% had developed evacuation plans (Linnabary, New, Vogt, Griffiths-Davies, & Williams, 1993).

Hall and colleagues (2004) cite Florida's 1992 Hurricane Andrew as the major impetus to developing disaster plans that explicitly included animals, for so many were affected. Florida became the first state to include pets in its disaster planning. In 1993, veterinary services were incorporated into the federal response plan. The American Veterinary Medical Association (AVMA) sponsors Veterinary Medical Assistance Teams (VMATs), which can be activated by the request of a state to the National Disaster Medical System (NDMS). The Humane Society has also developed Disaster Animal Rescue Teams (DARTs). In 2006, the Pets Evacuation and Transportation Standards (PETS) Act was signed into law, which requires all states to include companion and service animals into their disaster plans; many states are also developing State Animal Response Teams (SARTs; Irvine, 2007).

Despite these efforts, difficulties still exist for effective intervention for animals during disaster. Although the PETS Act requires a plan, these plans may not be effectively implemented. For example, a cross-sectional study of Ohio agencies demonstrated a continued lack of preparedness for animals (Decker et al., 2010). This survey of animal care and control agencies in Ohio (n = 115) found that while most (68%) agreed that emergency and disaster preparedness for pets was important to their organization, only 13% had completed a written emergency and disaster response plan. The majority (80%) indicated that they would be available to provide resources and assistance during a disaster, but only 33% were even aware of the existence of the PETS Act of 2006. Another study involved potential problems with adequate training for animal evacuation during a mock disaster drill (Irvine, 2007). Here, the scenario involved an explosion at a natural gas facility at a metropolitan animal shelter involving 38 dogs and 11 cats. A temporary evacuation facility was set up 5 miles away. The drill utilized 35 volunteers, most from a local training program for veterinary technicians. The volunteers were organized into four squads with two or three teams each and were briefed to stay with their squad or team. However, in the drill, the volunteers were not consistent in staying with their team/squad and were unclear about from whom to take directions. Another problem that emerged is that although the volunteers had training in animal handling, they did not have experience with shelter animals that had unknown histories and temperaments. One dangerous situation occurred where a bottleneck occurred in a narrow hallway where volunteers and dogs were trapped, and two dogs began to fight with one another. Irvine suggests that situations such as these could be exacerbated when well-meaning volunteers from the general public attempt to assist with evacuation of animals and may find themselves in a dangerous situation, particularly when animals may be frightened. Such volunteers are referred to as spontaneous untrained (or unsolicited) volunteers (SUVs).

At the federal level, the National Veterinary Response Team (NVRT) is part of the NDMS and includes professional volunteers with expertise in veterinary medicine and public health (HHS, 2013). NVRT members are private citizens who are activated and temporarily hired as federal employees during a disaster. They provide a number of services including assessing the medical needs of animals, support for horses and livestock, treatment of injured animals, veterinary support for sheltered animals, support for laboratory animals, and assessment of potential environmental hazards and zoonotic disease. An important nonprofit involved in caring for animals in disaster is the National Animal Rescue and Sheltering Coalition (NARSC; Engelke, 2009). A coalition of partners meet bimonthly to work to find collaborative solutions for animals in disaster. Partners include the American Society for the Prevention of Cruelty to Animals (ASPCA), the American Humane Association, the Best Friends Animal Society, Code 3 Associates, the Humane Society of the United States, the National Animal Control Association, the United Animal Nations/Emergency Animal Rescue Services, and the Society of Animal Welfare Administrators. One additional organization is the National Animal Health Emergency Response Corps (NAHERC), which is activated in the event of a major outbreak of foreign animal disease (Engelke, 2009).

Response and Recovery for Persons With Animals and Pets

Significant psychological effects can result in individuals who are separated from pets during a disaster. Loss of a companion animal can exacerbate the losses already experienced in a disaster, depending on the role of the pet in a person's life, the length or ownership, shared experiences with the pet, and the circumstances surrounding the loss (Evans, 2011). In a study of the aftermath of Hurricane Katrina in 2005, a number of psychological effects of pet loss were examined (Hunt et al., 2008). Online questionnaires were administered to 65 pet owners who lived in affected regions using several instruments: the Beck Depression Inventory (BDI-II), the PTSD Symptom Scale Self-Report (PSS-SR), the Peritraumatic Dissociative Experiences Questionnaire Self Report (PDEQ-SR), the Stanford Acute Stress Reaction Questionnaire (SARSQ), and the Pet Attachment Questionnaire (PAQ). Comparisons were made between those who lost pets and those who were able to keep their pets. Pet loss was found to be a significant predictor of depressive symptoms, peritraumatic dissociation, posttraumatic stress disorder (PTSD), and severity of symptoms. Moreover, the authors found that people who had lost both their homes and their pets had similar psychopathological outcomes as those who had only lost their pets. Another study examining psychological effects involved survey data from a random sample of 1,510 Hurricane Katrina survivors conducted by Gallup in 2005 (Zottarelli, 2010). The study found that women, younger adults, and people who evacuated were more likely to have lost a pet. Those who lost pets were statistically different from their counterparts in that they were more likely to have been separated from their families, to have evacuated to an emergency shelter, or had been hurt or injured during the disaster.

The best way for disaster personnel to assist individuals with pets to respond is in educating the public to make preparations ahead of time. Table 9.1 presents recommendations from a number of sources involved in animal care, including

TABLE 9.1 Preparedness for Persons With Animals and Pets

BE INFORMED
<ul><li>Be aware of the types of disasters that occur in your area and county warning procedures, evacuation plans, and shelters before disaster strikes</li><li>Be aware of evacuation procedures in your workplace; know the location of fire extinguishers and emergency alarms</li><li>Monitor television, radio, Internet, and social media news reports as able for information from authorities on local conditions and official instructions</li><li>Know your community's response and evacuation plans</li></ul>

MAKE A PLAN
General
Pets and Service Animals
<ul><li>Take pets with you if possible and never leave them chained outside</li><li>Make sure your pet or service animal's vaccinations are up to date, and it is wearing a collar and identification tag that includes your cell phone number; consider having your pet or service animal microchipped; you may want to consider a secondary contact number of a friend or relative not in your disaster area</li><li>Contact your local office of emergency management to determine if you will be allowed to evacuate with your pets and if there will be shelters that take people and their pets/service animals in your area</li><li>Contact hotels and motels outside your immediate area to determine whether or not they accept pets</li><li>Investigate other options for care and/or boarding of pets, including: a kennel or vet's office, friends or relatives outside your area, or as a last resort, your local animal shelter</li><li>Include your pets in evacuation drills so that they become used to entering and traveling in their carriers calmly</li><li>If you live in an apartment, make sure animals are on record with management and are able to evacuate via the stairwell; dogs should be taught to go up and down stairs to better assist rescue personnel</li><li>In case you are not home, provide a list near your evacuation supplies of the number, type, and location of your animals, including favorite hiding spots</li><li>Consider providing muzzles, handling gloves, catch nets, and animal restraints where rescue personnel can find them since animals may become unpredictable when frightened</li></ul>
Horses and Other Livestock
<ul><li>All animals should have some form of identification</li><ul><li>○ Horses can be marked with a microchip, tattoo, halter tag, neck collars, leg band, brand, mane clip, luggage tag braided into tail or mane, clipper-shaved information in the animal's hair, livestock marking crayon, nontoxic/waterproof marker or paint, or permanent marker to the hooves</li><li>○ Other livestock can be marked with a neck chain, leg band, ear tag, brand, livestock marking crayon, nontoxic/waterproof paint or markers, wattle notching, ear tattoo, or back or leg tag</li></ul><li>Assess the stability of barn and other livestock housing; remove dead trees and minimize debris in the immediate environment</li><li>Have well-maintained backup generators for use in food-animal production operations</li><li>Make sure that animals are familiar with being loaded onto a trailer</li></ul>

SHELTERING IN PLACE AND EVACUATION
Develop a Plan to Stay
<ul><li>Identify a safe area in your home that is appropriate for both you and your pets and keep emergency supplies there</li><li>Close off or eliminate unsafe nooks and crannies where small, frightened pets may attempt to hide</li><li>Bring pets indoors as soon as authorities provide information that a disaster is on its way</li></ul>

(continued)

TABLE 9.1 Preparedness for Persons With Animals and Pets (*continued*)

Develop a Plan to Evacuate

- Do not leave pets or service animals behind if you evacuate your home
- Evacuate early: this provides the best chance of you being able to evacuate with your pet
- If you have to leave your pet or service animal at home, take the following precautions: keep your pet in a safe area inside; never leave your pet chained outside; place notices outside in a visible area saying what pets are in the house and where; provide a phone number where you can be reached (or a contact) and the name and number of your vet
- Get a Rescue Alert Sticker to let people know that pets are inside your home, which is visible to rescue workers, that includes: the number and types of pets that are in your home; the name of your veterinarian; and your veterinarian's phone number. If you evacuate with your pets, write "evacuated" across these stickers

Evacuating Pet Birds

- Transport using small, secure, covered carriers
- If traveling in cold weather, warm the interior of your vehicle before moving from house and cover cage with a blanket
- In warm weather, carry a spray bottle to periodically moisten your birds' feathers
- Transfer bird(s) to a standard cage upon arrival at the evacuation site; covering the cage may help to decrease stress; make transfer in a small, enclosed room to reduce the risk of escape
- Birds should be kept in quiet areas and not allowed out of a cage in unfamiliar surroundings
- Provide fresh food and water daily; if you must leave your bird unexpectedly, a timed feeder will ensure its feeding schedule
- If your bird appears ill, lower the cage perch, food dish, and water bowl and consult a veterinarian as soon as possible

Evacuating Pet Reptiles

- Transport small reptiles using a pillowcase, cloth sack, or small transport carrier
- If possible, promote defecation before transporting (e.g., allow tortoises, lizards, or snakes to soak in a shallow water bath before bagging or caging)
- Transfer your pet to a secure cage at the evacuation site as soon as possible
- Since most reptiles do not eat daily, feeding during evacuation may increase stress; determine if feeding is in the animal's best interest, especially if the container may be fouled
- Provide a sturdy bowl for soaking and a heating pad, hot water bottle, or other warming devices
- House pet at evacuation facility in a controlled environment, away from noise and vibrations if possible

Evacuating Pet Amphibians

- Transport amphibians using watertight plastic bags or plastic containers with snap-on lids
- Small ventilation holes should be placed in upper wall or plastic lid; smooth inner surface of the holes with a file or sandpaper to prevent injury to the animal
- For terrestrial or semiaquatic amphibians, use a tiny amount of water, or moistened paper towels, clean foam rubber, or moss as a substrate
- For aquatic species, fill plastic bag one-third full of water, then inflate the bag with fresh air, and close with a knot of rubber band; it is best to use clean water from the animal's enclosure to minimize psychological stress
- Care must be taken to monitor the water and air temperature, humidity, lighting, and nutrition during the time that the animal will be in the evacuation facility
- If possible, place the enclosure in a controlled environment, away from noise and vibrations
- Take an extra container of clean, moist paper towels of clean moss in case the pet container breaks or leaks
- Feeding during evacuation may increase stress, so it may not be in the animal's best interest to supply food, especially if the water may become fouled

(*continued*)

TABLE 9.1 Preparedness for Persons With Animals and Pets (*continued*)

Evacuating Horses and Livestock
- Evacuate livestock whenever possible
- Evacuation sites for livestock would have food, water, veterinary care, handling equipment, and facilities (possible sites include veterinary or land grant colleges, racetracks, showgrounds, pastures, stables, fairgrounds, equestrian centers, livestock corrals, stockyards or auction facilities, or other boarding facilities)
- Trucks, trailers, and other vehicles for transporting livestock should be available with experienced handlers and drivers; if you do not have enough trailers to transport all your animals quickly, contact neighbors, local haulers, farmers, producers, or other providers to establish a network of available and reliable resources that will provide transportation in the event of a disaster
- If evacuation is not possible, move animals to shelter or turn them outside, based on the type of disaster and the safety and location of the shelter

Communication—Family, Friend, and Neighbor Communication Plan
- Make arrangements in advance for a friend, neighbor, or family member to take your pets if a disaster strikes and you are not home (they should bring your pets to the location you have evacuated to)
- Keep a pre-signed letter that releases the person designated to keep your animal from responsibility if one of your animals becomes injured

BUILD A KIT

Emergency Kit
Pets and Service Animals
- Food and water for a minimum of 3 days (2 weeks if possible) for each pet, including food bowls, waterproof food containers, and a manual can opener
- Medications and veterinary records: stored in a waterproof container with a first aid kit (may want to include a pet first aid manual)
- Cat litter box, litter scoop, and garbage bag to collect all pet's wastes
- Sturdy leashes, harnesses, and carriers to transport pets safely and prevent their escape; label carriers
- Current photo of you with your pet or service animal for identification purposes
- Pet beds or blankets and toys, if easily transported
- Written information about your pet or service animal's feeding schedule, medical conditions, list of medications, and behavior issues along with the name and phone number of your veterinarian
- Additional items for pet birds: cage perch, materials to line bottom of cage, bird toys, hot water bottle for warming birds in cold weather, any necessary dietary supplements
- Additional items for pet reptiles: water bowl for soaking, essential dietary supplements, spray bottle for misting, extra bags or newspapers, heating pad, battery-operated heating source and extra batteries, appropriate handling gloves, and supplies
- Additional items for small mammals (such as hamsters and gerbils): necessary dietary supplements, extra bedding materials, appropriate exercise equipment, salt lick, extra water bottle

Horses and Livestock
- Seven- to ten-day supply of food and water
- Make copies of registration information, adoption papers, proof of purchase, and microchip information
- List each one of your animals and its species, breed, age, sex, color, and distinguishing characteristics
- Keep current photographs of your animals
- Information on the diet of all animals
- Medications, including information on the dose and frequency of each medication and veterinary and pharmacy contact for refills
- Additional supplies: nose leads; plastic trashcans with lids (can be used to store water); portable livestock panels; rope; shovel; water buckets; prods; wire cutters

(*continued*)

TABLE 9.1 Preparedness for Persons With Animals and Pets (*continued*)

Animal First Aid Kit
Suggested items for animal first aid kit from the American Veterinary Medical Association (AVMA):
• Bandages and dressings: cotton bandage rolls; cotton-tipped swabs; elastic bandage rolls; bandage tape; gauze pads and rolls; nonadherent bandage pads
• Medications and treatments: prescribed medications; liquid activated charcoal; antidiarrheal medication; antibiotic ointment for wounds; antibiotic eye ointment Betadine® (povidone-iodine) or Nolvasan® (cholrhexadine), scrub and solution; sterile eye rinse; flea and tick prevention and treatment; isopropyl alcohol/alcohol prep pads; liquid dish detergent (mild wound and body cleanser); preventatives (such as heartworm prevention) with clearly labeled instructions, include veterinary and pharmacy contact information for refills; saline solution (for rinsing wounds); sterile lubricant; styptic powder (clotting agent)
• Medical supplies: bandage scissors; popsicle sticks for splints; latex gloves or nonallergic gloves; measuring spoons; syringe or eyedropper; digital thermometer; tourniquet; towel and washcloth; tweezers

Sources: ARC (2013); ASPCA (2013); AVMA (2010); CDPH (2013); CVHS (2011); FEMA (2012a, 2012b, 2013, 2014); HSUS (2013).

ASPCA, AVMA, the Humane Society, as well as FEMA and ARC. As previously mentioned, federal rescue vehicles cannot transport any animals except service dogs, and many shelters, including the ARC, will not take pets. Responders may be able to provide assistance in evacuating pets if they are able to provide information about local hotels that can take pets, shelters that will allow pets, or designated disaster animal shelters. If pets must be left behind, responders should let owners know never to tie up a pet.

Responders may also be faced with the problem of loose and frightened pets during an evacuation effort. As noted above, a significant source of injury for individuals responding to a disaster is a serious bite from an animal, primarily dogs. If VMATs or DARTs or SARTs are available locally, it is safest to allow these trained teams to assist with handling animals.

SUMMARY AND CONCLUSIONS

In the United States, 62% of households have one or more pets. More American households have pets than children. In the past, disaster planning did not include making accommodations for animals, particularly pets. Recent disasters, such as Hurricanes Andrew and Katrina, pointed to the need for greater attention to inclusion of pets in disaster planning. In both of these hurricanes, large numbers of animals were lost or abandoned. But perhaps more importantly, recent disasters have demonstrated the problem of individuals being unwilling to evacuate without their beloved pets. In a number of documented cases, individuals have attempted to return to their homes in unsafe conditions due to concern for a pet that has been left behind.

The PETS Act of 2006 requires all states to include companion and service animals in their disaster plans. However, the literature demonstrates that such plans may not be elaborated adequately or tested sufficiently to determine their effectiveness. Several ad hoc animal response units have been developed in recent years, including VMATs, DARTs, and SARTs. Here, too, the effectiveness of these volunteer units has been little studied.

The most important measure for effective disaster response for animals is the same as it is for humans: planning ahead. In the chaos of a disaster, it is difficult to find emergency shelters for pets, particularly given that many shelters for humans do not allow pets. Loose, frightened animals are a danger to both themselves and to others. Further research is needed to better understand the obstacles that prevent many families from making adequate preparations for their pets. Studies have demonstrated that the loss of a pet can be devastating, particularly when compounded with other losses experienced in a disaster. Additional empirical research is also needed to address disaster preparedness and response for the special conditions of livestock and farm animals.

REFERENCES

Adair, R. L. (2010). Monkeys and horses and ferrets . . . oh my-non-traditional service animals under the ADA. *Northern Kentucky Law Review, 37*(4), 415–439.

American Humane Association (AHA). (2013). *U.S. Pet (Dog and Cat) Population Fact Sheet.* Retrieved March 24, 2013, from http://www.americanhumane.org/assets /pdfs/pets-fact-sheet.pdf

American Kennel Club (AKC). (2006). *AKC survey finds majority of owners would defy emergency evacuation orders and stay with pets.* Retrieved February 1, 2014, from http://images.akc.org/pdf/press_center/press_releases/2006/Hurricane_Survey .pdf

American Red Cross (ARC). (2009). *Be Red Cross ready: Pets and disaster safety checklist.* Retrieved October 27, 2013, from http://www.redcross.org/images/MEDIA _CustomProductCatalog/m3640126_PetSafety.pdf

American Red Cross (ARC). (2013). *Pets.* Retrieved September 19, 2013, from http:// www.redcross.org/prepare/location/home-family/pets

American Society for the Prevention of Cruelty to Animals (ASPCA). (2013). *Disaster preparedness.* Retrieved October 29, 2013, from http://www.aspca.org/pet-care /disaster-preparedness

American Veterinary Medical Association (AVMA). (2010). *Saving the whole family: Disaster preparedness series.* Retrieved October 29, 2013, from https://ebusinesss .avma.org/ebusiness50/files/productdownloads/saving_familiy_brochure.pdf

Americans with Disabilities (ADA) National Network. (2012). *Service animals.* Retrieved March 24, 2014, from http://adata.org/factsheet/service-animals

Austin, J. A. (2013). Shelter from the storm: Companion animal emergency planning in nine states. *Journal of Sociology & Social Welfare, 40*(4), 185–210.

California Department of Public Health (CDPH). (2013). *Disaster planning tips for pet/livestock owners.* Retrieved September 17, 2013, from http://www.bepreparedcalifornia .ca.gov/BePrepared/IndividualsAndFamilies/Pages/DisasterPlanningTipsfor PetLivestockOwner.aspx

Casteel, M. J., Sobsey, M. D., & Mueller, J. P. (2006). Fecal contamination of agricultural soils before and after hurricane-associated flooding in North Carolina. *Journal of Environmental Science and Health Part A, 41*, 173–184.

Central Vermont Humane Society (CVHS). (2011). The companion connection. Retrieved October 29, 2013, http://cvhumane.com/wp-content/uploads/2011/08/CC-Final-8.11.pdf

Chaffee, M. (2009). Willingness of health care personnel to work in a disaster: An integrative review of the literature. *Disaster Medicine and Public Health Preparedness, 3*(1), 42–56.

Cohen, S. P. (2002). Can pets function as family members? *Western Journal of Nursing Research. Special Issue: Human Animal Interaction, 24*, 621–638.

Coren, S. (2012). *The dogs of Hurricane Katrina. Modern Dog Magazine.* Retrieved March 24, 2014, from http://moderndogmagazine.come/articles/dogs-hurricane-katrina/151

Decker, S. M., Lord, L. K., Walker, W. L., & Wittum, T. E. (2010). Emergency and disaster planning at Ohio animal shelters. *Journal of Applied Animal Welfare Science, 13*, 66–76.

Engelke, H. T. (2009). Emergency management during disasters for small animal practitioners. *Veterinary Clinics of North America: Small Animal Practice, 39*(2), 347–358.

Evans, N. (2011). We are all in this together: The dynamics of animal-human relationships during and following a natural disaster. *Te Awatea Review, 9*(1–2), 19–25.

Federal Emergency Management Agency (FEMA). (2008). *Mass evacuation incident annex.* Retrieved March 24, 2014, from https://www.fema.gov/pdf/emergency/nrf/nrf_massevacuationincidentannex.pdf

Federal Emergency Management Agency (FEMA). (2012a). *Preparing your pets for emergencies makes sense.* Retrieved September 19, 2013, from http://www.ready.gov/sites/default/files/documents/files/pets_brochure.pdf

Federal Emergency Management Agency (FEMA). (2012b). *Livestock in disasters.* Retrieved February 8, 2014, from http://emilms.fema.gov/is111a/index.htm

Federal Emergency Management Agency (FEMA). (2013). *Caring for animals.* Retrieved September 19, 2013, from http://www.ready.gov/caring-animals

Federal Emergency Management Agency (FEMA). (2014). *Ready. Prepare. Plan. Stay informed.* Retrieved March 5, 2014, from http://www.ready.gov

Gallup®. (2006). *Americans and their pets.* Retrieved February 1, 2006, from http://www.gallup.com/poll/25969/americans-their-pets-aspx

Garde, E., Pérez, G. E., Acosta-Jamett, G., & Bronsvoort, B. M. (2013). Challenges encountered during the veterinary disaster response: An example from Chile. *Animals, 3*(4), 1073–1085. doi:10.3390/ani3041073

Glassey, S., & Wilson, T. (2011). Animal welfare impact following the 4 September 2010 Canterbury (Darfield) earthquake. *Australian Journal of Disaster and Trauma Studies, 2*, 49–59.

Hall, M. J., Ng, A., Ursano, R. J., Holloway, H., Fullerton, C., & Casper, J. (2004). The psychological impact of the animal-human bond in disaster preparedness and response. *Journal of Psychiatric Practice, 10*(6), 368–374.

Heath, S. E., Kass, P. H., Beck, A. M., & Glickman, L. T. (2001a). Human and pet-related risk factors for household evacuation failure during a natural disaster. *American Journal of Epidemiology, 153*(7), 659–665.

Heath, S. E., Voeks, S. K., & Glickman, L. T. (2001b). Epidemiologic features of pet evacuation failure in a rapid-onset disaster. *Journal of the American Veterinary Medical Association, 218*(12), 1989–1904.

Hill, D. R., King, S. A., & Mrachko, A. A. (2013). Students with autism, service dogs, and public schools: A review of state laws. *Journal of Disability Policy Studies.* Retrieved March 24, 2014, from http://dps.sagepub.com/content/early/2013/03/04/1044207313477204.full.pdf+html. doi:10.1177/1044207313477204

Humane Society of the United States (HSUS). (2013). *Make a disaster plan for your pets*. Retrieved September 17, 2013, from http://m.humanesociety.org/issues/animal _rescue/tips/pets-disaster.html

Humane Society of the United States (HSUS). (2014). *Pets by the numbers*. Retrieved February 1, 2013, from http://www.humanesociety.org/issues/pet_overpopulation /facts/pet_ownership_statistics_html

Hunt, M., Al-Awadi, H., & Johnson, M. (2008). Psychological sequelae of pet loss following Hurricane Katrina. *Anthrozoös, 21*(4), 109–121.

Hunt, M. G., Bogue, K., & Rohrbaugh, N. (2012). Pet ownership and evacuation prior to Hurricane Irene. *Animals, 2*, 529–539. doi:10.3390/ani2040529

Irvine, L. (2007). Ready or not: Evacuating an animal shelter during a mock emergency. *Anthrozoös, 20*(4), 355–364.

Levy, J. K., Lappin, M. R., Glaser, A. L. Birkenheuer, A. J., Anderson, T. C., & Edinboro, C. H. (2011). Prevalence of infectious diseases in cats and dogs rescued following Hurricane Katrina. *Journal of the American Veterinary Association, 238*(3), 311–317. doi:10.2460/javma.238.3.311

Linnabary, R. D., New, J. C., Vogt, B. M., Griffiths-Davies, C., & Williams, L. (1993). Emergency evacuation of horses: A Madison County, Kentucky survey. *Journal of Equine Veterinary Science, 13*, 153–158.

Malamud, R. (2013). Service animals: Serve us animals: Serve us, animals. *Social Alternatives, 32*(4), 34–40.

Mori, J., Tusbokura, M., Sugimoto, A., Tanimoto, T., Kami, M., Oikawa, T., & Kanazawa, Y. (2013). Increased incidence of dog-bite injuries after the Fukushima nuclear accident. *Preventive Medicine, 57*(4), 363–365.

Murphy, R. G. L., & Knight, A. P. (2009). Carcass disposal following a veterinary disaster. In W. E. Wingfield & S. B. Palmer (Eds.), *Veterinary disaster response* (pp. 391–400). Ames, IA: Wiley-Blackwell.

Nolen, R. S. (2005). Hurricane Katrina. Katrina's other victims. *Journal of the American Veterinary Association, 227*(8), 1215–1216.

Paul, B. K., Che, D., & Tinnon, V. L. (2007). Emergency responses for high plains cattle affected by the December 28–31, 2006, Blizzard. Quick Response Research Report 191. Boulder, CO: University of Colorado Natural Hazards Center. Retrieved February 8, 2014, from http://www.colorado.edu/hazards/research/qr/qr191 /qr191.html

Pew Research Center. (2006). *Gauging family intimacy*. Retrieved February 1, 2014, from http://www.pewsocialtrends.org/2006/03/07/gauging-family-intimacy

Schmidt, C. W. (2000). Lessons from the flood: Will Floyd change livestock farming? *Environmental Health Perspectives, 108*(2), A74–A77.

Thompson, C. N., Brommer, D. M., & Sherman-Morris, K. (2012). Pet ownership and the spatial and temporal dimensions of evacuation decisions. *Southeastern Geographer, 52*(3), 253–266.

Thompson, K. (2013). Save me, save my dog: Increasing natural disaster preparedness and survival by addressing human-animal relationships. *Australian Journal of Communication, 40*(1), 123–136.

United States Department of Health and Human Services (HHS). (2013). National veterinary response team (NVRT). Retrieved February 8, 2014, from http://www .phe.gov/Preparedness/responders/ndms/teams/Pages/nvrt.aspx

Warner, G. S. (2010). Increased incidence of domestic animal bites following a natural disaster due to natural hazards. *Prehospital and Disaster Medicine, 25*(2), 188–190.

Wilson, T., Cole, J., Johnston, D., Cronin, S., Stewart, C., & Dantas, A. (2012). Short- and long-term evacuation of people and livestock during a volcanic crisis: Lessons from the 1991 eruption of Volcán Hudson, Chile. *Journal of Applied Volcanology, 1*(2). Retrieved February 1, 2014, from http://www.appliedvolc.com/content/1/1/2

Zottarelli, L. K. (2010). Broken bond: An exploration of human factors associated with companion animal loss during Hurricane Katrina. *Sociological Forum, 25*(1), 110–122. doi:10.1111/j.1573-7861.2009.00159.x

Responder Self-Care

Throughout this book, the authors have taken special care to provide responders with guidelines for working with multiple vulnerable populations. While it is true that such populations include children, older adults, persons with disabilities, and even pets, there is also one additional population that cannot be overlooked. It seems fitting to end this discussion of vulnerable populations by reviewing the needs of responders, providing a framework for support and intervention for those who are on the front lines.

After the attacks on the World Trade Center (WTC) on September 11, 2001, 90,000 disaster workers participated in the rescue, recovery, and cleanup at the massive destruction site known as "ground zero" (Ekenga & Friedman-Jimenez, 2011). This group of disaster workers was not unlike others, comprising persons from all professions and walks of life. Responders included fire, police, emergency medical services, city workers, government organizations, Voluntary Organizations Active in Disaster (VOADs), community agencies, and nonaffiliated volunteers. Nonaffiliated volunteers are those who respond based on their personal desire to help, without being affiliated with an agency or organization. Nontraditional responders may also answer the call to help, and like nonaffiliated volunteers, may not have had any previous thoughts about working in a post-disaster environment. These workers include construction engineers, heavy equipment operators, carpenters, and laborers. Although critical to the response, recovery, and cleanup efforts, these responders rarely receive training in disaster work, even though they are exposed to the same physical and psychological hazards (Benedek, Fullerton, & Ursano, 2007).

Responders as a general rule can be reluctant to focus on their own needs, and instead place attention on the needs of others. Literature speaks to a "culture" of responders, which includes ideals that make it challenging for the responder to seek help, or be able to effectively assess when help is needed. Due to the nature of the work, responders often disregard their own needs, focusing efforts outwards. Community membership is based on shared experiences that provide support to those who have common history. This culture is protective in nature, consisting of rigid value systems and a tight-knit fellowship that is not always easy to penetrate. Oftentimes defense mechanisms result in a reluctance to seek help from those outside the community, protecting members from sharing events with those who may misunderstand their experience (Kronenberg et al., 2008).

Responders, especially those at their first disaster, often arrive with a specific skill set. When met with the realities of the diverse needs, it is necessary to adjust previous thoughts about necessary skills and adapt to the environment. Rogers (2007) discusses such a transition in thoughts about his response to the WTC attacks. He explains that as a psychiatrist trained in emergency psychiatric response he felt more than equipped to respond to the mental health needs of victims. Instead, he realized that he needed to shift his interventions to include basic principles of human connection and compassion, instead of utilizing his more advanced training in psychiatric assessment. While there is no doubt that his formal training was useful, his ability to adjust his approach to meet the needs of others was the critical skill. Flexibility in response is a key characteristic for those in the disaster field, although at times such an adjustment may be stressful.

CASE STUDY: World Trade Center

"This big, brawly FBI guy had his shield around his neck. And, you know, I looked up at him and he's telling, there was about six officers there with me, and he's like, 'If you want to live, you, you might as well leave now.' He said, 'We're all gonna die,'" Paulkner recalled.

"And I'm like, 'I can't, we can't leave. I'm, I'm not leaving.' And the officers that I were there with, 'We're not leaving either.' And we continued to evacuate and do our jobs, but, you know, we were all like, 'Wow, we're gonna die,'" she said.

Quote from Carol Paulkner, police officer responding to attacks on WTC. (Peterson, 2013)

Disaster responders by nature are a resilient group of people. Aware of the hazards of the work, they are exposed to physical and emotional stressors, often for prolonged periods of time. This exposure consists of sensory stressors including sights, smells, and sounds. Viewing loss of life and human suffering, smelling odors from areas that have suffered destruction and loss of sanitation systems, and hearing sounds of emergency response and cries for help are all possibilities. Threat of death or injury, hazardous working conditions, and environmental toxins are ever-present realities. When these stimuli are combined they can become overwhelming, resulting in health and mental health effects.

Dass-Brailsford (2010) acknowledges that there are many areas of the responder environment contributing to overall stress levels, including direct exposure to traumatic events and witnessing trauma exposures to others. In addition, the organizational environment may or may not be an additional source of stress. Depending on the structure of the organization there may be a lack of resources, lack of administrative structure, and frequently changing leadership, all of which can be stressful. Responders who are new to the field or unaccustomed to working in a quickly changing environment may find such variables personally challenging.

The combination of these stressors, along with personal characteristics, can result in negative health and mental health effects for the responder. Literature has documented that first responders are not immune to health and mental health effects similar to other disaster victims, including symptoms of depression, increase in drug or alcohol use, and symptoms of posttraumatic stress disorder (PTSD; Benedek et al., 2007). Lengthy and numerous deployments, lack of support, and resistance to seek help can lead to stress, compassion fatigue, and burnout. Once responders reach the point of burnout or compassion fatigue they may find themselves suffering from secondary health issues due to exhaustion, a decreased ability to maintain empathy, and feelings of psychological stress. Responders with prolonged exposure to hazards and risks find subsequent negative health effects, injuries, and complications of pre-existing conditions.

HEALTH EFFECTS

Numerous studies have documented the immediate and long-term health effects for first responders. These effects are often disaster specific as a result of the unique composition of the disaster and accompanying response and recovery tasks. Ample literature has reviewed the health effects of responders in relation to the attacks on the WTC in 2011. The WTC response was unique in that the collapse of the buildings, along with the burning of the jet fuel, resulted in an environment filled with smoke, dust, debris, and other environmental toxins. Rescue and recovery efforts lasted for weeks and months, prolonging exposure.

Studies have found that respiratory illness is common in responders and cleanup workers after the WTC attacks, including short- and long-term effects (Ekenga & Friedman-Jimenez, 2011). Several health surveillance programs have been put in place to track health effects of responders and citizens, including the WTC Health Registry. Friedman et al. (2013) reviewed a sample of over 14,000 responders from the WTC disaster and found comorbid disorders that included lower respiratory symptoms and PTSD. The authors discuss that the existence of concurrent issues may have cumulative effects, resulting in increases in psychological and physical distress, as compared to those without coexisting conditions. Lucchin and colleagues (2012) report that longitudinal data (10 years post-event) continues to support the evidence of long-term health problems, including respiratory illness, gastroesophageal reflux disease, obstructive sleep apnea, and musculoskeletal injuries.

Herbert and colleagues (2006) surveyed 9,443 first responders 5 years after the WTC disaster and additionally found high rates of respiratory illness. Thirty-two percent reported new-onset lower respiratory illness, with 44% reporting development of new symptoms of upper respiratory illness, especially among those arriving early to the disaster site who were engulfed in the dust cloud related to the building collapse. These results are supported in the literature comparing WTC-exposed employees with nonexposed employees (Mauer, Cummings, & Hoen, 2010).

Health effects of the WTC attacks are not only limited to respiratory illness. Jordan and colleagues (2013) found increased risk of hospitalization due to cardiovascular disease among male rescue and recovery workers. In addition, increased risk for certain types of cancers has also been found. Solan and colleagues (2013) found that WTC rescue workers were exposed to environmental pollutants containing carcinogens, including asbestos, silica, hydrocarbons, and metals. A survey of almost 21,000 participants found increased incidence of thyroid and prostate cancer among responders with high levels of exposure during response. An earlier study by Jiehul and colleagues (2012) also found increased risk of thyroid and prostate cancers and multiple myeloma, but did not find an association related to intensity of exposure. Both studies caution that cancer may take years to develop, indicating a need for longer term follow-up studies.

The attacks on the WTC exposed rescue and recovery workers to specific hazards; however, other disasters also bring unique risks. After Hurricanes Katrina and Rita, investigators found health effects different from those witnessed after the WTC attacks. Noe and colleagues (2007) explored such effects when they surveyed construction workers aiding in the recovery efforts following Hurricane Katrina. The authors found that sleeping in areas that had once been flooded contributed to an increase in acute skin disease. The Centers for Disease Control and Prevention (CDC, 2006) found multiple health effects in their survey of fire and police responders active after Hurricane Katrina. Physical injuries such as cuts and sprains were common, but upper respiratory illnesses and skin rashes were also evident. These findings were confirmed in a study of firefighters after Hurricane Katrina. Tak, Bernard, Driscoll, and Dowell (2007) also found increased reporting of new-onset respiratory symptoms, throat irritation, and skin rashes. Exposure to contaminated floodwater appeared to be the associated hazard. Such findings of the above studies speak to the fact that each disaster brings its own set of unique health hazards, and precautions should consider potential differences.

MENTAL HEALTH EFFECTS

Along with health effects, literature suggests that mental health effects are also a possibility for responders, ranging from minimal, short-term symptoms to more significant long-term illness (Bills et al., 2008). This is not unlike what is found in the general population; however, responders are at risk for longer and more intense exposure to psychological hazards. Persons who are trained responders as opposed to nontraditional or untrained responders are more likely to demonstrate resiliency, a characteristic that can protect against symptoms of PTSD (Pietrzak, 2014).

Studies are clear that symptoms of PTSD are not uncommon in responders. Perrin and colleagues (2007) found PTSD prevalence rates ranging from 6.2% to 21.2% in responders 2 to 3 years after the disaster. Authors found that exposure early in the crisis and prolonged duration of response work increased risk. West and colleagues (2008) found similar symptoms in their study of 912 police officers 8 weeks after Hurricane Katrina. Symptoms included depression (26%) and PTSD (19%) for a significant proportion of the population. Many of the officers had significant events related to the disaster, including witnessing death and severe injury and harm to family members. Higher symptoms of depression were associated with having a home that was uninhabitable and having no or minimal contact with family members. Response personnel that are called to respond in their hometowns are faced with the challenge of balancing the requirements of their position with concern for their own family and friends. This can be a difficult balancing act, especially when communication is compromised.

Osofsky and colleagues (2011) sampled 1,382 first responders at two points, 6 to 9 months and 13 to 18 months after Hurricane Katrina. Not unlike other disaster victims, first responders reported multiple losses including home-related losses, family separation, and stressful working conditions. Of the sample, 69% witnessed injury or death, 52% suffered uninhabitable home damage, and 25% witnessed the death of a friend or family member. Symptoms of PTSD were evident in the population over both assessment periods, with 20% to 30% reporting some symptoms of PTSD and 26.4% reporting depression symptoms at the initial screening, dropping to 24.9% at the later time period. In addition to symptoms of PTSD and depression, participants reported increase in the frequency and amount of alcohol consumption as well as increase in partner conflict. For all indicators, there was no significant decrease in symptoms over time.

Soo and colleagues (2011) found slightly less prevalence rates of possible PTSD in responders from the WTC attacks. The authors found that symptoms decreased from 10% 1 year after the WTC attacks to 7% 9 years after the attacks in a sample of over 11,000 exposed firefighters. Similar to other studies, persistent direct exposure and early arrival to the disaster scene increased risk. Negative coping behaviors such as increase in alcohol use and amount, smoking of tobacco products, and lack of self-care such as exercise contributed to higher incidence. The incidence of symptoms months to years after the event has significant implications for providing long-term support. McCaslin and colleagues (2005) found that disaster responders who had a negative life event in the year following the disaster had high rates of depression, suggesting that not only is long-term care important, but that the effects of the disaster may make it more difficult for responders to deal with subsequent stressors later on.

The literature also indicates that those with prior training in disaster response fare better and are more resilient to coping with negative effects (Debchoudhury et al., 2011; Pietrzak, 2014). Lay volunteers, or those unaffiliated with an organization, are at greater risk for acute exposures. Deploying within an organization structure allows for monitoring of safety hazards as well as symptoms of distress within responders. Lay volunteers are at higher risk for probable symptoms of PTSD, depression, and anxiety. In addition, support services are not as available as they may be for affiliated responders (Debchoudhury et al., 2011).

INTERVENING

Once it is identified that a responder needs psychosocial support or assistance, special care should be given to the process of intervening. Kronenberg and colleagues (2008) reiterate recognizing the culture of first responders. As discussed earlier, the culture is based on group norms consisting of group cohesion, trust, and self-reliance. Important components include (a) focusing on resiliency, (b) establishing trust, and (c) providing services in alternate settings. The authors discuss that focusing on the resiliency of the client, or utilizing a strengths-based perspective, allows the responder to draw on his or her own social supports, freeing the interventionist to meet more concrete needs. Establishing trust is universal, speaking to all mental health interventions. Establishing trust and building rapport provide a context for the therapeutic relationships. This includes being flexible in service delivery, perhaps meeting persons in places outside of clinical settings. Meeting the responder at his or her workplace, in a neutral location, or at a park or public center helps to remove any stigma associated with receiving help. Keeping the intervention in a causal context can sometimes be beneficial in reducing anxiety.

As outlined in Chapter 3, crisis intervention and mental health support should be delivered from an evidence-based perspective. While a more in-depth discussion is available in previous chapters, evidence-guided intervention such as psychological first aid can be very effective in helping persons initiate recovery. In instances where long-term interventions are indicated, cognitive behavioral therapy or psychopharmacology could be considered (Benedek et al., 2007). Psychological first aid is effective when utilized as an individual intervention; however, it may also be applied in group settings with responders (Johnstone, 2007).

Psychological debriefing, sometimes referred to as critical incident stress debriefing, has limitations when utilized in some post-disaster settings. A comprehensive review of the empirical literature on psychological debriefing revealed that it does not prevent the onset of PTSD symptoms nor reduce psychological distress. In addition, in certain circumstances it was found to be no more effective than an education intervention for relieving distress (Rose, Bisson, Churchill, & Wessely, 2009). Regehr (2001) also discussed concerns in a review of offering crisis debriefing for emergency responders, although components of the model, including social support and the use of psychoeducation, appear to be effective. Other components, such as graphic review of details, appear to be less effective, and even harmful at times. A better model is to allow for free flow of details at the responder's discretion, and at a time of his or her choosing.

Regehr and Bober (2005) provide guidelines on which components are important to include in interventions for responders. Those guidelines include:

1. Providing timely and accurate information
2. Establishing an organizational climate that supports workers
3. Teaching stress management skills as a part of training
4. Providing access to individualized mental health services
5. Recognizing the value of the social support of family, friends, and networks

Social support is again mentioned as an important component of healing and emotional recovery post-event. Herberman, Fullerton, Kowalski-Trakofler, Reissman, and Scharf (2013) confirmed this notion when discussing the importance of the presence of social support to mediate symptoms of PTSD.

Managers can play a pivotal role in creating an environment that supports responders before the deployment, at the scene, and after work is completed. This can be accomplished by providing adequate training including hazard mitigation, and ensuring scene safety and security, minimizing stressors at the scene, and providing frequent information briefings. Partnering new responders with seasoned responders solidifies training concepts and provides a sense of social support during deployment. Rotating workers through tasks of high and low stress, monitoring and enforcing breaks, establishing respite areas, and ensuring the safety and security of workers help buffer negative effects. After assignments are complete, managers can continue to support workers by providing time off, offering educational in-services, providing information on stress management and self-care activities, and providing access to mental health assessment and services as needed (Katz, 2010).

SELF-CARE

As mentioned in previous literature, one of the most effective ways to help offset the negative effects of disasters is through adequate training. Training, including elements of crisis intervention, is imperative to equip responders with the tools needed to effectively respond. Perhaps the most essential aspect of this training is self-care. Self-care involves being able to access positive coping mechanisms, recognizing signs of stress and fatigue, and daily caring for body and mind in a way that promotes good physical and mental health. Self-care includes self-awareness, taking breaks between assignments and during assignments when suggested, being aware of other commitments, setting boundaries, seeking support, and maintaining a good work/life balance (Dass-Brailsford, 2010; Herberman et al., 2013; Kaul, 2002).

Self-care encompasses three principles according to Dass-Brailsford (2010). It should be (a) attainable, concrete, and tasks should be easily available; (b) related to the reactions of the responder; and (c) should utilize positive coping mechanisms.

There are specific self-care strategies that are appropriate at all times, including before, during, and after the response (DHHS, 2005; ISTSS, 2014; SAMHSA, n.d.). The following responder guidelines (Table 10.1) provide an overview of practical ways to deal with the stressors of events, including ways to prepare

TABLE 10.1 Responder Self-Care Guidelines

BEFORE THE EVENT
• Practice good health and mental health behaviors • Be familiar with signs of stress and stress reactions (see Chapter 3) • Learn positive methods to cope with stress • Involve family and significant other in emergency planning • Develop plans for covering home and work obligations in case of response
DURING THE EVENT
• Practice good stress management techniques (deep breathing, meditation, stretching) • Adhere to safety policies and procedures • Encourage and support coworkers • Recognize that there may be periods of inactivity or "waiting" during the disaster response • Avoid use of alcohol, tobacco, drugs, and excessive caffeine • Eat regular, nutritious meals • Seek out support via family, friends, other networks • Take regular breaks
AFTER THE EVENT—RETURNING HOME
• Allow time to recharge and reconnect with family and friends • Continue leisure activities—hobbies and interests • Continue with stress management techniques • Seek spiritual support if needed, draw on support system • Avoid use of alcohol, tobacco, and drugs to cope • Seek professional help if needed • Maintain adequate diet and exercise • Reframe experience to restore meaning and hope • Recognize emotions that may easily arise
WHEN TO SEEK HELP
Seek professional help if you experience any of the following: • Disorientation, memory loss • Depression, pervasive feelings of hopelessness and despair • Withdrawal from persons and activities • Anxiety, restlessness • Obsessive fear, especially of disasters • Acute psychiatric symptoms, including hearing voices and delusions • Disinterest in caring for basic needs • Thoughts of harming self or others • Excessive use of alcohol or illegal substances • Violence toward others

Sources: U.S. Department of Health and Human Services (DHHS, 2005); International Society for Traumatic Stress Studies (ISTSS, 2014); Substance Abuse and Mental Health Services Administration (SAMHSA, n.d.).

ahead of time. These guidelines are presented to complement general disaster preparedness recommendations addressing all-hazards readiness.

SUMMARY AND CONCLUSIONS

Being on the front line of a disaster presents physical and psychological challenges to all responders. Responders are obligated to ensure that they have the proper training and emotional resiliency to meet those challenges. Training before an event lays the foundation for preparing responders to accomplish their tasks without becoming another disaster victim. Managers, organizations, and governing bodies share in the responsibility of providing safe environments, adequate resources, and clear and effective supervision, equipping responders with the necessary tools and support. Responders should be aware of possible hazards and take the initiative to obtain training that will support them in their efforts.

When the psychological aspects of response take their toll, responders should be able to recognize the need for immediate and ongoing mental health support and intervention. Processes should be put in place that provide effective and confidential counseling, and supervisors should encourage the use of such supports. Responders should be aware of signs of stress and engage in self-care activities that promote resiliency. Available resources, such as the Responder Self-Care mobile app (University of Minnesota, http://sph.umn.edu/ce/perl/mobile/selfcare) should be utilized and shared with other responders. Social support networks should also be able to recognize signs of stress in responders and provide support as needed.

Disasters will continue to be a reality in the years to come. Recognizing the health and mental health effects of disasters for responders provides the foundation for implementing supportive services and access to medical and mental health care. Helping those who help should be viewed as a priority for all those involved in rescue, response, and recovery.

REFERENCES

Benedek, D. M., Fullerton, C., & Ursano, R. J. (2007). First responders; mental health consequences of natural and human-made disasters for public health and safety workers. *Annual Review of Public Health, 28*, 55–68. doi:10.1146/annurev.publichealth.28.021406.144037

Bills, C., Levy, N. A., Sharma, V., Charney, D. S., Herbert, R., Moline, J., & Katz, C. L. (2008). Mental health of workers and volunteers responding to the events of 9/11: Review of the literature. *Mt. Sinai Journal of Medicine, 75*(2), 115–127. doi:10.1002/msj.20026

Centers for Disease Control and Prevention. (2006). Health hazard evaluation of police officers and firefighters after Hurricane Katrina-New Orleans, Louisiana, October 17–28 and November 30–December 5, 2005. *Morbidity and Mortality Weekly Report, 55*(16), 456–458.

Dass-Brailsford, P. (2010). Secondary trauma among disaster responders. In *Crisis and disaster counseling* (pp. 213–228). Thousand Oaks, CA: Sage.

Debchoudhury, I., Welch, A. E., Fairclough, M. A., Cone, J. E., Brackbill, R. M., Stellman, S. D., & Farfel, M. R. (2011). Comparison of health outcomes among affiliated and lay disaster volunteers enrolled in the World Trade Center Health Registry. *Preventive Medicine, 53*(6), 359–363. doi:10.1016/j.ypmed.2011.08.034

Ekenga, C. C., & Friedman-Jimenez, G. (2011). Epidemiology of respiratory health outcomes among World Trade Center disaster workers: Review of the literature 10 years after the September 11, 2001 terrorist attacks. *Disaster Medicine and Public Health Preparedness, 5*(2), s189–s196.

Friedman, S. M., Farfel, M. R., Maslow, C. B., Cone, J. E., Brackbill, R. M., & Stellman, S. D. (2013). Comorbid persistent lower respiratory symptoms and post traumatic stress disorder 5–6 years post 9/11 in responders enrolled in the World Trade Center health Registry. *American Journal of Industrial Medicine, 56*(11), 1251–1261. doi:10.1002/H/22217

Herberman, H. B., Fullerton, C. S., Kowalski-Trakofler, Reissman, D. B., & Scharf, T. (2013). Florida Department of Health worker's response to 2004 hurricanes: A qualitative analysis. *Disaster Medicine and Public Health Preparedness, 7*(2), 153–159. doi:10.1017/dmp.2013.13

Herbert, R., Moline, J., Skloot, G., Metzger, K., Baron, S., Luft, B., . . . Lewing, S. M. (2006). The World Trade Center disaster and the health of workers: Five-year assessment of a unique medical screening program. *Environmental Health Perspectives, 114*(12), 1853–1858.

Higgins, L. (2012). First responder: Worst tragedy I've ever seen. Retrieved March 12, 2014, from http://www.usatoday.com/story/news/nation/2012/12/15/horrific-scene-haunts-first-responder/1771725/

International Society for Traumatic Stress Studies. (ISTSS). (2014). Treating trauma: Self-care for providers. Retrieved March 12, 2014, from http://www.istss.org/SelfCareForProviders.htm

Jiehul, L., Cone, J. E., Kahn, A. R., Brackbill, R. M., Farfel, M. R., Greene, C. M., . . . Stellman, S. D. (2012). Association between World Trade Center exposure and excess cancer risk. *Journal of the American Medical Association, 308*(23), 2479–2488. doi:10.1001/jama.2012.110980

Johnstone, M. (2007). Disaster response and group self-care. *Perspectives in Psychiatric Care, 43*(1), 38–40.

Jordan, H. T., Stellman, S. D., Morabia, A., Miller-Archie, S. A., Alper, H., Laskaris, Z., . . . Cone, J. E. (2013). Cardiovascular disease hospitalizations in relation to exposure to September 2011 World Trade Center and posttraumatic stress disorder. *Journal of the American Heart Association, 2*(5). doi:10.1161/JAHA.113.00431

Katz, C. L. (2010). Understanding and helping responders. In F. J. Stoddard, C. L. Katz, & J. B. Merlino (Eds.), *Hidden impact: What you need to know for the next disaster.* Boston, MA: Jones and Bartlett.

Kaul, R. E. (2002). A social worker's account of 31 days responding to the Pentagon disaster: Crisis intervention training and self-care practices. *Brief Treatment and Crisis Intervention, 2*(1), 33–37.

Kronenberg, M., Osofsky, H. J., Osofsky, J. D., Many, M., Hardy, M., & Arey, J. (2008). First responder culture: Implications for mental health professionals providing services following a natural disaster. *Psychiatric Annals, 38*(2), 114–118. doi:10.3928/00485713-20080201-05

Lucchin, R. G., Crane, M. A., Crowley, L., Globina, Y., Milek, D. J., Boffetta, P., & Landrigan, P. J. (2012). The World Trade Center health surveillance program: Results of the first 10 years and implications for prevention. *Giornale Italiano di Medicina del Lavoro ed Ergonomia, 34*(3), 529–533.

Mauer, M. P., Cummings, K. R., & Hoen, R. (2010). Long-term respiratory symptoms in Word Trade Center responders. *Occupational Medicine (Lond), 60*(2), 145–151.

McCaslin, S. E., Jacobs, G. A., Meyer, D. L., Johnson-Jimenez, E., Metzler, T. J., & Marmar, C. R. (2005). How does negative life change following disaster response impact distress among Red Cross responders? *Professional Psychology: Research and Practice, 36*(3), 246–253. doi:10.1037/0735-7028.36.3.246

Noe, R., Cohen, A. L., Lederman, E., Gould, L. H., Alsdurf, H., Vranken, P., . . . Mott, J. (2007). Skin disorders among construction workers following Hurricane Katrina and Hurricane Rita: An outbreak investigation in New Orleans, Louisiana. *Archives of Dermatology, 143*(11), 1393–1398.

Osofsky, H. J., Osofsky, J. D., Arey, J., Kronenberg, M. E., Hansel, T., & Many, M. (2011). Hurricane Katrina's first responders: The struggle to protect and serve in the aftermath of a disaster. *Disaster Medicine and Public Health Preparedness, 5*(2), s214–s219.

Perrin, M. A., DiGrande, L., Wheeler, K., Thorpe, L., Farfel, M., & Brackbill, R. (2007). Differences in PTSD prevalence and associated risk factors among World Trade Center disaster rescue and recovery workers. *American Journal of Psychiatry, 164*(9), 1385–1394.

Peterson, R. (2013). Ground Zero Responders Remember 9/11. Retrieved March 12, 2014, from http://www.cbsnews.com/news/ground-zero-responders-remember-9-11/

Pietrzak, R. H., Feder, A., Singh, R., Schechter, C. B., Bromet, E. J., Katz, C. L., . . . Southwick, S. M. (2014). Trajectories of PTSD risk and resilience in World Trade Center responders: An 8-year prospective cohort study. *Psychological Medicine, 44*(1), 205–219. doi:10.1017/S0033291713000597

Regehr, C. (2001). Crisis debriefing groups for emergency responders: Reviewing the evidence. *Brief Treatment and Crisis Intervention, 1*(2), 87–100.

Regehr, C., & Bober, T. (2005). *In the line of fire: Trauma in the emergency services.* New York, NY: Oxford University Press.

Rogers, J. R. (2007). Disaster response and the mental health counselor. *Journal of Mental Health Counseling, 29*(1), 1–3.

Rose, S. C., Bisson, J., Churchill, R., & Wessely, S. (2009). Psychological debriefing for preventing post traumatic stress disorder (PTSD) (Review). Retrieved March 12, 2014, from http://www.cochranelibrary.com

Substance Abuse and Mental Health Services Administration. (SAMHSA). (n.d.). A Post-deployment Guide for Emergency and Disaster Response Workers. Retrieved March 12, 2014, from http://store.samhsa.gov/shin/content/SMA11-DISASTER /SMA11-DISASTER-04.pdf

Solan, S., Wallenstein, S., Shapiro, M., Teitelbaum, S. L., Stevenson, L., Kochman, A., . . . Landrigan, P. J. (2013). Cancer incidence in world trade center rescue and recovery workers, 2001-2008. *Environmental Health Perspectives, 121*(6), 699–704. doi:10.1289 /ehp.1205894

Soo, J., Webber, M. P., Gustave, J., Hall, C. B., Cohen, H. W., Kelly, K. J., & Prezant, D. J. (2011). Trends in probable PTSD in firefighters exposed to the World Trade Center Disaster, 2001-2010. *Disaster Medicine and Public Health Preparedness, 5*(2), s205–s213.

Tak, S., Bernard, B. P., Driscoll, R. J., & Dowell, C. H. (2007). Floodwater exposure and the related health symptoms among firefighters in New Orleans, Louisiana 2005. *American Journal of Industrial Medicine, 50*(5), 377–382.

U.S. Department of Health and Human Services (DHHS). (2005). *A guide to managing stress in crisis response professions*. Rockville, MD: Center for Mental Health Services, Substance Abuse and Mental Health Services Administration.

West, C., Bernard, B., Mueller, C., Kitt, M., Driscoll, R., & Tak, S. (2008). Mental health outcomes in police personnel after Hurricane Katrina. *Journal of Occupational and Environmental Medicine, 50*(6), 689–695.

Final Considerations: Ethnic and Economic Diversity and Disasters

CASE STUDY: Cuban Immigrant, Conditions in Waterplace Apartments in Mississippi After Katrina

There was two or three apartments of Latinos, and the others were African American and White. And the owner was charging the Latinos rent, but not charging anybody else rent after the storm. . . . They were having to pay rent and there was no doors on their apartments, the windows were busted out. All their furniture had been lost, the mold was growing in there. . . . They were paying I think $50 a week each, and there was like seven in one apartment and then five in another apartment . . . $350 on one apartment weekly! . . . and then the other apartment was like five people in it so he made a good bundle. (Weil, 2009)

Ethnicity is a broad term that is based on one's self-identification with any number of groups based on affiliation with other individuals sharing a common heritage, history, culture, language, geography, religion, or other socially important dimensions (Cormier & Jones, 2010). It is difficult to make generalizations involving specific guidelines for such diverse populations. However, ethnic minorities do share some things in common. For one, ethnic minorities are more likely to have low incomes, which can complicate the ability to prepare for and respond to a disaster. Recent immigrants may have low English literacy skills, which can create communication difficulties in all aspects of a disaster.

It should also be pointed out that the categories used to define members of a particular ethnic group are inconsistent and vary over time. Some terms for ethnic groups used by researchers change over time, may fall into political incorrectness, or may lump individuals into categories that are not necessarily socially meaningful. For example, the term "Hispanic" or "Latino" groups together Spanish-speaking people from a large number of cultures and regions who may see themselves as having little in common apart from a shared language. The term "Asian" groups together people who speak many different languages and who are from a wide variety of cultures and geographic regions. Ethnic categorization is also limiting in that it fails to distinguish among individuals or families who have recently immigrated to the United States and those whose families have been long established. Despite those caveats, it is still important to attempt to address issues of cultural and economic diversity and how it relates to preparation and intervention in disaster. In this chapter, the ethnic terminology used by the researchers is preserved. For example, if the term "Black," "White," or "Hispanic" is used in a study, it has not been changed to alternate terms such as "African American," "Caucasian," or "Latino." The primary reason is that it is important to preserve the categories used by the study so that the reader may best critically evaluate the information.

ETHNIC MINORITIES AND LOW ECONOMIC STATUS PERSONS IN DISASTERS

"No contact anywhere with an illegal alien!" conservative talk show host Michael Savage advised his U.S. listeners this week on how to avoid the swine flu. "And that starts in the restaurants" where, he said, you "don't know if they wipe their behinds with their hands!" (Alexander, 2009)

According to Andrulis, Siddiqui, and Ganter (2007), there has been a general lack of diversity in the disaster preparedness literature. However, a few studies are available that suggest that ethnic minorities and lower income persons in the United States tend to be less likely to develop a disaster plan or build an emergency kit. A study involving a review of the literature on race, ethnicity, and disaster found that Asians were less likely than Blacks, Whites, or Hispanics to develop an emergency plan for earthquakes (Fothergill, Darlington, & Maestras, 1999). One qualitative study involving 51 Latino immigrants in Montgomery County, Maryland, found that only four had an emergency plan (Carter-Pokras, Zambrana, Mora, Aaby, 2007). In a survey of 935 Katrina evacuees, it was found that an emergency plan had been prepared prior to the event by 49.1% of Caucasians, 31.4% of African Americans, and 38.4% of other non-Whites (Spence, Lachlan, & Griffine, 2007). Contrary to what might be expected, this study found that those in higher income brackets were less likely to have an evacuation plan or an emergency kit. Another broad study was conducted using Behavioral Risk Factor Surveillance System (BRFSS) data from five states that use preparedness modules developed by the Centers for Disease Control and Prevention (CDC; Arizona, Connecticut, Montana, Nevada, and Tennessee; Ablah, Konda, & Kelley, 2009). Respondents were defined as prepared if they were deficient in no more than one of six actionable preparedness measures: evacuation planning, water supply, food supply, medication supply, radio, and flashlight. The study results indicated that people who were prepared were more likely to report incomes greater than $50,000 (50.9% vs. 46.2%) and less likely to be Hispanic (6.9% vs. 10.9%). A study involving focus groups among Latino migrant and seasonal farm workers in North Carolina found that few had emergency kits or had developed an emergency plan (Burke, Bethel, & Britt, 2012). Of the participants, 84% identified lack of information in Spanish as a significant barrier for preparedness.

In part due to language barriers, ethnic minorities tend to rely on social networks to receive disaster information. A study involving a sample of 165 Latino and 1,069 non-Latino single-family homeowners from the Florida Statewide Mitigation Survey found that Latino homeowners prefer to utilize friends and families as sources of disaster preparation information (Peguero, 2006). One qualitative study involving interviews with 65 Latino survivors of Hurricane Katrina found that they perceived social networks to have been important in gathering information, making decisions, and accessing resources (Hilfinger Messias, Barrington, & Lacy, 2012). A review of research studies found that before Hurricane Andrew, Black and Hispanic families were more likely than Anglo families to have been helped by relatives in preparing for a disaster (Fothergill et al., 1999).

Ethnic minorities and low-income-status persons tend to be more vulnerable in disasters. During the 1995 Chicago heat wave, it was found that mortality rates were higher among Blacks than among other ethnic groups (Kaiser et al., 2007). Ethnic differences among Hurricane Katrina victims were widely reported in the popular media, but studies do verify the news reports. Deaths from Hurricane Katrina affected ethnic groups disproportionately. One study documented that Katrina deaths were 51% Black, 42% White, and 2% Hispanic/Latino (Brunkard, Namulanda, & Ratard, 2008). When adjusting for the ethnic percentages in the area, the mortality rate among Blacks was found to be 1.7 to 4 times higher in Blacks than Whites for people 18 years of age and older. Another study involving a multiple-additive regression tree indicated that African Americans experienced disproportionate structural exposure (flood height, building damage) and personal exposure (locations of 911 calls) during Hurricane Katrina (Curtis, Li, Marx, Mills, & Pine, 2011). The researchers identified factors affecting increased vulnerability of African Americans as living in more vulnerable areas, disproportionately higher neighborhood and social stressors, overall poor health including high chronic diseases (such as diabetes and hypertension), and the burden of infectious diseases. During Katrina, African Americans were less able to evacuate and more likely to wind up in shelters. One study estimates that among evacuees in American Red Cross shelters in Louisiana, 76.4% were African American (Greenough et al., 2008).

Economic status may be a more crucial factor in disasters than ethnicity. A study based on data from the World Bank and the Center for Research on the Epidemiology of Disasters found that globally, poor people are two times more exposed to natural disasters than the nonpoor in the 21st century (Kim, 2012). One study of flood events in Texas involved analysis of 832 flood events at the county level in Texas from 1997 to 2001 (Zahran, Brody, Peacock, Vedlitz, & Grove, 2008). The researchers found that localities with higher-than-average numbers of poor and minority residents were more likely to experience injury and death. In a population-based cohort study from the 1999 Taiwan earthquake, it was found that the degree of vulnerability increased with decreasing monthly wage (Chou et al., 2004). In addition, a study of residents in an urban Hispanic area in El Paso County that experienced a flood disaster in 2006 showed a number of adverse outcomes (Collins, Jimenez, & Grineski, 2013). Health impacts were assessed in 475 individuals using a mail survey. Many had one or more physical (43%) or mental (18%) health problems in the 4 months following the flood, and 28% had one or more injuries or acute affect related to the post-flood cleanup. Lower socioeconomic status was significantly associated with negative post-flood health outcomes. Predictors of negative outcomes included lack of English proficiency, non-U.S. citizenship, and lack of access to health care.

Historically, ethnic minorities have often been scapegoated during disasters. In the United States, immigrants have been associated with germs, with the social perception that exposure to an immigrant brings exposure to disease (Markel & Stern, 2002). Alexander (2009) describes several examples of such ethnic blaming. During the Medieval Black Plague, Europeans blamed the Jews, claiming that they had poisoned the wells, causing the outbreak of the disease. In a 1982 cholera pandemic in the United States, the immigrant European Jews were blamed. In the United States, the 1918 influenza pandemic was referred to as the "Spanish flu." The Spanish blamed the Italians and the Italians blamed the Spanish. More recently, Mexicans were blamed in the early stages of the 2009 H1N1 pandemic (Schoch-Spana, Rambhia, & Norwood, 2010). This influenza was termed by some the "Mexican flu" or the "fajita flu." Mexican immigrants were viewed as disease agents who were a danger to the country and even Mexican commodities were avoided. In reality, Mexican immigrants were more vulnerable to influenza and its complications due to poor health and limited access to health care.

At the very lowest rung of the economic ladder are homeless people, who are often overlooked in disaster preparedness. There are approximately 610,000 homeless people in the United States (HUD, 2013). The homeless often suffer from mental and physical illness. Between 20% and 25% of people who are homeless have some form of severe and persistent mental illness (NCH, 2006). Among the sheltered homeless, 38.6% have some form of disability; 19.4% have a physical or developmental disability (Solaria, Cortes, Brown, Khadduri, & Culhane, 2013). For all homeless people, it is estimated that 38% are dependent on alcohol and 26% abuse other drugs (NCH, 2009). In addition, one-third of the homeless are children (under 18) or youths (18 to 24); 12% of the adult homeless are veterans (HUD, 2013). Many of the information outlets are not accessible to the homeless. Even if the message to "shelter in place" is received, approximately two-thirds of the homeless are unsheltered (HUD, 2013). Edgington (2009) has outlined some of the problems the homeless face in disaster. Disaster preparedness is difficult to achieve, for homeless persons have limited resources to stockpile food, store medications, and shelter in place. Evacuation is difficult, for the homeless have limited access to transportation. They also have limited channels of communication for receiving vital disaster information due to lack of access to television, radio, and Internet due to their social isolation.

Ethnic minorities may be more vulnerable to fraud than the general population. Unfortunately, various forms of fraud are common during a disaster. According to a Congressional report, as much as 1.4 billion dollars in disaster aid to victims of Hurricanes Katrina and Rita, nearly one-fourth the total, may have been used fraudulently (Lipton, 2006; United States, 2007). Disaster assistance money was used to purchase items including a $450 tattoo, $400 massages, a $1,100 engagement ring, a $1,300 handgun, a $200 bottle of Dom Perignon, $5,000 to a divorce attorney, gambling expenses, football tickets, condoms, tax payments, a house down payment, bail bonds, and "Girls Gone Wild" videos. The Federal Emergency Management Association (FEMA) paid for luxury hotel rooms in New York City and on beachfront property. FEMA also provided cash or funds for housing assistance to more than 1,000 prison inmates. Another con involves extracting fraudulent donations. Two Texas brothers, Steven and Bartholomew Stephens, created a fake Salvation Army website purporting to take donations for Hurricane Katrina victims (Blanton, 2012). They received hundreds of donations amounting to tens of thousands of dollars before the operation was discovered and shut down.

Ethnic minorities with limited English language skills or knowledge of governmental services and regulations may be more prone to be taken in by fraud. Caribbean immigrants recounted a con artist who went through the neighborhood, impersonating a FEMA official with a FEMA jacket and badge after Hurricane Katrina (Munton & McLeod, 2011). He had residents fill out a form to receive disaster assistance, including name, social security number, and back account information for electronic transfer of finds. He was able to use this information to divert funds from these claims to himself. Another study described housing discrimination after Hurricane Katrina (Weil, 2009). Here, focus groups were conducted with 25 Latinos. They described discriminatory practices including denial of housing units or rejection from homeless shelters. Contributing factors identified were legal status, occupational status, and limited English language familiarity. Older adults are also often targets of fraud post-disaster (Banks, 2013; Oriol, 1999). Contractor fraud is also commonly directed at older adults and immigrants (Davila, Marquart, & Mullings, 2005; Munton & McLeod, 2011).

SUMMARY AND CONCLUSIONS

Ethnic minorities and persons with low incomes have increased vulnerability to disasters and tend to be less prepared for disasters. Ethnic minorities who are recent immigrants may have limited English language skills, which can create a number of communication barriers affecting disaster planning, response, and recovery. Language barriers and lack of familiarity with laws and governmental regulations can make immigrant populations a target of con artists and other forms of post-disaster exploitation. Ethnic minorities also often have low incomes. Individuals with low incomes are at increased risk because they tend to live in lower quality housing that is more vulnerable to some types of disasters and they often have increased health concerns linked with low income. At the lowest end of the socioeconomic spectrum are the homeless. Many of the homeless are doubly vulnerable because they suffer from mental illness, addictive disease, or disability. Many of the homeless are unsheltered and have no place to stockpile resources and lack the ability to protect themselves from the environmental effects of a disaster. Limited studies are available that address diversity at this time; it will be an important area for further research in the future.

REFERENCES

Ablah, E., Konda, K., & Kelley, C. L. (2009). Factors predicting individual emergency preparedness: A multi-state analysis of 2006 BRFSS data. *Biosecurity and Bioterrorism: Biodefense Strategy, Practice, and Science, 7*(3), 317–330.

Alexander, B. (2009). Amid swine flu outbreak, racism goes viral. *NBC News.* Retrieved February 18, 2014, from http://www.nbcnews.com/id/30467300/ns/health-cold_and_flu/t/amid-swine-flu-outbreak-racism-goes-viral.

Andrulis, D. P., Siddiqui, N. J., & Ganter, J. L. (2007). Preparing racially and ethnically diverse communities for public health emergencies. *Health Affairs, 26*(5), 1269–1279.

Banks, L. (2013). Caring for elderly adults during disasters: Improving health outcomes and recovery. *Southern Medical Journal, 106*(1), 94–98.

Blanton, K. (2012, February). The rise of financial fraud: Scams never change but disguises do. *The Center for Retirement Research, 12*(5). Retrieved July 12, 2014, from http://develop.fafo.no/files/news/8746/IB_12-5.pdf

Brunkard, J., Namulanda, G., & Ratard, R. (2008). Hurricane Katrina deaths, 2005. *Disaster Medicine and Public Health Preparedness, 2*(4), 215–223. doi:10.1097/DMP.0b013e31818aaf55.

Burke, A., Bethel, J. W., & Britt, A. F. (2012). Assessing disaster preparedness among Latino migrant and seasonal farmworkers in Eastern North Carolina. *International Journal of Environmental Research and Public Health, 9,* 3115–3133. doi:10.3390/ijerph9093115 Retrieved October 21, 2013, from http://www.mdpi.com/1660-4601/9/9/3115/pdf

Carter-Pokras, O., Zambrana, R. E., Mora, S. E., & Aaby, K. A. (2007). Emergency preparedness: Knowledge and perceptions of Latin American immigrants. *Journal of Health Care for the Poor and Underserved, 18,* 465–481.

Chou, Y. J., Huang, N., Lee, C. H., Tsai, S. L., Chen, L. S., & Chang, H. J. (2004). Who is at risk of death in an earthquake? *American Journal of Epidemiology, 160*(7), 688–695. doi:10.1093/aje/kwh270

Collins, T. W., Jimenez, A. M., & Grineski, S. E. (2013). Hispanic health disparities after a flood disaster: Results of a population-based survey of individuals experiencing home site damage in El Paso, Texas. *Journal of Immigrant and Minority Health, 15*(2), 415–426.

Cormier, L. A., & Jones, S. R. (2010). *Introductory cultural anthropology: An interactive approach.* El Cajon, CA: National Social Science Press.

Curtis, A., Li, B., Marx, B. D., Mills, J. W., & Pine, J. (2011). A multiple additive regression tree analysis of three exposure measures during Hurricane Katrina. *Disasters, 35*(1), 19–35. doi:10.1111/j.0361-3666.2010.01190.x

Davila, M., Marquart, J. W., & Mullings, J. L. (2005). Beyond Mother Nature: Contractor fraud in the wake of natural disasters. *Deviant Behavior, 26*(3), 271–293. doi:10.1080 /01639620590927623

Edgington, S. (2009). *Disaster planning for people experiencing homelessness.* National Health Care for the Homeless Council (NHCHC). Retrieved March 27, 2014, from http:// www.nhchc.org/wp-content/uploads/2011/10/Disaster-Planning-for-People -Experiencing-Homelessness.pdf

Fothergill, A., Darlington, J. D., & Maestras, E. G. M. (1999). Race, ethnicity and disasters in the United States: A review of the literature. *Disasters, 23*(2), 156–173. doi:10.1111 /1467-7717.00111

Greenough, P. G., Lappi, M. D., Hsu, E. B., Fink, S., Hsieh, Y., Vu, A., . . . Kirsch, T. D. (2008). Burden of disease and health status among Hurricane Katrina-displaced persons in shelters: A population-based cluster sample. *Annals of Emergency Medicine, 51*(4), 426–432.

Hilfinger Messias, D. K., Barrington, C., & Lacy, E. (2012). Latino social network dynamics and the Hurricane Katrina disaster. *Disasters, 36*(1), 101–121.

Kaiser, R., Le Tertre, A., Schwartz, J., Gotway, C. A., Daley, W. R., & Rubin, C. H. (2007). The effect of the 1995 heat wave in Chicago on all-cause and cause-specific mortality. *American Journal of Public Health, 97*(Suppl. 1), S158–S162. doi:10.2105/AJPH .2006.10008

Kim, N. (2012). How much more exposed are the poor to natural disasters? Global and regional measurement. *Disasters, 36*(2), 195–211. doi:10.1111/j1467-7717.2011.01258.x

Lipton, E. (2006). Study finds huge fraud in the wake of hurricanes. *New York Times (June 14),* p. A20.

Markel, H., & Stern, A. M. (2002). The foreignness of germs: The persistent association of immigrants and disease in American society. *The Milbank Quarterly, 80*(4), 757–788.

Munton, J., & McLeon, J. (2011). *The con: How scams work, why you're vulnerable, and how to protect yourself.* Lanham, MD. Rowman & Littlefield.

National Coalition for the Homeless (NCH). (2006). Mental illness and homelessness. Retrieved March 27, 2014, from http://www.nationalhomeless.org/factsheets /Mental_Illness.pdf

National Coalition for the Homeless (NCH). (2009). Substance abuse and homelessness. Retrieved March 27, 2014, from http://www.nationalhomeless.org/factsheets /addiction.pdf

Oriol, W. (1999). *Psychosocial issues for older adults in disasters.* U.S. Department of Health and Human Services, Substance Abuse and Mental Health Services Administration, Center for Mental Health Services. Retrieved on March 1, 2014, from http://store .samhsa.gov/shin/content/SMA11-DISASTER/SMA11-DISASTER-03.pdf

Peguero, A. A. (2006). Latino disaster vulnerability. The dissemination of hurricane mitigation information among Florida's homeowners. *Hispanic Journal of Behavioral Sciences, 28*(1), 5–22.

Schoch-Spana, M., Rambhia, K. J., & Norwood, A. (2010). Stigma, health disparities, and the 2009 H1N1 influenza pandemic: How to protect Latino farmworkers in future health emergencies. *Biosecurity and Bioterrorism: Biodefense Strategy, Practice, and Science, 8,* 243–254.

Solaria, C., Cortes, A., Brown, S., Khadduri, J., & Culhane, D. P. (2013). *The 2012 annual homelessness assessment report (AHAR) to congress, Volume 2, Estimates of homelessness in the United States.* Retrieved March 27, 2014, from http://works.bepress.com/cgi /viewcontent.cgi?article=1169&context=dennis_culhane

Spence, P. R., Lachlan, K. A., & Griffine, D. R. (2007). Crisis communication, race, and natural disasters. *Journal of Black Studies, 37*(4), 539–554. doi:10.1177/002193470 6296192

United States Department of Housing and Urban Development (HUD). (2013). *The 2013 Annual Homeless Assessment Report (AHAR) to Congress. Part 1: Point-in-time estimates of homelessness.* Retrieved March 27, 2014, from http://www.onecp.info/resources /documents/ahar-2013-part1.pdf

United States Congress House Committee on Homeland Security. Subcommittee on Investigations. (2007). *Waste and fraud in the aftermath of Hurricane Katrina: Hearing before the Subcommittee on Homeland Security, House of Representatives, One Hundred Ninth Congress, second session, June 14, 2006* (Vol. 4). Government Printing Office. http://gpo.gov/fdsys/pkg/CHRG-109hhrg37291/html/CHRG-109hhrg37291.htm

Weil, J. H. (2009). Finding housing: Discrimination and exploitation of Latinos in the Post-Katrina rental market. *Organization and Environment, 22*(4), 491–502.

Zahran, S., Brody, S. D., Peacock, W. G., Vedlitz, A., & Grover, H. (2008). Social vulnerability and the natural and build environment: A model of flood casualties in Texas. *Disasters, 32*(4), 537–560. doi:10.1111/j.0361-3666.2008.01054.x

Resources and Tools

RESOURCE KEY

A	Animals/Pets	**G**	Government agency	**O**	Older adults
App	Mobile apps	**I/C**	Infants and children	**P**	Preparedness
D	Disabilities	**MH**	Mental health	**R**	Response
SA	Substance abuse				

GENERAL

American Red Cross (ARC)

Comprehensive site offering resources for disaster preparedness, response, and training with multiple populations. Offers "Safe and Well" website registry to assist in reunification. Multiple mobile apps available for hazard-specific preparedness, first aid, pet (animal) first aid, and shelter locator.

Website: http://www.redcross.org

P	R	I/C	D	O	A	MH	App		SA

Centers for Disease Control and Prevention

Online preparedness information for all hazards and all populations. Includes information for general public and professionals. Available mobile apps for medical field triage and companion app for Centers for Disease Control and Prevention (CDC) main page.

Main website: http://www.cdc.gov

Emergency Preparedness and Response website: http://www.emergency.cdc.gov

P	R	I/C	D	O	A	MH	App	G	

Federal Emergency Management Agency (FEMA)

Online source for information related to preparedness, response, and special populations. Available mobile app for disaster safety, emergency information, and shelter map.

Main website: http://www.fema.gov

Preparedness website: http://www.ready.gov

P	R	I/C	D	O	A	MH	App	G	

Illinois Terrorism Task Force

Advisory body to the State of Illinois that makes recommendations regarding homeland security. Includes publications and videos (some in Spanish) involving general disaster preparedness, emergency planning, and information on dealing with terrorist threats.

Disaster resources page: http://www.iema.illinois.gov/iema/ittf/publications/

P	R							G	

National Center for Disaster Preparedness

Website offers information, research clearinghouse, online training, policy statements, and resources about preparedness with multiple populations.

Main website: http://ncdp.columbia.edu/

P	R	I/C	D	O		MH			

United States Department of Veterans Affairs

Online source for information for benefits and services to veterans and their families. Provides preparedness information as well as mental health information and resources. Mobile apps available for public and professionals on suicide prevention and posttraumatic stress disorder (PTSD).

Main website: http://www.va.gov

Mental health website: http://www.mentalhealth.va.gov

P	R		D	O		MH	App		

MENTAL HEALTH AND SUBSTANCE USE

American Psychological Association

Information for general public and professionals on disaster mental health topics, including natural disasters, education, stress, and emotional health. Links are provided to online disaster mental health training opportunities. Provides mobile apps on general information as well as psychological tests.

Main website: http://www.apa.org

P	R	I/C	D	O	A	MH	App	G	

Mental Health America

Online resource for information about mental health disorders. General information, policy statements, and fact sheets.

Main website: http://mentalhealthamerica.net

	R	I/C		O		MH			SA

National Alliance on Mental Health

Organization that provides general information on mental illness. Includes education on types of mental illness, health care, treatment, and recovery; education for individuals, caregivers, teachers, and families; support groups; and advocacy.

Home page: http://www.nami.org

					MH			

National Child Traumatic Stress Network

Online resource focusing on traumatic stress. Offers *Psychological First Aid Field Guide* and mobile app for responders. Provides information for schools on preparedness, response, and recovery.

Main website: http://www.nctsn.org

P	R	I/C			MH	App		

National Institute of Mental Health

Information and resources for a wide range of mental health disorders. Appropriate for general public and professionals.

Main website: http://www.nimh.nih.gov

	R	I/C		O		MH		G	

Substance Abuse and Mental Health Services Administration (SAMHSA) Disaster Behavioral Health Information Series (DBHIS) Resource Collections

Website includes resources about disaster behavioral health. Topics cover different populations, specific disaster types, and general preparedness and response.

Main website: http://www.samhsa.gov/dtac/

Alcohol and substance abuse indicators: http://store.samhsa.gov/shin/content/NMH05-0212/NMH05-0212.pdf

P	R	I/C	D	O	A	MH		G	SA

United States Department of Veteran's Affairs

Online source for information for benefits and services to veterans and their families. Provides preparedness information as well as mental health information and resources. Mobile apps available for public and professionals on suicide prevention and PTSD.

Main website: http://www.va.gov

Mental health website: http://www.mentalhealth.va.gov

P	R		D	O		MH	App	G	SA

World Health Organization

Provides online guide for psychological first aid for fieldworkers. The handbook is geared toward dealing with individuals in crisis across cultures.

Online psychological first aid guide: http://whqlibdoc.who.int/publications/2011/9789241548205_eng.pdf

Yale Center for Public Health Preparedness

Webpage hosted by Yale Center for Public Health Preparedness (YCPHP) on disaster preparedness for individuals with serious mental illness. Provides information on challenges and vulnerabilities, preparedness, and recovery of people with chronic mental illness.

P	R					MH			

INFANTS AND CHILDREN

American Academy of Child and Adolescent Psychiatry (Disaster Resource Center)

Resources for parents and professionals on helping children and adolescents post-disasters. Includes information on grief reactions and identifying symptoms of PTSD.

Main website: http://www.aacap.org

	R	I/C				MH			

American Academy of Pediatrics

Information for parents and professionals about child health. Includes articles, fact sheets, and policy statement on topics related to the care of children. Mobile apps available for parents and adults on child health, including health information and tools for medical professionals.

Main website: http://www.aap.org

P	R	I/C	D			MH	App		

Child Care Aware of America

Resources for parents, caregivers, schools, and child care agencies for helping children cope following a disaster. Also provides resources for finding emergency child care after disasters.

Main website: http://www.childcareaware.org

P	R	I/C	D			MH			

FEMA for Kids

Website hosted by FEMA specifically targeting information for children and families. Includes kid-friendly activities to assist in preparedness, as well as information for parents and educators.

Main website: www.ready.gov/kids

P	R	I/C	D			MH	App	G	

March of Dimes

Information for parents and professionals related to the health of pregnant women and newborns. Includes guidelines for preparedness response, information for evacuation, health issues post-disaster, and infant feeding. Available mobile app on healthy pregnancy information.

Main website: http://www.marchofdimes.com

P	R	I/C				MH	App		

National Child Traumatic Stress Network

Online resource focusing on traumatic stress. Offers *Psychological First Aid Field Guide* and mobile app for responders. Provides information for schools on preparedness, response, and recovery.

Main website: http://www.nctsn.org/

P	R	I/C				MH	App		

University of Massachusetts Medical School Shriver Center

The Emergency Preparedness and Response Initiative provides information for professionals and parents on preparedness and response for children with disabilities. Resources include parent toolkits, online training for first responders, planning for sheltering and evacuations, and consultation for drills and training exercises.

Main website: http://www.umassmed.edu

Initiative website: http://www.umassmed.edu/shriver/service/emergency-preparedness-initiative.aspx

P	R	I/C	D							

National Center for Missing and Exploited Children

Website for information on missing children. Includes disaster preparedness and family reunification information, as well as the Unaccompanied Minors Registry to help locate missing children post-disaster. Information includes resources for families, law enforcement, and media.

Disaster website: http://www.missingkids.com/Disasters

P	R	I/C				MH	App		

OLDER ADULTS

Administration on Aging

Website providing information on special needs of older adults. Includes special needs of older adults in disaster. Includes information on preparedness for The State Unit on Aging and disaster social services.

Disaster website: http://www.aoa.gov/aoaroot/preparedness/Resources_Network/manual/disaster_assist_manual.aspx

P	R		O				G	

American Red Cross: Seniors

Webpage hosted by the ARC website targeting information for older adults in disasters. Includes information to assist in disaster preparedness, particularly steps in developing a personal support network.

Seniors and disaster webpage: http://www.redcross.org/prepare/location /home-family/seniors

P	R			O					

California Department on Aging

Website providing disaster preparedness tip sheets for seniors. Includes information on floods, hot weather, cold weather, pets, earthquakes, power outages, and wildfires. Tip sheets are available in Chinese, English, Hmong, Japanese, Russian, Spanish, and Vietnamese.

Disaster website: http://www.aging.ca.gov/ProgramsProviders/AAA /Disaster_Preparedness/Disaster_Tip_Sheets/

P	R			O	A			G	

Centers for Disease Control: Older Adults

Webpages hosted by the CDC with links and information on disaster preparedness. Includes information on personal preparedness tools and information for older adults and their caregivers. Also includes information on resources for media professionals to increase attention to unique needs of older adults in emergencies.

Disaster and older adult webpages: http://www.cdc.gov/aging/emer gency/; http://www.cdc.gov/aging/emergency/preparedness.htm

P	R			O				G	

FEMA: Seniors

Website hosted by FEMA. Provides guidelines targeting older adults for planning for a disaster.

Main disaster and seniors website: http://www.ready.gov/seniors

P	R			O				G	

National Association of Area Agencies on Aging: Eldercare Locator

Webpage hosted by the National Association of Area Agencies on Aging. Provides information on the Eldercare Locator Call Center. Includes information on aging and disability and general links to other local resources on aging. Spanish-speaking specialists are available.

Eldercare Locator webpage: http://www.n4a.org/programs/eldercare-locator/?fa=fast-facts

Toll-free number: 1-800-677-1116

P	R			O					

National Institute on Aging: Alzheimer's Disease

Webpage hosted by the National Institute on Aging focusing on the special needs of individuals with Alzheimer's disease. Provides information on disaster preparedness for both individuals with Alzheimer's disease and their caregivers. Links provided to Alzheimer's resources.

P	R			O				G	

State of Florida Department of Elder Affairs

Webpage hosted by the Department of Elder Affairs (DOEA) provides information on disaster preparedness for older adults. Includes links to disaster preparedness guides for elders in English and Spanish, information on making a family disaster plan and supply kit, and a disaster online library.

Disaster website: http://elderaffairs.state.fl.us/doea/disaster.php

P	R			O				G	

PHYSICAL DISABILITIES

American Red Cross: People With Disabilities

Online booklet, *Preparing for Disaster for People with Disabilities and Other Special Needs*. Provides information and tips on getting informed, making a plan, assembling a kit, and keeping plans up to date.

Link to disaster booklet: http://www.redcross.org/images/MEDIA_CustomProductCatalog/m4240199_A4497.pdf

P	R		D	O					

CDC: Persons With Disabilities

Webpages hosted by the CDC that provide disaster information and links for people with chronic conditions and disabilities. Includes videos with American Sign Language (ASL) for the hearing impaired and some information in Spanish.

Disaster information for people with chronic diseases and disabilities: http://emergency.cdc.gov/disasters/chronic.asp

Disabilities (emergency preparedness training): http://www.cdc.gov/features/emergencypreparedness/index.html

P	R		D				G	

Disability.Gov: Emergency Preparedness

Website provides clearinghouse with hundreds of links on disaster preparedness and resources for individuals with disabilities, their caregivers, responders, and employers. Includes information relevant for older adults with disabilities.

Disaster resources page: https://www.disability.gov/?s=&fq=topics_taxonomy:%22Emergency+Preparedness%5E%5E%22

P	R			D	O			G	

FEMA: Access and Functional Needs

Website hosted by FEMA targeting individuals with physical disabilities. Provides information on special needs for making plans to evacuate/shelter in place and items in emergency kit for individuals with physical disabilities.

Disaster website: http://www.ready.gov/individuals-access-functional-needs

P	R		D				G	

National Fire Protection Agency

Website that provides information targeting individuals with disabilities. Includes home safety information and emergency evacuation planning guide for persons with disabilities.

Disability and fire safety website: https://www.nfpa.org/safety-information/for-consumers/populations/people-with-disabilities

P	R		D					

National Organization on Disability

Website hosted by the National Organization on Disability (NOD) providing numerous resources on disaster preparedness, response, and recovery. Includes information for individuals with disabilities, caregivers, responders, and employers related to disasters. Specific disaster readiness tips provided in brochures include: mobility disabilities, sensory disabilities, developmental/cognitive disabilities, and owners of pets or service animals.

Main disaster website: http://nod.org/disability_resources/emergency _preparedness_for_persons_with_disabilities

P	R		D	O	A				

Nobody Left Behind: Disaster Preparedness for Persons With Mobility Impairments

Website provides clearinghouse of links to information concerning disasters and individuals with physical disabilities provided by the University of Kansas Research and Training Center on Independent Living and the Kansas Department of Health and Environment. Includes information on disasters for individuals, employers, health professionals, and policy makers.

Disaster website: http://www.nobodyleftbehind2.org/resources/index .shtml

P	R		D					G	

Oregon Office on Disability and Health

Online "Ready Now" toolkit provides information for people with disabilities emphasizing independence and focus on an individual's unique needs. Includes information about being informed, making a plan, and building a kit, targeted toward special concerns of persons with disabilities.

Disaster booklet: http://www.ohsu.edu/xd/outreach/occyshn/upload /ReadyNowToolkit.pdf

P	R		D						

Office of Disability Employment Policy

Online link to an employer's guide for disaster preparedness and evacuation of individuals with disabilities. The Office of Disability Employment Policy is under the U.S. Department of Labor.

P	R		D				G	

ANIMALS AND PETS

American Humane Association

General website of the American Humane Association (AHA). Mission is to ensure the welfare, wellness, and well-being of children and animals, including protecting pets and farm animals from abuse and neglect.

Website: http://www.americanhumane.org/about-us/who-we-are/

		I/C			A				

American Red Cross: Pets

Website hosted by the ARC providing information on pets. Provides information on disaster preparedness, assembling an emergency kit, and ways to help emergency workers to help pets.

Disaster website: http://www.redcross.org/prepare/location/home-family /pets

P	R				A				

American Society for the Prevention of Cruelty to Animals

Webpage hosted by the website of the American Society for the Prevention of Cruelty to Animals (ASPCA). Provides information on disaster preparedness and response for pets. Includes special considerations for birds, reptiles, and small animals.

Disaster webpage: http://www.aspca.org/pet-care/disaster-preparedness

P	R				A				

American Veterinary Medical Association

Webpage of the American Veterinary Medical Association (AVMA) on disaster preparedness and response. Includes links to downloadable guides for families and pets and livestock, first responders, and veterinarians.

Disaster webpage: https://www.avma.org/KB/Resources/Reference /disaster/Pages/default.aspx

P	R				A				

Americans With Disabilities National Network

Webpage of the Americans with Disabilities (ADA) National Network. Provides a fact sheet with information about current laws regarding service animals.

Webpage: http://adata.org/factsheet/service-animals

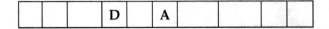

California Department of Public Health

Webpage of the California Department of Public Health (CDPH). Provides disaster planning tips for pet and livestock owners; includes information on evacuation of livestock.

Disaster webpage: http://www.bepreparedcalifornia.ca.gov/BePrepared/IndividualsAndFamilies/Pages/DisasterPlanningTipsforPetLivestockOwner.aspx

P	R				A			G	

FEMA: Caring for Animals

Website hosted by FEMA. Provides information on caring for pets and large animals. Includes pet and animal care disaster preparedness, caring for animals during a disaster, and caring for animals after a disaster.

Disaster website: http://www.ready.gov/caring-animals

P	R				A			G	

Humane Society of the United States

Website of the Humane Society. Provides links to information on disasters and animals. Includes disaster planning for pets, farm animals, and horses. Also includes special considerations for tornados.

Disaster website: http://www.humanesociety.org/about/departments/disaster_preparedness.html

P	R			D		A				

ASSESSMENT TOOLS

Centers for Disease Control Shelter Assessment Tool

Environmental health assessment tool to conduct rapid assessment of shelter conditions during disasters. Covers general areas of environmental health from food and water safety to health and medical, handicap accessibility, and child-care areas.

Available from: http://www.bt.cdc.gov/shelterassessment/

Psychological Simple Triage and Rapid Treatment (PsySTART)

Provides a framework and rapid triage assessment tool for disaster mental health. Emphasis on exposure to stressors, not symptoms.

Available from: http://www.cphd.ucla.edu/ (UCLA Center for Public Health and Disasters)

Abbreviations

AAA	Area Agency on Aging
AAO	American Academy of Opthalmology
AAP	American Academy of Pediatrics
ABM	Academy of Breastfeeding Medicine
ACT	Assertive Community Treatment
ADA	Americans with Disabilities Act of 1990
ADL	Activities of Daily Living
ADRD	Alzheimer's Related Disorder
AHA	American Humane Association
AHAR	Annual Homeless Assessment Report
AKC	American Kennel Club
ARC	American Red Cross
ASL	American Sign Language
AOA	U.S. Administration on Aging
ASPCA	American Society for the Prevention of Cruelty to Animals
AT	Alcohol and Tobacco
AVMA	American Veterinary Medical Association
BDI-II	Beck Depression Inventory
BRFSS	Behavioral Risk Factor Surveillance System
CCP	Crisis Counseling and Assistance and Training Program (by FEMA)
CDC	Centers for Disease Control and Prevention
CDIHP	Center for Disability Issues and the Health Professions
CDPH	California Department of Public Health
CDR	California Department of Rehabilitation
CDV	Canine Distemper Virus
CERT	Community Emergency Response Team
CGI	Clinical Global Impression
CIDNY	Center for Independence of the Disabled in New York
CISD	Critical Incident Stress Debriefing

CMS	Consumable Medical Supplies
CPR	Cardiopulmonary Resuscitation
CRED	Center for Research on the Epidemiology of Disasters
CRIS	Case Register Interactive Search
CSAT	Center for Substance Abuse Treatment
CVHS	Central Vermont Humane Society
CY-PAS	Cornell-Yale Panic Attack Scale
DART	Disaster Animal Rescue Team
DBHIS	Disaster Behavioral Health Information Series
DHS	Department of Homeland Security
DMAT	Disaster Medical Assistance Team
DME	Durable Medical Equipment
DOEA	Department of Elder Affairs (State of Florida)
DOL	Department of Labor
DSM-IV	The *Diagnostic and Statistical Manual of Mental Disorders,* Fourth Edition
DTAC	Disaster Technical Assistance Center
EEOC	United States Equal Opportunity Commission
ED	Emergency Department
EMS	Emergency Medical Services
EOC	Emergency Operations Center
FEMA	Federal Emergency Management Agency
FNSS	Functional Needs and Supports Services
GAI	Geriatric Anxiety Inventory
GHO	General Health Questionnaire
GP	General Practitioner
HAMA	Hamilton Anxiety Rating Scale
HAMD	Hamilton Anxiety Depression Rating Scale
HHS	The United States Department of Health and Human Services
HHS-AOA	Health and Human Services Administration on Aging
HKCAG	Hurricane Katrina Community Advisory Group
HSUS	Humane Society of the United States
HUD	The United States Department of Housing and Urban Development
ICC	Interagency Coordinating Council on Emergency Preparedness and Individuals with Disabilities
ICE	In Case of Emergency
ID	Illicit Drug
IDDC	International Disability and Development Consortium
IES	Impact of Event Scale
IES-R	Impact of Event Scale-Revised
IFE Core Group	Infant and Young Child Feeding in Emergencies Core Group
ISTSS	International Society for Traumatic Stress Studies
ITTF	Illinois Terrorism Task Force
JAN	Job Accommodation Network

LAPS	Lexington Attachment to Pets Scale
LLS	Liverpool Stoicism Scale
MRE	Meal, Ready-to-Eat
NAHC	National Association of Home Care and Hospice
NAHERC	National Animal Health Emergency Response Corps
NARSC	National Animal Rescue and Sheltering Coalition
NCD	National Council on Disability
NCDP	National Center for Disaster Preparedness
NCH	National Coalition for the Homeless
NCMEC	National Center for Missing and Exploited Children
NDMS	National Disaster Medical System
NFPA	National Fire Prevention Association
NGO	Nongovernmental Organization
NHCHC	National Health Care for the Homeless Council
NIA	National Institute on Aging
NICU	Neonatal Intensive Care Unit
NIDCD	National Institute on Deafness and Other Communication Disorders
NIMH	National Institute of Mental Health
NIMS	National Incident Management System
NIST	National Institute of Standards and Technology
NOAA	National Oceanic and Atmospheric Administration
NOD	National Organization on Disability
NPF	National Pain Foundation
NRF	National Response Framework
NSDUH	National Survey on Drug Use and Health
NSHAP	National Social Life, Health, and Aging Project
NVOAD	National VOAD
NVRT	National Veterinary Response Team
OCD	Obsessive–Compulsive Disorder
ODEP	Office of Disability Employment Policy
OODH	Oregon Office on Disability and Health
PAS	Panic and Agoraphobia Scale
PAQ	Pet Attachment Questionnaire
PBQ	Pet Bereavement Questionnaire
PETS	Pet Evacuation and Transportation Standards Act of 2006
PD	Panic Disorder
PDEQ-SR	Peritraumatic Dissociative Experiences Questionnaire-Self-Report
PPD-8	Presidential Policy Directive 8
PFA	Psychological First Aid
PSS-SR	PTSD Symptom Scale Self-Report
PsySTART	Psychological Simple Triage and Rapid Treatment
PTSD	Posttraumatic Stress Disorder
SAMHSA	Substance Abuse and Mental Health Services Administration
SARSQ	Stanford Acute Stress Reaction Questionnaire

SART	State Animal Response Team
SES	Socioeconomic Status
SILC	State (California) Independent Living Council
SLAM	South London & Maudsley Foundation NHS Foundation Trust
SMI	Severe Mental Illness
SOAR	Searchable Online Accommodation Resource
SUV	Spontaneous Untrained (or Unsolicited) Volunteers
SWiFT	Seniors Without Families Team
SWLS	Satisfaction With Life Scale
TOS	Toxic Oil Syndrome
UAB	University of Alabama at Birmingham
USGS	U.S. Geological Survey
VOADs	Voluntary Organizations Active in Disaster
VMAT	Veterinary Medical Assistance Team
WCST	Wisconsin Card Sorting Test
WNV	West Nile Virus
WTC	World Trade Center
YBOC	Yale-Brown Obsessive Compulsive Scale
YCPHP	Yale Center for Public Health Preparedness

Index

ACT. *See* Assertive Community Treatment

ADA. *See* Americans with Disabilities Act

Administration on Aging, 216

ADRD. *See* Alzheimer's disease/ Alzheimer's related disorder

Alzheimer's disease/Alzheimer's related disorder (ADRD), 128–129

American Academy of Child and Adolescent Psychiatry, 214–215

American Academy of Pediatrics, 215

American Humane Association, 221

American Psychological Association, 213

American Red Cross (ARC), 75, 178, 211, 217, 218, 221

American Society for the Prevention of Cruelty to Animals (ASPCA), 221

Americans with Disabilities Act (ADA), 96, 140, 179, 221–222

American Veterinary Medical Association (AVMA), 221

ARC. *See* American Red Cross

ASPCA. *See* American Society for the Prevention of Cruelty to Animals

Assertive Community Treatment (ACT), 49, 144

AVMA. *See* American Veterinary Medical Association

Behavioral Risk Factor Surveillance System (BRFSS), 103, 107, 204

breastfeeding, 67–68

breast milk, 68

BRFSS. *See* Behavioral Risk Factor Surveillance System

California Department of Public Health (CDPH), 222

California Department on Aging, 217

CDC. *See* Centers for Disease Control and Prevention

CDPH. *See* California Department of Public Health

Center for Research on the Epidemiology of Disasters, 205

Centers for Disease Control and Prevention (CDC), 107, 159, 194, 211–212, 217–218, 222

CERTs. *See* Community Emergency Response Teams

Child Care Aware of America, 215

children
emotional disturbance, 71
families of children with disabilities, 73–74
medical perspective, 70
modeling adaptive coping skills, 81
rescue and recovery issues, 72–73
responder guidelines
  overview of, 84
  psychosocial issues, 85–87
  training and planning, 83–85
reunification, 74–75
schools and preschools, 75–76
with special needs, 72–74